Praise for *Poison Spring*

"In this riveting indictment, Vallianatos and Jenkins valiantly divulge the blinding greed and unfathomable stupidity behind the unconscionable lies and travesties—assaults against the very fabric of life. A resounding call for genuine and sustained environmental responsibility."

—*Booklist*, starred review

"Vallianatos, former staff scientist at the Environmental Protection Agency (EPA), and Jenkins sound the alarm about toxins in common use . . . An indictment that implicates pesticides in wildlife and livestock die-offs, as well as in human maladies and deaths."

—*Library Journal*

"Written with a strong dose of moral urgency, *Poison Spring* is a tragic and deeply troubling insider's account of the EPA that will raise the hair on the back of your neck. This is a book for all Americans who need to be aware that an agency set up to regulate chemicals has vilified some of its own employees for carrying out that mission, falsely classified toxic substances as 'inert,' undermined the laboratories of scientists producing evidence inconvenient to industry, and relied on faked studies by a rogue, privately run lab—in the paid service of chemical companies themselves—to register and license hundreds of chemicals. A brave book about a chilling chapter in U.S. environmental history."

—Ted Steinberg, author of *Down to Earth: Nature's Role in American History* and *Gotham Unbound: The Ecological History of Greater*

"*Poison Spring*, an insider's look at a failed federal agency, should alarm every citizen who believes the EPA's middle name ought to mean something. This is an important, clear-eyed, and carefully documented story of how the EPA, once so full of promise, is played by the industries it is supposed to regulate and weakened by the allies of those same industries in government."

—William Souder, author of *On a Farther Shore: The Life and Legacy of Rachel Carson*

"[Fifty-three years after *Silent Spring*], we are no better off. In fact, as shown in this remarkable new book, *Poison Spring*, we are worse off . . . *Poison Spring* is an extraordinary account that required courage to relay."

—*Truthout*

Poison Spring

POISON SPRING

THE SECRET HISTORY OF POLLUTION AND THE EPA

E. G. Vallianatos with McKay Jenkins

BLOOMSBURY

NEW YORK · LONDON · OXFORD · NEW DELHI · SYDNEY

Bloomsbury Press
An imprint of Bloomsbury Publishing Plc

1385 Broadway	50 Bedford Square
New York	London
NY 10018	WC1B 3DP
USA	UK

www.bloomsbury.com

First published 2014
This paperback edition published 2015

ISBN: HB: 978-1-60819-914-3
PB: 978-1-60819-926-6
ePub: 978-1-60819-925-9

Library of Congress Cataloging-in-Publication Data

Vallianatos, E. G.
Poison spring : the secret history of pollution and the EPA / by E. G. Vallianatos with McKay
Jenkins.—1st U.S. edition.
pages cm
Includes bibliographical references and index.
ISBN 978-1-60819-914-3 (alk. paper hardcover)
1. Pollution—Research—United States. 2. United States. Environmental Protection Agency.
3. Corporate power—United States. 4. Environmental responsibility—United States.
I. Jenkins, McKay, 1963– II. Title.
TD170.93.V35 2013
363.730973—dc23
2013041923

2 4 6 8 10 9 7 5 3

Typeset by Hewer Text UK Ltd, Edinburgh
Printed and bound in the U.S.A. by Thomson-Shore Inc., Dexter, Michigan

To find out more about our authors and books visit www.bloomsbury.
com. Here you will find extracts, author interviews, details of forthcoming
events, and the option to sign up for our newsletters.

Bloomsbury books may be purchased for business or promotional use. For
information on bulk purchases please contact Macmillan Corporate and
Premium Sales Department at specialmarkets@macmillan.com.

Contents

A Country Bathed in
Man-Made Chemicals

I wrote this book to tell the story of what I learned at the Environmental Protection Agency, where I worked from 1979 to 2004. This story—secret, exasperating, and tragic—explains why and how the chemical and other industries have captured the EPA and turned it from an environmental protection agency into a polluters' protection agency.

Both Democrats and Republicans, in Congress and the White House, have been responsible for this dangerous subversion. Taken in by the strategies and the financial clout of global industries, they have in turn facilitated the practical and moral breakdown at the agency. This story—how the EPA became a target of polluters, and how industrial polluters and their supporters in the White House and Congress remade EPA in their own image—is of immense importance both to the health of Americans and to the integrity of the natural world.

I spent most of my career in the EPA's Office of Pesticides Programs, where the regulation of powerful toxins is debated—and where the chemical pipeline that leads directly onto our food (and into our bodies) is opened or shut. While I touch on other causes of pollution of air and water, the primary focus of this book is on pesticides, herbicides, and other chemicals used on farms and in homes, on lawns and in forests—and which collectively have frightful effects on human and ecological health that are still largely hidden from public view. This fact should be very troubling to all Americans.

It is simply not possible to understand why the EPA behaves the way it does without appreciating the enormous power of America's industrial farmers and their allies in the chemical pesticide industries, which currently do about $40 billion per year in business. For decades, industry lobbyists have preached the gospel of unregulated capitalism, and Americans have bought it. Today, it seems, the entire government is at the service of the private interests of America's corporate class. In January 2007, the EPA even approved a promotional slogan that pesticide companies inserted onto the label of their sprays: "This insecticide is dedicated to a healthier world."

Far from simply making a narrow case against pesticides, this book offers a broad overview of the failure of environmental protection in the United States over the last seventy-five years—the same period, ironically, that some consider to have been the heyday of environmental regulation. This is environmental history our government and the industries don't want us to know. But here it is, constructed with the help of secret government documents.

Pesticides simply unify the story: the EPA offered me the documentary evidence to show the dangerous disregard for human health and the environment in the United States government, and in the industries it has sworn to oversee. *Poison Spring* makes public a secret history of pollution in the United States.

The EPA is an agency with the legal, and I would say sacred, responsibility of safeguarding our health and the health of the natural world. The decisions the EPA makes—or does not make—affect our lives in deep and subtle ways. These decisions are often more important and longer lasting than decisions made by any other part of the government.

To say the least, the troubles within the EPA mirror the troubles that have bedeviled our government from its very beginning. Then as now, powerful economic interests have worked tirelessly to handcuff government oversight. Two hundred fifty years ago, Alexander Hamilton denounced this state of affairs; in Hamilton's mind, a government bought and sold is worthless.[1]

In recent decades, from the 1940s to the dawn of the twenty-first century, it has seemed as if government has been working for industry rather than overseeing it. Most government and academic scientists working on agricultural practices and pest control have obdurately ignored research into nature's intricate and subtle workings. Instead, they have smoothed the way for the poisonous (and hugely profitable) concoctions of the chemical industry, and they are now doing the same for the rapidly growing field of genetic crop engineering, another Trojan horse of agribusiness.

In the mid-twentieth century, the Cold War provided the ideological context for the government's push for expanding agribusiness at the expense of the family farm. Facing the Communist Soviet Union, which wrecked peasant agriculture for its own version of state agribusiness, the United States adopted its own imperial form of farming, focusing on maximizing production and profit on ever-larger industrial-scale farms. Pesticides became more than just a gargantuan industry of their own; they became the very glue of this imperial system.

Such a tectonic shift—from small, family-run, and largely nontoxic farms to industrial-scale, intensely toxic industrial farms—had ecologists and health experts worried from the beginning. Margery W. Shaw, a scientist and physician writing in 1970 (the year the EPA came into being), feared that the introduction of hundreds of chemicals into the environment would result in a "genetic catastrophe."[2]

Six years later, at a conference in Washington on "Women and the Workplace," three American scientists (Eula Bingham, Marvin S. Legator, and Stephen J. Rinkus) warned of the high price we were likely to pay for the use of the "miracles" of the chemical age. Scientists, they wrote, "can only speculate on the detrimental effects on the genetic pool from injurious chemical exposure. In terms of ourselves as a population of living organisms, we are suffering chemical shock."[3]

A few years after this, my EPA colleague George Beusch reflected on his early years in the chemical business, including a New Jersey factory he knew where workers were manufacturing explosives. "Their skin would turn yellow and at that moment they knew it was time to die, which they did without much protest," Beusch recalled to me. "We called them the 'yellow canaries.'

"In other jobs I had with chemical companies, I learned to breathe—almost instinctively—with only the upper part of my lungs. Trying to make a workplace safe isn't easy, for it takes a lot of dollars. Money, not human health and welfare, is the heart and soul of that corporate business. People are cheap these days. The chemical industry can kill as many workers as they have at any one time, yet there are still more workers waiting outside to take their place. And the government always looks the other way while the worker gasps for breath."

Writing in 1994, two scientists of the United Nations University, Robert Ayres and Udo Simonis, described the spread of industrialization in the nineteenth and twentieth centuries as "a cancer." Industrialization in its present form, they said, "is a process of uncontrolled, unsustainable 'growth' that eventually destroys its host—the biosphere."[4]

Like other synthetic petrochemicals, and like radiation, pesticides affect life processes all the way down to the genes. And since Americans have been eating food contaminated by pesticides for more than seventy years, the genetic impact of pesticides must be correspondingly large.

Indeed, underlying most of the problems discussed in this book is the overwhelming power over ecological and human health held by this country's agricultural economy, which is controlled by fewer and fewer companies. For example, IBP, ConAgra Beef, Excel Corporation (Cargill), and Farmland National Beef Packing Company slaughtered 79 percent of cattle in the United States in 1998. Six companies— Smithfield, IBP, ConAgra (Swift), Cargill (Excel), Farmland Industries, and Hormel Foods—slaughtered 75 percent of all pigs in the country in 1999. Four companies—Cargill (Nutrena), Purina Mills (Koch

Industries), Central Soya, and Consolidated Nutrition (ADM and AGP)—controlled all feed plants in the United States by 1994. Also, by 1997, four companies (Cargill, ADM Milling, Continental Grain, and Bunge) controlled America's grain trade: they managed 24 percent of the grains, 39 percent of the facilities for storing grain, and 59 percent of the grain export facilities in the country.[5]

The EPA has been standing alongside and (mostly) cheering these industries for nearly fifty years. Like most administrative and policy functions of EPA, funding for research and regulatory work is shrouded in secrecy and ambiguity. A very small number of officials have enormous control over what gets funded. If a political appointee sees a chance to increase his prestige or the influence of a corporation, he will divert money from one activity to another, close a government laboratory, and hire a private laboratory more sympathetic to the desires of his clients in industry. During the last years of the George W. Bush administration, the EPA dismantled its libraries, the very foundation of its institutional memory. Why? Because the libraries were full of EPA-funded studies documenting the adverse effects of chemicals made by companies that had supported Bush's candidacy.

As a rule, these industries lobby tirelessly for the dissolution of the country's environmental bureaucracy and for a return to a nineteenth-century version of unregulated "free enterprise." Their representatives arrive for EPA meetings well dressed and well prepared to defend their interests. They know how to play the game: they come to meetings with slides, computer programs, fancy jargon, and colorful handouts, pretending to deliver a scholarly exercise in the manner of a college seminar or a defense of a doctoral thesis. Taking their cue, EPA staffers behave like students eager to learn from their chemical masters, allowing them to go on with their spurious presentations and never challenging their outrageous claims.

This entire book is, in a sense, about a bureaucracy going mad. The EPA bureaucracy is "civilized," and it may appear far removed from the darker Soviet forms written about by people like Alexander

Solzhenitsyn. Indeed, along with so many scientists, economists, lawyers, and experts in many other important disciplines of useful knowledge, the EPA might easily fit in Plato's Republic: their work—protecting the natural world and the health of people—is, in theory at least, entirely virtuous.[6]

The trouble is, as Solzhenitsyn knew too well, both individual people and entire bureaucracies are susceptible to corruption. Appoint a corrupt administrator at EPA, as Ronald Reagan appointed Anne Gorsuch, and the disease spreads fast through the entire bureaucratic system. This does not mean bureaucrats are more prone to corruption than other people; bureaucrats are just trying to make a living, and like everyone else, they want promotions and higher salaries. They follow the leadership of their organizations, which in the case of the EPA always mirrors the desires of the White House and Congress—and thus, inevitably, of the industries that control the country's politics.[7]

By 1979, America already had 7,500 manufacturers producing 47,000 industrial chemicals in amounts totaling more than 500 billion pounds per year. A great many of those substances had the potential for trouble. Among the most well known, asbestos threatened not merely a quarter million workers in its mining and manufacture, but also endangered some 5 million children because their schools had asbestos in their classrooms. Benzene exposed 110 million urban Americans to chronic levels of poisoning, and thirty thousand workers to far more intense hazard. The list of industrial chemicals and their historical effects on people is very long indeed.[8]

In the 1970s, William Carl Heinrich Hueper, a renowned scientist at the National Institutes of Health, described the world's industrial chemicals as a "global disaster." "It is in the best interest of mankind that industry makes the proper adaptations for eliminating and/or reducing environmental and occupational cancer hazards," Hueper wrote in 1976. Human beings "lack the ability to make the appropriate biologic adaptations for effectively combating the growing wave of toxic and carcinogenic risks propagated by modern industry, which represent biologic death bombs with a delayed time fuse and which may prove to be, in the long run, as dangerous to the existence of mankind as the arsenal of atom bombs."[9]

Hueper paid a heavy price for his honesty and independence. He was hounded incessantly by the chemical industry and his own agency. And if anything, voices like Hueper's have only become harder to hear. Today, the chemical industry operates behind front organizations including the American Chemical Society; the Toxicology Forum; the American Crop Protection Association (once known as the National Agricultural Chemicals Association); the Iowa Corn Growers Association; and a group known as Vision 2000. Each of these groups spends a great deal of money cozying up to EPA regulators as they shepherd their products through the regulatory pipeline.

Toxic pesticides, of course, are a tremendous source of pollution, and not merely on farms and lawns. By 1987, the EPA list of businesses that contaminate the environment with poisonous sprays included 6,300 sawmills; more than 500 wood treatment plants; 21,000 sheep dip pits; 95,000 storage sheds on large farms; 500,000 on-farm grain storage sheds; 13,000 greenhouses; 19,000 food processors; 6,900 slaughter-houses; 6,500 hospitals; 9,000 golf courses; 560 paper and pulp mills; 217,000 drinking water plants; 15,000 sewage treatment plants; 636,000 oil wells; 22,400 morgues; 13,000 photo processing labs; 5,200 textile mills; and 53,000 printing and publishing companies.[10]

A tremendous quantity of toxic pesticides ends up in homes as well. A 1984 EPA survey of home chemical use is instructive about our society's mind-boggling addiction to biocides: by this time, Americans were using 32 different chemicals at home, among them 20 million pounds per year of pine oil for bacteria, 30 million pounds of ethanol for bacteria, 45 million pounds of naphthalene for moths, 10 million pounds of pentachlorophenol for fungi and insects, and 200 million pounds of sodium hypochlorite for bacteria and fungi.[11]

By 1983, the EPA had evidence that 30 percent of 75,000 gas storage stations leaked gasoline, contaminating groundwater and having other toxic ecological effects. That condition would rise to about 75 percent by the end of the decade.[11]

In all, since World War II, we have been living inside an explosion of synthetic chemicals: from 1 billion pounds in the 1940s to more than 400 billion pounds in the late 1980s. Even these numbers barely hint at the ubiquity of chemicals in our synthetic century. By 2004, the U.S. chemical industry was producing more than 138 billion pounds of seven petrochemicals—ethylene, propylene, butylenes, benzene, toluene, xylenes, and methane—from which companies make tens of thousands of consumer products. Today, industries worldwide generate 300 billion pounds of plastics a year.[13]

It is only in this context—a country bathed in man-made chemicals—that one can understand why the United States is in the midst of a cancer epidemic. The cancer establishment (made up by the National Cancer Institute, the American Cancer Society, trade associations like the Chemical Manufacturers Association, and the chemical industry) has fundamentally misled the American people into searching for a miraculous "cure." Rather than vigorously examining the myriad poisons we are forced to encounter every day, these groups warn people to be careful about their "lifestyle." Blame for cancer falls on consumers, not on the poisons that cause illness. From the perspective of the industries that make these chemicals, it's a brilliant strategy. For the rest of us, it's a tragedy.

In 1989, William Lijinsky, a government cancer specialist, wrote that something like a quarter to a sixth of the population of America and other industrialized countries suffer and die from cancer, a condition comparable to the great epidemics of the eighteenth and nineteenth centuries. "The solution to the epidemics of infectious disease," he says, is "prevention rather than cure, and so it is with cancer."[14]

Samuel Epstein, professor of occupational and environmental medicine at the University of Illinois, estimated in 1987 that the cancer epidemic in the United States was striking one in three persons, killing one in four.[15] In 2000, Janette Sherman, physician, toxicologist, and author of *Life's Delicate Balance: Causes and Prevention of Breast Cancer*, spoke about "the carnage of endocrine-disrupting chemicals, nuclear radiation, and chemical carcinogens, alone and in combination, invading nearly every family with cancer." In 2007, Devra Davis, another first-rate cancer specialist and author of *The Secret History of the War on Cancer*, complained that "cancer has become the price of modern life." In today's United States and England, Davis says, one out of two men will get cancer. So will one in three women.

This book has emerged from my personal experience with the EPA and from information I gleaned from thousands of government documents, some of them rescued from destruction.

Before coming to Washington, I was trained in zoology (at the University of Illinois), earned a doctorate in history (from the University of Wisconsin, in 1972), and did postdoctoral studies in the history of science at Harvard. Throughout my training, I was taught to ask questions about how and why things come into being and how they develop. It was this combination of humanistic and science background that has helped me make sense of the EPA.[16]

EPA hired me as a "generalist," a person with broad training in and understanding of science. My official title was "program analyst." I was expected to employ my skills in researching and analyzing science issues relevant to environmental protection. I quickly understood why the EPA's mission was fatally compromised: bad scientific practices within the agency, and corrupting influences without.

I spent twenty-five years with EPA, from 1979 to 2004, primarily as an analyst of issues relating to pesticides and agriculture. Over the years, I took part in countless meetings and did many other mundane things one does in a huge bureaucracy—all in the interest of helping shape policy that, I wanted to believe, would protect public health and nature.[17]

In the course of my work, I routinely monitored congressional actions and outside scientific reports and articles. I also read thousands of letters, memos, notes, briefs, and reports. Not all of them dealt with pesticides, but the documents that most caught my attention examined policy issues about the regulation, health effects, and environmental impact of pesticides. I did not have access to documents that contained "confidential business information" because only people with clearance were allowed to handle such documents. But from the rumors circulating about such documents, I gathered that there was not much trustworthy information in them: chemical formulas and estimates of how many pounds of active ingredient of a certain chemical were produced per year came from industry, not from independent monitors.

I collected my data from all kinds of sources. I attended meetings at which scientists and managers were making policy or discussing important issues and kept notes from those encounters. I met with colleagues for lunch or in their offices, and discussed their work and experience. A number of these people not only talked to me extensively about the problems they faced in their organizations, but also handed me hundreds of key documents illustrating the reasons for their discontent. In this way I was able to examine countless memoranda, issue papers, briefings, letters, studies, reports, and notes detailing the vast panorama of the EPA's pesticide swamp. Some of the documents mentioned here were generated by the EPA; others were created by other scientists studying environmental and toxicological issues who were supported by EPA funds. I have provided source citations for hundreds of these documents.[18]

 Many sources

From among these documents, I have chosen those that best summarize the science and effects of EPA policy. I studied most carefully those documents that draw connections between science and policy. As official paperwork, these documents are rarely personal, and they rarely examine or describe the ways policy actually gets made. These subtleties I absorbed by talking to many colleagues over the course of several decades. It is from this material that I have compiled a picture of the pesticide empire: its power, its abuses, and its effect on human health and the natural world.

Throughout this book, I cite examples of the dilemmas the EPA has faced as it has confronted the country's ecological crises, most of them relating to toxic chemical sprays. I often quote my sources (drawing on my notes of conversations with them) to give the reader a taste of the style, vigor, and ideas of those caught up in the country's environmental upheavals.

Although the book's structure is largely concerned with well-documented events from the 1970s and 1980s, nearly all chapters foreshadow problems running straight through the Obama administration. In all cases I concentrate on events that I knew about from direct experience or have been able to personally document. Over time, the EPA has become less and less transparent—not merely in what it did, but how it did what it did. Access to information has been another casualty of the dismantling of the EPA.

The agency's oversight of pesticides is monitored by agricultural committees in Congress, which—in a government dedicated to protecting industries rather than people—means that efforts to regulate agricultural poisons are often cast as "attacks on farmers" rather than as "efforts to protect consumers from toxic chemicals." More frustrating, the Department of Agriculture's interminable process of assessing the dangers of "problem pesticides" has left little chance that dangerous toxins can even be *evaluated* before they impact our "grandchildren's grandchildren," according to David Menotti, the EPA's former deputy associate general counsel.[19]

What have been the repercussions of this resistance? As far as Aldo Leopold could tell, American civilization was already failing in the 1930s. The country was already being remade through the power and influence of increasingly larger corporations. For decades, rural America had been losing its character, becoming an alien landscape: empty of people, a colossus of one-crop agriculture, huge ranches, and animal factories. "A harmonious relation to land is more intricate, and of more consequence to civilization, than the historians of its progress seem to realize," said Leopold, one of America's great scientists and environmental philosophers. "Civilization is not, as they seem to assume, the enslavement of a stable and constant earth. It is a state of mutual and interdependent cooperation between human animals, other animals, plants, and soils, which may be disrupted at any moment by the failure of any of them."[20]

In the 1940s, Leopold described this condition as "clean farming," which translated as "a food chain aimed solely at economic profit and purged of all non-conforming links, a sort of *Pax Germanica* of the agricultural world."[21]

If only Leopold knew what would befall his beloved American landscape following his death in 1948. Spraying DDT on marshes and tidelands in the 1950s and 1960s killed many billions of fish and aquatic invertebrates and drove fish-eating birds such as the nation's iconic bald eagle to the very brink of extinction. DDT-like sprays including dieldrin and heptachlor killed about 80 percent of songbirds in affected areas, wiping out game birds and decimating wild mammals. Just the runoff of cotton insecticides "caused staggering losses of fish," according to senior EPA ecologists David Coppage and Clayton Bushong; they once calculated the harm of farm poisons at more than $1.25 trillion per year in lost recreational, commercial, personal food, and aesthetic values.[22]

It boggles the mind to think that we have continued to put up with such destruction for so many years with complete indifference.[23] The social and cultural costs of this practice are simply incalculable. Aside from their damaging effects on health and ecological systems, these chemicals are an integral part of the industrialization of our farms, depopulating rural America as family farms continue to be swallowed by corporate giants. Once out of the laboratory, pesticides destroy the beautiful yet vulnerable links—the affection, the real symbiosis—that bind people to the land. It is my hope that this book will go some distance, however small, toward reversing this dire trend.

CHAPTER 1

The EPA Nobody Knows

A SAD fact of contemporary life is that most of us have come to accept that we spend our lives swimming in a chemical soup. Our lives are built on synthetic chemicals: in our food, in our cosmetics, in our water bottles, on our lawns. Here are just a few of the soup's ingredients—the words are hard to pronounce, and harder to trace: methoxychlor, chlorpyrifos, amitrole, glyphosate, dibromochloropropane, polychlorinated biphenyls, polybrominated biphenyls, dichlorodiphenyltrichloroethane (DDT), vinclozolin, 1,3,-butadiene, petroleum distillates, di-(2-ethylhexyl)-phthalate, fonofos, parathion, malathion, coumaphos, permethrin, atrazine, alachlor, metolachlor, trifluralin, simazine, 2,4-D, carbaryl, dieldrin, diazinon, endosulfan, glasswool (fiberglass), ethylene thiouria, asbestos, acrylonitrile, chloroform, aflatoxins, lead, nickel, mercury, cyanide, arsenic, beryllium, benzene, and chlorine.

The words are not exactly name brands. They are not widely advertised. But they are here, they are in us, and they will remain—in our food and water, in our air, and in our bodies—for a long time to come, because their use has been approved by the EPA. Consumers may not know what these chemicals are, but they implicitly trust that someone—if not the companies, then surely the EPA—is keeping their health and safety in mind.

That, at least, is the hope. The EPA is charged with setting standards for environmental and health safety, and then with monitoring industries that threaten to violate those standards. The public is aware that a (very) few chemicals, such as DDT, have been banned. But they have no idea that close molecular relatives of even these dangerous chemicals are still produced in great quantities.

Here's how it works: A company coming to EPA for the "registration" of a pesticide either conducts (or contracts out) several tests of its product on laboratory animals. Each laboratory test costs lots of money, sometimes more than a hundred thousand dollars. When all or part of the tests show that the product does not cause "unreasonable adverse effects on man and the environment," the EPA approves the product, and the company begins selling it. But this process is far from a guarantee that these products, or their chemical ingredients, are safe.[1]

EPA labs can (and do) check on the validity of the information that chemical companies give the government. When a new chemical enters the market (and thereby ends up in our water or our food), the chemical company and EPA discuss how much of the toxin should be allowed in human food. Theoretically, such an amount should in no way harm us. These amounts are measured in parts per million (ppm), parts per billion (ppb), and parts per trillion (ppt). A part per million is like dissolving an ounce of salt into 7,500 gallons of water. One part per billion is like putting an ounce of chocolate syrup in 1,000 tank cars of milk. And a part per trillion is the equivalent of a pinch of salt over 10,000 tons of potato chips.

This "legal" amount of a poison permitted in food is an artifice known as human "tolerance," which—if we are talking about pesticides—is really just a cover meant to protect farmers from lawsuits filed by people sickened by the food they eat. To detect "tolerable" poison in apples, for example, EPA looks over the experiments conducted by the industry that makes the poison. Animal studies testing the toxicity of sprays, assuming they are done honestly, reveal the real (or potential) danger of the pesticides or drugs fed to experimental animals such as mice, rats, rabbits, and dogs. Once these results are in hand, EPA then disseminates them to state agencies and foreign countries.

Tests are designed to detect both immediate and long-term danger. You want to know whether, say, 7 parts per million of a certain chemical will poison someone eating corn sprayed with that chemical. But you also want to know about eating this chemical over a long time. This is where the "chronic toxicity" testing comes in: dosing animals for two years to see how the animal reacts. Does the animal become blind or paralyzed? Does it stop eating or develop cancer tumors? These would be clear signs the chemical is not fit for human consumption and therefore inappropriate for EPA approval.

Congress can cut funding for labs, but such action is unusual. Instead, Congress cuts funding for the EPA itself, and—depending on the politics of the administration—the EPA then cuts funding for the labs or turns testing over to private labs. As we will see in due course, private labs do the testing for chemicals; nevertheless, EPA labs are critical in monitoring the activities of private companies and labs. If EPA management cuts funding for EPA labs—which it has done—it becomes difficult to detect, much less control, industry corruption.

Since lab tests are so critical to protecting our health and the environment, you would think they would be used widely to help monitor the eighty thousand synthetic chemicals in common use today. Nothing could be further from the truth. My first supervisor, Bill Preston, a good scientist with extensive experience in the federal government, lamented that the number of laboratories serving the Office of Pesticide Programs of the EPA had dropped from a dozen in 1971 to a half dozen in 1979. By the time I retired from the EPA in 2004, there were two.

For the majority of politicians and executives in corporate America, effective environmental protection and the safeguarding of public health—the legal mission of the EPA—has rarely been a compelling priority. To understand this fact, one has only to look back at the EPA's history during its first three decades. I was there, increasingly incredulous, watching that mission being betrayed.

The Office of Pesticide Programs, the largest organization of the EPA, within which I did most of my work, is essentially owned by the global chemical-pesticide industry, and this has been true under both Democratic and Republican administrations. EPA became a place where honest science has been replaced by dishonest "risk assessments" and "cost-benefit analyses," both of which serve as thin bureaucratic covers for putting the interests of industry ahead of the environment and public health.

At its foundation, the EPA inherited much of its work from the U.S. Department of Agriculture and, to a lesser extent, from the Department of the Interior and the Department of Health, Education and Welfare (now Health and Human Services). This inheritance led to a disastrous impact on the EPA's noble mission, which was—and remains—not the coddling of industry, but the protection of the country's environment and human health.

Congress has given the EPA the authority to implement more than a dozen environmental laws designed to keep air, water, and food relatively clean and safe; trash properly disposed off; radiation away from people; and the environment relatively unharmed by industrial pollution or manufacturing practices.

The most important of our environmental laws administered by the EPA include the Federal Insecticide, Fungicide, and Rodenticide Act of 1947, which evolved from the 1910 Insecticide Act that was supposed to do away with fraudulent pesticide products.[2]

The EPA also oversees the Toxic Substances Control Act (TSCA) of 1976, which brought commercial chemicals under the purview of the law. The benefits of this law have been nominal at best, since the EPA has failed miserably to regulate the spread of industrial chemicals—which is exactly how the chemical industry wants it. From the outset, industry has neutered the TSCA law, forbidding the EPA from requiring premarket health and environmental testing of the massive amounts of chemicals the agency is charged with "regulating."

The Clean Air Act of 1970 gave the EPA the authority to set national air quality standards and air pollution limits. The Clean Water Act of 1972 authorized the EPA to issue pollution discharge permits to those who would otherwise continue to dump unlimited wastes into streams and rivers, and enabled the EPA to fund wastewater treatment plants throughout the country.[3]

Although these laws have been of incalculable benefit (at least compared to the way things would look had they not been implemented), the EPA remains a timid imitation of what it could have become. Sometimes the agency doesn't even bother to enforce its own rules. Other times it takes years for the EPA to publish its regulations. Even when regulations are posted promptly, they are routinely watered down by the White House Office of Management and Budget, or by congressional or industry demands. These forces often order EPA to rewrite its regulations to benefit industry, a cynical process that grinds down even the most thick-skinned scientists.

Worst of all, the EPA—like all government agencies—is infected with political appointees, a great many of them with strong ties to the very industries they have been hired to regulate. Once these people have been confirmed to senior posts by the Senate, they divide the agency budget and staff among themselves and then mold regulations as they see fit to satisfy their former (and often future) industry employers. Always, of course, industry is there on the other side of the thin line, watching, influencing, and disciplining both legislators and administrators of the country's laws.[4]

What does this industry influence mean in practice? With few exceptions, environmental statutes allow chemicals to be dumped on the market without ever having been tested. In the case of the pesticides law, for instance, the EPA is authorized to demand premarket health and environmental testing of new products. But in practice, the chemical industry plays a major role in writing those regulations and has a powerful

hand in restraining the EPA from enforcing its rules. The chemical industry's allies in Congress and the White House raise no objections.[5]

The truth is, most toxic chemicals enter the market without ever
being tested for health and environmental effects, and this is just the
way the chemical industry likes it. The Occupational Safety and
Health Act, the Toxic Substances Control Act, the cosmetic provisions
of the Food, Drug and Cosmetics Act, and all other federal laws
require no testing for the chemicals or other products entering the
market. Only the pesticides act and the food sections of the Food,
Drug and Cosmetics Act require testing of chemicals likely to enter
the food we eat. This does not prevent industry marketers from saying
that their products "meet EPA standards."

How does this happen? EPA staffers routinely cut and paste studies
conducted by the very industries they are supposed to be regulating—
and rubber-stamp industry conclusions with the imprimatur of
government. They fund studies no one reads; they pay for travel for political appointees; and—as political administrations change—they grease
the revolving door that barely separates the agency and industry.[6]

When political men and women leave the government for positions in industry—or when industry people move into government—
they carry their influence with them. Pesticide companies hire senior
EPA officials because those officials know how to craft strategies that
will ensure the flow of toxins into the market and the profits derived
from them. Former government officials are able to persuade their
former colleagues to be more lenient in their scrutiny of data provided
by industry, which ensures that new and more dangerous pesticides
continue to be "registered" and to enter the market. The former "government insiders" become the mirror image of what they once were—they
are now industry insiders. This revolving door is a fundamental fact in
the continuing hegemony of corporations over would-be regulators.

Long after tobacco was proven to be deadly dangerous, cigarette
companies continued to make billions of dollars because the industry
manipulated science and hid from the government what industry knew

about the hazards of cigarettes. The chemical industry has enthusiastically adopted this model of deception, manipulating the EPA the way Big Tobacco manipulated the Food and Drug Administration. The EPA has always claimed there was "good science" behind its approval of the chemical industry's products. As became tragically evident in the case of Big Tobacco, the truth about the safety of products hawked by Big Chemical is far less convincing.

Companies hire professional writers to compose articles favoring their products. Company bosses then find doctors and scientists to attach their names to the articles to make it appear as if their own research supported the findings. Such fake "scientific" articles then somehow pass the "peer review" process of scientific journals and become the very texts influencing public policy.[7]

For example, scientists for several years have been documenting the health effects of mixtures of two pesticides: the fungicide maneb and the weed killer paraquat. Researchers find that both mice and people exposed to maneb-paraquat mixtures increase their risk of Parkinson's disease. The companies manufacturing these chemicals don't like what this evidence might mean for their gold-minting toxins; paraquat alone earns something on the order of $1 billion per year. (The world's largest producers of paraquat are companies based in China; the Swiss company Syngenta also manufactures it, though Switzerland has banned it for home use.)

So the owners of these two poisons hired Exponent, Inc., a scientific consulting company, to prepare a campaign to protect paraquat and maneb from scrutiny. Exponent went straight to the federal government and agreed to donate $60,000 to fund a study of the chemicals by the National Institute for Occupational Safety and Health, a branch of the Centers for Disease Control and Prevention. The money went to the Centers for Disease Control Foundation, which accepts private money for private research.[8]

Such a system raises obvious worries that the "partnership" between industry and government will blur the line between "the monitor and those who are being monitored," said Craig Holman, a lobbyist for Public Citizen, a consumer advocacy organization based in Washington, D.C. With industry pressing to "reduce the size of government"—that is, to reduce any oversight at all—such "partnerships" are becoming all too common. For decades, companies have lobbied hard to shrink the size of agencies prepared to scrutinize their products. They call this being "fiscally conservative." What it really is, of course, is being self-serving. And there, at the end of the toxic pipeline, is the American public.[9]

By the 1960s (before the EPA was founded), it was clear that the federal organizations set up to protect human health and the environment—including the USDA, the Department of the Interior, and the Department of Health, Education and Welfare (now Health and Human Services)—had already failed miserably in their mission. These departments did little more than defend industry, often more blatantly than they do today. The situation was so bad that President Richard Nixon—hardly an environmentalist when he came into office—was forced to address the issue in his 1970 State of the Union speech.

"The great question of the seventies is, shall we surrender to our surroundings, or shall we make our peace with nature and begin to make reparations for the damage we have done to our air, to our land, and to our water?" Nixon said. "Clean air, clean water, open spaces—these should once again be the birthright of every American. I see an America in which we have made great strides in stopping the pollution of our air, cleaning up our water, opening up our parks, continuing to explore in space."[10]

Less than a year later, Nixon founded the EPA, charging the agency with protecting our natural environment—and the public health—from the insults of industrial pollution. Fundamentally, the EPA was formed as a keeper of the public trust, to safeguard American citizens from threats they themselves might not even understand.

Change takes time, and change for the better takes both time and virtuous leadership. In 1970, the year of the birth of the EPA, the

United States was already full of chemicals, and full of industries accustomed to cutting corners for competition and profit.

In other words, from the moment of its inception in December 1970, the EPA was caught in a trap. It could not honestly protect "human health and the environment" (the slogan on EPA's logo) from the perpetual onslaught of toxins and outright pollution of the industrial behemoth of the United States. Industries had already begun mastering the art of "externalizing" their pollution—they found ways to dump it or spew it and get someone else to pay for the damages. And for many decades, we have.

"Part of the trouble with talking about something like DDT is that the use of it is not just a practical device, it's almost an establishment religion," Gary Snyder, the environmental philosopher and Pulitzer Prize–winning poet wrote in *Turtle Island*, a 1974 book of poems. Indeed, by the 1970s, the most the EPA could do was to try to "regulate" pollution—that is, it set levels at which factories were "allowed to pollute" and prohibit, at least on paper, the most life-threatening practices of companies making poisons and other dangerous products.

At first, there was some basic consensus: Americans ought not to drop dead from breathing air or drinking water or eating food poisoned by chemicals. Rivers (like Cleveland's Cuyahoga) ought not to catch on fire. Richard Nixon and the EPA's first administrator, William Ruckelshaus, banned DDT in 1972, not a small achievement. The passage of the Clean Air Act of 1970 and the Safe Drinking Water Act of 1972 were designed with similar purposes in mind: the EPA imposed some limits on the sources of our most obvious pollution. After a time, American rivers were no longer catching fire, and the air became somewhat less burdened by visible pollution—though people in cities still suffer from smog and soot from the pipes of cars, trucks, airplanes, incinerators, large farms, and factories. These microscopic particles still cause inflammation and injury to the lungs and the blood, killing some twenty thousand people in the United States every year and hurting many more.[11]

But even as he formed the EPA in 1970, Nixon was too preoccupied with fighting the terrible war in Vietnam to concern himself with domestic environmental protection. At the heart of his presidency was a dark paradox: Nixon formed the EPA to do something about pollution, but he also allowed chemical warfare in the jungles of Vietnam. The legacy of this paradox—most vividly displayed in the effects of the hideous Agent Orange—would come back to haunt both American soldiers and the country as a whole.

"I have concluded that in a very real sense we are all Vietnamese to the chemical companies, who feel their annual profits are more important than the health of human beings," wrote Fred A. Wilcox, the author of *Waiting for an Army to Die: The Tragedy of Agent Orange.* "America, like Vietnam during the war years, is a testing ground for the chemical companies and their vested interests. We have allowed ourselves to be used as guinea pigs, permitted our land and water to be poisoned, and accepted the notion that the average citizen is powerless to stop the ecological devastation of our nation and our world."[12]

At the EPA, Nixon's first move, in 1970, was a good one: he appointed Ruckelshaus to head the agency. Ruckelshaus had grown up in Indiana, studied law at Princeton and Harvard, and been elected in the Indiana House of Representatives, from which President Richard Nixon picked him to become the EPA's first administrator.

Ruckelshaus started right off rallying the troops to set the foundations of institutional environmental protection. From the beginning, EPA was an extremely well-educated bureaucracy: men and women skilled in science, law, engineering, agriculture, water, physics, and economics, among many other technical subjects.

Ruckelshaus made the agency's goal of environmental protection noble and real. With words, appointments, rewards, and above all good policies, he gave a mission to the EPA: clean up the country's environmental mess and protect our natural treasures and people's health from the visible and invisible pollution of the industry. Banning DDT in 1972, for example, showed how a well-motivated EPA could start righting the wrongs of past decades while sending an unmistakable message to industry to mend its toxic ways.

"[F]or most crops, including cotton, which in the past accounted for 80 percent of DDT use, production has been maintained," the EPA wrote in a press release. Nationally, the cost of switching to alternative chemicals "has cost cotton farmers slightly more than $1.00 per acre per year. In the southeastern U.S., however, this figure increases to an additional $6.00 per acre per year. For the consumer, the cost of buying cotton goods produced with other pesticides increased 2.2 cents per person per year."[13]

Industry got the message, and they did not like it at all. It put up vociferous opposition to the abolition of DDT. It denounced the EPA in the same ways it had excoriated Rachel Carson when her book *Silent Spring* appeared in 1962. It sent its agents to the White House and Congress to undermine the EPA and henceforth take charge of dictating America's "environmental protection." The effects of this campaign filtered down to the bureaucracy and in time dramatically recast—and contaminated—the mission of the EPA.

Ruckelshaus served the EPA with distinction, at least at first. But after leaving the agency, he became a pioneer of the "revolving door" policy between government and industry that would plague the EPA for decades. Ruckelshaus was hired as senior vice president of Weyerhaeuser, the giant timber and paper company that has been causing environmental destruction and pollution for decades. He returned to the EPA as a Reagan appointee ten years later, then left the agency again for lucrative jobs at Monsanto, Cummings Engine Company, the American Paper Institute, and a group of companies, the Coalition on Superfund, that lobbied for the weakening of the country's toxic waste laws. Ruckelshaus also became the CEO of Browning-Ferris, a huge waste management company in Houston, Texas. When Ruckelshaus resigned from the EPA in 1985, he was earning $72,000 a year. Browning-Ferris Industries hired him at a minimum salary of $1 million.[14]

The "revolving door" between government and industry could not help but compromise Ruckelshaus or the numerous other outstanding (and less than outstanding) men and women who moved in and out of public service. Few could resist the temptation of earning huge sums for selling their government experience to the very corporations they had once regulated.

The Carter administration's EPA administrator, Douglas Costle, became chairman of Metcalf and Eddy, a company offering consulting services on hazardous wastes. Steven Jellinek, assistant EPA administrator under President Carter, joined a pesticide lobbying firm and for years used his strong connections with EPA scientists and managers to get expedited approval of toxic sprays, especially those made in Japan. Lee Thomas, the EPA administrator in the second Reagan administration, became president of Law Environmental, another hazardous waste consultant. Rita Lavelle, who compromised EPA's hazardous waste program in the early 1980s, also became a consultant to the industry dealing with hazardous wastes. The revolving door worked the other way as well: Clarence Thomas worked as a lawyer for Monsanto before joining the Supreme Court, and he has been widely criticized for ruling in favor of Monsanto in landmark cases involving the company's genetically modified seeds.[15]

Intimately connected to the revolving door is the corrupting tradition of industry-sponsored junkets. Deep-pocketed companies spend a great deal of time and money wining and dining the very government employees who are supposed to be regulating them. These "retreats" and "conferences" are hosted at luxurious hotels, resorts, and other pleasure domes all over the world. Between October 1997 and March 2006, for example, EPA officials took more than ten thousand trips to countries including Australia, Korea, France, Germany, Italy, China, Thailand, Taiwan, and Cuba, and to American vacation destinations in the United States such as Atlantic City, Las Vegas, and Reno. All of these trips were paid for by industry: toxic waste companies, contractors, petroleum companies, and other business organizations lobbying the federal government for favors. These firms almost invariably secure lucrative contracts and other benefits.

Such mutual back-scratching made some at the EPA more than a little queasy. John Quarles, a Nixon man who became a deputy administrator of the EPA in the early 1970s, found industry influence, disinformation, and propaganda against the EPA so insulting he wore his title of "bureaucrat" with pride. "I am part of the faceless, gray government machine, one of those government officials whom cartoonists make fun of and editorialists stick pins in, who are blasted with criticism by public leaders from Barry Goldwater to Ralph Nader," Quarles wrote. "I am also an environmentalist, a chief official of the United States Environmental Protection Agency since its creation in December 1970, and in that capacity, too, I have been the object of heated criticism. The agency has been the target of the power industry, the steel industry, the auto industry, labor unions, farmers, editorialists, and private citizens. Its actions have been attacked as arbitrary, unreasonable, narrow-minded, impractical, and un-American. Much of this condemnation has been based on misunderstanding."[16]

In its day-to-day work, the EPA most resembles a kind of giant emergency room. The staff constantly triages crises and moves a great deal of paper around, but it never gets the chance to address the systemic problems that create the crises the agency deals with every day.

Like most large government departments and agencies, the EPA is a labyrinth—organizationally and physically. It is a version of "Dilbert's World"—each employee stuck in his or her own cubicle and narrowly defined function. My colleagues worked in an environment that was antithetical to science: in the absence of debate, research data, or field investigations, they did monotonous analyses, mundane work that bore little resemblance to their scientific training. Field scientists morphed into office technicians. Since they rarely got out into the field, EPA scientists didn't really know much about how industrial agriculture worked. They assumed, for example, that

farmers followed the warnings on pesticide labels. That was a fundamental mistake.

A 1981 government survey of agricultural practices in Florida
showed, for example, that in about 40 percent of the cases, farmers
used the wrong spray on a given crop, or simply used too much.[17]
Such basic, misinformed behavior destroys any chance of producing
safe food and essentially renders EPA's regulations meaningless.

The situation has been made worse by the weakening—or
outright elimination—of the EPA's monitoring capabilities. In 1982,
the EPA shut down the only national laboratory responsible for checking the efficacy of disinfectants. This was done at a time when those
chemicals were failing at a rate between 50 and 66 percent.[18]

In addition, the EPA's risk assessment was fundamentally flawed.
So enamored was the agency of synthetic chemicals that EPA biologists and economists rarely even bothered comparing the risks of
chemical sprays to a less toxic system of pest control such as crop rotations, disease-resistant crops, beneficial insects, or organic farming
methods. The emerging practice of "integrated pest management"—
let alone organic farming—received little more than token attention.

Yet integrated pest management had started with the EPA. A
small number of early IPA specialists collected data in search of alternatives to pesticides, sponsored several studies showing the benefits
of biological control of pests, and cheered when the EPA banned
DDT. The EPA's IPA staff formed a lively link with the rest of the
government and the nonprofit environmental community on all issues
of farming and pest control. And when interest in organic farming
began to sprout in the 1970s, the agency's IPM experts were prepared
to offer their knowledge and support.

Tragically, the EPA put its IPM staff in a box. Outstanding policy
documents (edited by the vigorous ecologist Charles Reese) remained
unread, conventional scientists ignored the unit's skepticism about
chemicals, and eventually the IPM unit became entirely co-opted by
the agency's chemical culture, which saw IPM as a threat. Big

Chemical set about defining IPM in a way guaranteed to keep farmers hooked on their pesticide products.[19]

In the best of circumstances, IPM encourages farmers to use smaller quantities of toxins on crops. But the IPM at EPA essentially became a do-nothing shop existing entirely for public relations, throwing dust in the eyes of the people about the EPA's toleration of the expansion of the pesticide and herbicide poison empire.[20]

In other words, the choice has always been between one chemical and another, never between a chemical and an alternative. And given the growing chronicle of our country's chemical saturation, the choices we have been making are clearly not serving us well. During my career at EPA, I saw this firsthand.

"EPA's developing cancer policy is progressively less oriented to public protection," a congressional report stated in 1976, four years before Ronald Reagan came to office. "In its regulation of pesticides, EPA is failing to perform its mandate to protect the public. EPA's developing pesticide program is increasingly solicitous of the pesticide industry at the expense of the public health and well-being."[21]

Two years later, another congressional report highlighted the failure of the government to protect Americans from eating food "tainted with potentially dangerous pesticide residues."

"Because of the nature of chemical contaminants, we are forced to rely on the Federal government to protect us against potentially dangerous chemicals we cannot see, smell, or taste," the report said. "Our examination leads us to believe that we cannot rely on the Federal government to protect us." Researchers found that the EPA "continues to approve tolerances for potentially carcinogenic, mutagenic, and teratogenic pesticides which result in residues in our food." The agency had set tolerance levels for pesticides without complete safety data, and it had "exempted some potentially dangerous pesticides from its tolerance requirements which end up in or on food."

In almost all cases, these chemicals had been certified by both industry and the EPA as having an "acceptable" impact on the environment, or posing only "acceptable" risks to people. Human beings, we were told, had a "tolerance level" for each of them. As long as we use the chemicals "properly," we would be safe.

The EPA uses the term "tolerance" to describe how much of a certain pesticide will be tolerated in a given amount of food. But there is very little science behind these tolerance levels; their sole purpose is to provide legal cover for the companies who make the chemicals, the farmers who use them, and the manufacturers who process food. As long as the government sets even bogus health standards, companies have legal cover if their products make people sick.

Yet these definitions of "tolerance" require an astonishing level of trust from the consumer. Who does the testing? Who determines what is safe and what is not? Who establishes the tolerance levels? If you think it is the EPA, you would be wrong. In most cases, the EPA bases its decisions to certify chemical products on the research and testing results provided by the very companies that make them.

By using an inadequate and outdated statistical base for setting tolerance levels, the EPA "often does not know what level of pesticide residue usually results from the use of a product, and bases its approval of pesticides merely on industry-supplied safety data."[22]

In other words, the EPA's tolerance setting program "is abysmal and needs a complete overhaul," one report concluded. "Even when meat was found to be contaminated with dangerously high levels of toxic pesticides, neither USDA nor FDA could stop these products from reaching the dinner table. This is an appalling state of affairs which cannot be allowed to continue."[23]

During the Reagan years, I spent several years with the EPA's "Benefits and Use" division—another ironic name, given that "benefits" meant the benefits (that is to say, "profits") that pesticides bring to industrial farms and pesticide companies, not the human or environmental health benefits the EPA is supposed to protect.[24]

To say the least, the staff of this division rarely thought about the adverse effects of pesticides. Cancer, especially cancer caused by pesticides, was not their concern. They listened to the producers of pesticides and their industry-funded academics who sought to "prove" that synthetic cancer-causing molecules in farm sprays were less dangerous than carcinogens that occur in nature. This led to an Orwellian situation in which the EPA was being asked on one hand to regulate processed foods in which these toxic chemicals showed up, and on the other hand being asked to formally allow "acceptable" levels of carcinogenic residuals in farmers' sprays. No one wanted to acknowledge, for example, that carcinogens sprayed on farms could actually end up in the carrots they grew. At the EPA, this became known as the "Delaney Paradox": the agency was stuck, essentially left to obscure the quality and potency of the chemicals that end up in the processed food we eat.

In May 1987, the prestigious National Academy of Sciences set out to make the EPA's job easier. In "Regulating Pesticides in Food: The Delaney Paradox," the academy concluded that the EPA ought to abandon the Delaney prohibition of carcinogens in food, and instead should regulate all pesticides under a single risk standard assessed during food production.

Whatever its intentions, the decision to abandon Delaney led to a disastrous outcome. Clearly, the more pesticide data companies collected, the more their products would be shown to be carcinogenic; under the Delaney provision, evidence of carcinogenic toxins turning up in processed food would mean that companies were breaking the law. By dropping the law—the only one prohibiting the presence of carcinogens in certain foods—the EPA was offering companies a way to avoid this oversight. Worse, the EPA was now essentially allowing the agricultural industry to regulate itself. Abandoning the Delaney Clause made it easier for chemical companies to hide data and meant that EPA scientists no longer felt obliged to investigate carcinogens in food.

In 1996, the Clinton administration brought this debate to a close when the president signed the so-called Food Quality Protection Act. The law amended a wide swath of chemical regulations, from pesticide and cosmetic oversight to the law establishing "tolerances" in food. Supporters said the new law established "a single health-based standard for all pesticides in all foods."

Beleaguered EPA scientists said something else: true, there was no more discrimination against processed foods; now all foods could legally be served with a daily dosage of poison.[25]

In September 1987, while I was writing a speech for Allen Jennings, my division deputy, a colleague suggested that my hard line on pesticide safety might be the result of a misunderstanding of the EPA's duty. EPA was not designed to keep chemicals that cause cancer, birth defects, or neurological disorders out of food and drinking water, he said. Rather, EPA existed only to ensure that the "risk" from those poisons was not "unreasonable."

My colleague asked me to study the speeches and congressional testimony of the two chiefs running EPA's pesticides empire, Jack Moore and Doug Campt. Reading this material would give me proper "guidance" in my assignment to rewrite the speech for Jennings. The message was clear: the EPA's main role was not to protect human health, but to determine just how much poison human beings can "tolerate."

The branch of EPA that oversees these "tolerance" decisions—the nerve center of EPA for all things relating to pesticides—is called the Registration Division. Its job is to decide how much poison can legally be present in the food we eat; it is where substantive decisions about pesticides are made. It is also where all data about pesticides receives an initial hearing before scientists examine the toxins in detail.

Over the years, my colleagues repeatedly told me that the Registration Division was in chaos, a madhouse of incompetence and lost or misdirected papers. Officials would mail documents to the wrong people. They would create lengthy documents known as "registration standards" but would rarely follow up to see whether their recommendations were actually being acted upon. When they received documents from chemical companies, they would dump them, misplace them, or simply do nothing. This black hole of paperwork made it far easier for chemical companies to register their products without even rudimentary oversight.[26]

In March 1987, the EPA hosted a two-day meeting of a group of special interests known by the fancy name Pesticide Users Advisory Committee. I was asked to help with this organization, which had essentially been formed to assure agribusiness that EPA would not get in the way of the pesticide industry.

The members of this committee could not disguise their contempt for the EPA and its attempts to protect wildlife and human health. So they must have been amused as they listened to an EPA ecologist explain the agency's (halfhearted) plans to protect endangered species from pesticides. I could see the smiles disappear when an EPA scientist described a well water survey seeking to detect traces of pesticides. These corporate representatives clearly felt the EPA had no business looking for poisons—which they used in huge volumes—in America's drinking water.

EPA scientists had also been troubled for many years that residues of ethylene bisdithiocarbamate (EBDC) fungicides ended up in food, and that these fungicides (which are still in use) degrade to ETU, or ethylene thiouria, which is known to cause thyroid cancer in experimental animals.

These fungicides had emerged as a major problem. The trouble for the agency, as usual, was that these compounds were extremely profitable: the half-dozen EBDC chemicals constituted half of the most popular fungicide sprays and 90 percent of the 120 million pounds of active ingredients used in American farming. EPA knew in September 1987 that some or most of these toxins presented "adverse affects to man or the environment," and for a time, EPA considered banning them from farming. Because of the resistance from agribusiness, however, nothing happened. Suddenly, in a dramatic turnabout, EPA were toeing the industry line, warning not about the dangers of fungicides but that banning these poisons would cost fruit and vegetable producers $5.6 billion in the first year alone and that food prices would rise by more than 16 percent.[27]

In October, a colleague asked me to review an EPA/USDA document dealing with the "benefits" of these fungicides. The 250-page document was full of evidence of scientists mouthing the propaganda of the chemical industry. The document was not an assessment or analysis, but a spirited defense of the fungicides from scientists from all over the government (and the country) who claimed that banning these compounds would have an adverse effect on food supplies. Despite the presence of chemicals that cause thyroid cancer in animals and humans, they reported, the fungicides were actually "safe."

During the Reagan years, working at the EPA meant living with a certain level of irony. The same month I was asked to acknowledge the "benefits" of dangerous fungicides, I went to a Capitol Hill reception honoring the twenty-fifth anniversary of the publication of Rachel Carson's *Silent Spring*. While there I spoke briefly to Congressman George E. Brown Jr., whom I had known for several years. He understood the difficulties I faced at the EPA and was supportive. The rest of the crowd was made up of environmental activists and congressional staff.

We listened to a moving speech by Carson's friend and disciple Shirley Briggs. Yet even as I was enjoying some good wine and canapés, I began to fear that Carson's warning had largely faded into history—and out of the public's consciousness. It was all too clear to me that—even with the EPA overseeing things—the volume of toxins used in America and their destructive impact had increased enormously since Carson's death in 1964.

Not long after this, I had breakfast with an EPA scientist colleague who told me that an elaborate and expensive EPA survey of pesticides in ground water was a disaster. This $10 million project's statistical design was fatally flawed, he said, since a large number of the study's water samples would come not from contaminated agricultural areas but from relatively clean forests and nonrural regions. This meant the results would be heavily diluted; the survey would inevitably "prove" that the contamination of groundwater with farm sprays was of no concern.

My friend also accused the laboratory, which had been hired by the EPA's water program, of using analytical methods so outdated that they would not even detect most poisons in the water. Within the Reagan administration, of course, this combination—incompetent lab practices and bad statistical design—meant the study would not be a failure, but a success: it would satisfy the administration's plan of showing there were no significant amounts of toxic substances in America's drinking water.[28]

CHAPTER 2

Pest Control: A Matter of Merchandising

I N July 1980, a young man from Cheektowaga, New York, named Thaddeus Jarzabek complained to the EPA that he had gotten "a good whiff" of a couple of pesticides, after which his life had never been the same. Jarzabek, just twenty-nine years old, said that he had been waking up "with a lot of tiny particles floating inside my eyeballs, and I developed haloes around lights at night." With no family history of eye trouble, Jarzabek was convinced the troubles had been caused by the "Insta-Fog" pesticides sprayed at the milk cooperative where he worked in upstate New York. Insta-Fog, it turned out, contained piperonyl butoxide, pyrethrins, and a substance called N-octyl-bicycloheptene dicarboxyme.

"On two shifts a week they sprayed over the production area with pesticides," he wrote. "I was required to sit in a small adjacent office and I still got a good whiff of this stuff. My eyesight has been permanently damaged. In all common sense and logic there must be some correlation between my exposure to these pesticides and this condition. There had to have been some causation. Things like this do not just happen!"

When Jarzabek tried looking up the medical hazards associated with the chemicals in question, he learned that they were "unknown."

"I would like to know how this stuff can be used around people if the health effects are unknown?" he wrote. "Aren't there supposed to be laws that require research to be done and to set exposure limits? I am hoping that you could help me find the answer to these questions."[1]

Rather than bringing some comfort to this injured man—rather than digging into those pesticides to find out how they had damaged Thaddeus Jarzabek's eyes—EPA rushed to the defense of the chemical industry, declaring the poisons innocent of all wrongdoing. "We have found no evidence of the three ingredients in question to cause the condition you described," the EPA declared on September 26, 1980. Jarzabek's condition could have been caused by "vitamin deficiency, high blood pressure and lack of sufficient sleep."

The story repeated itself a couple of years later, when a sixty-three-year-old man from Iowa nearly killed himself—in less than two hours—by using four cans of Ortho Indoor Plant Insect Spray. Here again, piperonyl butoxide, petroleum distillates, pyrethrins, and rotenone were among the ingredients in that product.

Within twenty-four hours of his exposure to this insecticide, both by inhalation and by getting it on both hands, the man experienced severe headache, urinary retention, and severe tremors of all four limbs. He was taken to the hospital, and within the next nine days he had developed peripheral neuropathy and was breathing only with the help of a machine. Doctors diagnosed the man with Guillain-Barre syndrome, a serious illness that can lead to paralysis.

"I realize that this Ortho product is not normally associated with producing toxic neuropathies," the man's lawyer wrote the EPA. "In view of this man's history, however, I am compelled to consider that he is suffering from such an acute toxic condition. Sixty days after the exposure he remains partly paralyzed."[2]

I discovered these two cases purely by accident, and I was left to wonder: Are such incidents of human poisoning by pesticides that include piperonyl butoxide common or rare? I wasn't sure. One thing

I did know was that dangerous pesticide ingredients are commonly deemed "safe" by agribusiness, bad science, and bad federal regulation. And some of the most dangerous ingredients are known by the benign (and entirely misleading) term "inert."

The EPA has long made a false distinction between so-called "active" ingredients and "inert" ingredients, or adjuvants. The first, of course, are responsible for the action of the toxic chemical. The role of the second set is less obvious. Inert ingredients are included in a chemical compound to aid in binding it together, or for making the pesticide more effective once it hits its target. From the adjective "inert," one would naturally assume that these chemicals would have no dangerous effects. Nothing could be further from the truth.

What the pesticide industry defines as "inert" ingredients are, in most cases, very toxic materials indeed. They can include poisons such as acetone, benzene, chlorobenzene, chloroform, ethylene oxide, formaldehyde, formic acid, methyl alcohol, naphthalene, ethylene thiouria, and petroleum distillates. But because of EPA's surreal "regulation" of both actives and inerts, a known toxic chemical like DDT can be branded "inert" and used in a pesticide. And because there are so many of these chemicals—about 1,800 inert ingredients, which can constitute up to 99 percent of an individual pesticide— their cumulative volume is a real concern. I will never forget the horror and disgust on the face of John Shaughnessy, a senior EPA scientist, whenever the words "petroleum distillates" came up. "We don't even bother to think about petroleum distillates," he would often say. "What's the use? They are carcinogens—all of them. What a terrible mess. And to think they are used as 'inerts' in so many pesticides."

Another EPA official, William Roessler, knew the absurdity of using the word "inert" to describe what are in fact highly toxic chemicals. Although these ingredients are used to make pesticides disperse or to stick to plants, they still show up as unwanted poisons both in the environment and in human food. "We are gradually beginning to realize that inert ingredients in pesticide formulations are not really inert; they could have an impact on the environment, on human and wildlife health, and may even contain toxic or otherwise undesirable contaminants," he said.[3]

Seven years later, in 1981, Kenneth Bailey, an EPA pharmacologist, put together a plan to regulate these misnamed "inert" ingredients. His logic was pure common sense: inert ingredients, being chemicals, are no more or less threatening than "active" ingredients, but in contrast to the active ingredients, which are tested for cancer and other life-threatening effects, inert ingredients are rarely, if ever, tested themselves. "If this regulatory trend continues," Bailey concluded, "inerts will ultimately present more of a potential health hazard than actives."

Bailey was no more successful than Roessler in changing the way millions of tons of "inert" pesticide ingredients are regulated. Some physicians, including epidemiologists like the EPA's Dr. John Kliewer, considered regulating inerts like the cancer-causing petroleum distillates "as important or perhaps in some cases even more important than the active ingredient."

A Canadian physician, John Crocker, discovered that these pesticide solvents, emulsifiers, and other such "inerts" turn the otherwise merely bothersome virus influenza B into the lethal Reye's syndrome, especially in children in the countryside who have the misfortune to be sprayed with a pesticide and to catch influenza. Some of these children die terrible deaths as their brains, viscera, and livers disintegrate.[4]

The EPA learned about Dr. Crocker's Reye's syndrome pesticide research but did very little to encourage, support, repeat, or initiate its own investigations into the etiology and pathology of that dreadful disease. In a March 11, 1980, memo, a senior EPA official described the possibility of any adverse effects on humans from solvents, emulsifiers, and drift control agents as "truly negligible." In 1982, another

EPA scientist gave the inert pesticide ingredients a clean bill of health. I asked him about the work of John Crocker. "Crocker's studies are worthless," he said.[5]

However, another EPA scientist, Jeff Kempter, was more astute when assessing the prevalence of inerts. "My guess is that the [Reagan] administration will not want to start digging into the inerts bucket-of-worms except perhaps for only the worst-worst bad actors" such as proven carcinogens, he wrote in a memo dated July 7, 1981. "We should probably offer a bare-bones minimum scenario, which at least would address the inerts we don't want to see in any pesticide product. [D]ealing with that many chemicals looks like a big job to me and the only alternative we have is to start chipping away at the [inerts] iceberg, but at the highest point where it counts."

Kempter was right. To this day, the bucket of worms remains untouched. This dangerous state of affairs essentially nullifies all reasonable efforts to know exactly the total volume of toxic chemicals farmers and lawn owners actually use.

Here's how the agency tries to guess: EPA economists prepare annual estimates of pesticide usage. They subscribe to a variety of company estimates. They also have access to EPA's "confidential business information," which includes companies' reports of the amounts of pesticides they manufacture. The EPA and USDA also fund surveys of pesticide usage. Out of all these numbers they come up with their own estimates, which they make public. But in no case do the EPA or USDA or private data companies include the massive numbers of pesticide "inerts" in their estimation of how much pesticide is used annually in the United States—or in the world.

For many at the EPA, inerts did not exist. They churned out color graphs that charted the annual volume of pesticide use and worked hard to convince themselves that pesticide use in the United States was in decline. These numbers were hard to believe.

In fact, inerts do more than hide the total impact of agrotoxins on the environment. Some of them are immediate threats to human health. Others—called synergists—are designed to increase the deadly effects of the active ingredients. They work by fouling the microsomal enzymes of the liver, which, left alone, would break highly toxic compounds into harmless molecules. But a pesticide with a synergist is like a killer with a machine gun rather than a pistol. With the synergist's ability to knock out the liver's lifesaving powers, the active ingredient—the killer gas, liquid, or dust—can cause a hundred times more devastation than it could alone.[6]

Piperonyl butoxide, the chemical that damaged Thaddeus Jarzabek's eyes, is a very popular synergist. Every year, consumers spray something like 25 to 30 million pounds of this chemical, via 4,200 pesticide products manufactured by about 900 companies. Piperonyl butoxide is especially mixed with pyrethrins, natural insecticides extracted from the flowers of chrysanthemum. Pyrethrins and piperonyl butoxide don't have a bad reputation, either separately or in combination, so mixing them is routine.

Chemists correctly guessed that this "inert" synergist would effectively destroy a pest's natural defenses against "active" poisons. The combination proved to be a spectacular success, with skyrocketing sales of aerosol sprays, fogging concentrates, emulsions, dusts, and wettable powders for homes, gardens, factories, institutions, farms, and food processing plants. Yet two known carcinogens—safrole and dihydrosafrole—are involved in the manufacture of this synergist. In addition, the synergist itself is a cocarcinogen: when piperonyl butoxide is mixed with freons (fluorocarbons, which were used as propellants of pressurized pesticide poison gases), it causes cancer in laboratory animals. Serious concerns also exist that this widely used poison may give rise to tumors, changing the genetic stuff of life and causing lethal defects to the newborn and even chemical castration.

These chemicals show up in surprising places, such as the standard multilayer supermarket paper bag. Which means that when you use that paper bag to store food or carry your groceries home, you risk contaminating your food with piperonyl butoxide.

In September 1981, buckling under pressure from industry and the Reagan administration, the EPA aborted a five-year effort to regulate piperonyl butoxide, claiming that farmers need not worry about how much piperonyl butoxide remains on crops when the synergist and its pesticide carrier are sprayed "in accordance with good agricultural practice."

Such policies inevitably kill; the only questions are when and how many. We don't know much about the victims of pesticide-powered agribusiness because as a society we often refuse to heed the warnings of some of our best scientists.

One such scientist is David Pimentel of Cornell University. He has been studying American agriculture for half a century, and his studies have long highlighted the environmental and social costs of pesticides. Using EPA data from the early 1990s, Pimentel figured out that in the United States, pesticides cause 300,000 poisonings per year; worldwide, the number is more than 26 million a year. Every year, worldwide, pesticides kill approximately 220,000 people and cause chronic disease in another 750,000.[7]

As troubling as these trends are, they are more infuriating because we have known about these poisons for close to seventy years. In 1949, thirteen years before Rachel Carson alerted the world to the unseen dangers of pesticides, A. D. Pickett, a field entomologist in Nova Scotia, Canada, blamed farmers for a chain of deadly ecological reactions. Posterity, he said, would condemn us "as despoilers on account of the indiscriminate dissemination of poisons." Man, he reminded us, is merely one in a vast multitude of species making a living on earth. "For thousands of years man accepted insects as part of the normal environment over which he had little or no control, and it is only within the last half century that we have actually made any real attempt to reduce their effectiveness as competitors," Pickett wrote.

A beetle in Colorado, for example, had survived forever by eating only its host plant, the buffalo burr. But when settlers arrived and planted long rows of potatoes, the bug—now known as the Colorado potato beetle—went "berserk." Farmers reacted by spraying their crops relentlessly, killing the bugs but damaging their soil in the process.

"Most people who know anything about natural history realize that in nature there are elaborate and intricately balanced mechanisms for limiting animal populations," Pickett wrote. "In the case of insects this balance is maintained in a variety of ways, but mostly by the pressures exerted by the physical environment such as weather, by the availability of food and biological control."

Pickett warned that the farmers' excessive reliance on toxic sprays to control insects could end up "creating agricultural and nutritional problems with such far-reaching results that we cannot simply return to some previous stage and start over again." Entire ecosystems, he said, were in danger of falling apart from "chain reactions that may have far-reaching results."[8]

Pickett urged North Americans to return to an agricultural and food system that would render farm chemicals obsolete. We could grow crops primarily for "the purpose of satisfying man's food requirements and not as a means of making particular human activities commercially profitable regardless of the overall effect on human welfare."

Pickett's prophetic words remain buried in the pages of a technical journal. Other scientists, however, continue to offer their own critiques of our country's love affair with poisons.

In his book *Pesticides and Politics*, Christopher Bosso described the 1950s as "the golden age of pesticides." I would never use "golden" to describe the period that gave rise to the pesticide industry. But such language does speak, perversely, to a time when America became infatuated—and then saturated—with the very poisons that made the work of industrial agribusiness possible.

For farm communities hooked on such destructive practices, the economic picture was just as dismal as their spraying habit. Some pesticides failed to work; others worked so well that they killed the crop along with everything else around the crop. Sometimes pesticides eliminate "pests," but most often they just disfigure natural cycles, giving rise to other pests.

This fact was well known even before the EPA came into existence. In Mexico, the national cotton industry failed after farmers concluded the only way to battle pests was to spray "broad-spectrum insecticides." What happened? The tobacco budworm became resistant to all available insecticides, and the cotton industry collapsed.[9]

Pesticide use is also causing agricultural systems to fail in the United States. Decades of pesticide abuse by potato farmers created storms of insects that devoured the potatoes—and far beyond the state that gave the bug its name. "The future for chemical control of the Colorado potato beetle on Long Island is not encouraging based on experiences of the past," wrote Maurie Semel of the Long Island Horticultural Research Laboratory in Riverhead, New York.[10]

Farmers, however, ignored these warnings, listening instead to the tireless chemical salesmen. They just sprayed and sprayed, and the companies that made the sprays became richer and more powerful. Inevitably, the power of these chemical industries reached straight into the halls of legislators—and the regulatory agencies they controlled.[11]

The chief enabling agents in this "golden age" were Congress—especially the agriculture appropriations subcommittee headed by Mississippi congressman Jamie Whitten—and the USDA, the mammoth federal establishment that both embraced and promoted industrial agriculture and the chemical industry on which it came to depend.

At its inception in 1970, the EPA inherited about 80 percent of its scientists from the USDA, which had long since been abandoned any pretense of controlling agricultural pesticides. The EPA scientists arrived at their new agency already fully indoctrinated into a culture comfortable doing the bidding of industry. The tradition of treating pesticides with reverence moved smoothly—lock, stock, and barrel—from USDA to EPA. In the 1970s and 1980s, the EPA approved between 450 and 500 new pesticides, nearly half of the total sprays licensed in the United States in the last century.

Despite discovering—throughout the 1970s—that many pesticides had won approval on the basis of fraud, deception, and bad science, the EPA dismantled ten of its research laboratories. This was a catastrophe. Like libraries, labs are the eyes of the responsible regulator. To say the least, the more power industry grabs, the more important oversight labs become in making sure the products industry is churning out are not harmful to the public. Independent lab tests tell you what chemicals end up in the soil, in harvested food, or in drinking water. Industry knows this, of course. They also know that the fewer the labs, the more they can get away with.

All but a very few EPA labs were closed in the late 1970s and 1980s, a natural outgrowth of a government that had no interest in speaking the truth about poisons.

By the early 1970s, it was becoming clear that corporate greed had fully corrupted pesticide science and the policy that emerged from it. Although pesticides were first formulated in the nineteenth century, in recent years they had evolved into compounds having "spectacular toxicity," wrote two University of California scientists, R. L. Doutt and Ray F. Smith. These new toxins "proliferated enormously. They spread over the entire globe. They are characteristic of our time and have confronted us with another environmental crisis, outstanding in terms of massiveness, extensiveness and rate of change."

"There is probably not a single square centimeter of the earth's surface that has not felt the impact of man," Doutt and Smith wrote. "The astounding advances of modern science and technology have put these powerful chemical weapons into the bristling arsenal of all pest control practitioners. The pesticide salesman has no natural enemy in the agribusiness jungle."[12]

Political support for Big Agriculture and Big Chemical made the explosive growth of pesticides inevitable—so much so that Bosso spoke of a "pesticides subgovernment" operating independently of the federal government as a whole. The political rhetoric used to press chemicals on the American public sounds familiar to contemporary ears: new technologies made a war on pests possible, Bosso wrote; national security made it "imperative."[13]

The image of a pesticide industry working in the shadow of the federal government did not go entirely unnoticed. The use of farm sprays in the United States is nothing but "a massive pesticide orgy in which expenditure, waste, and pollution spiral while pest-control efficiency dwindles," according to Robert van den Bosch, a distinguished biology professor at the University of California, Berkeley, and an astute observer of the pest control business. Van den Bosch had particularly harsh things to say about the collusion between chemical companies and the scientists and administrators of land grant universities, whom he compared to a pro-pesticide "mafia."

This culture "has its *famiglie*, its *capi*, its *consiglieri*, its *soldati*, its *avvocati*, its lobbyists, its front organizations, its PR apparatus, and its 'hit men,'" Van den Bosch wrote. "It owns politicians, bureaucrats, researchers, county agents, administrators, and elements of the media, and it can break those who don't conform."[14]

Paul Ehrlich, an eminent professor of biological sciences at Stanford University, considers pesticides "an ideal product"—like heroin. "They promise paradise and deliver addiction," Ehrlich wrote. "And dope and pesticide peddlers both have only one cure for addiction: use more and more of the product at whatever cost in dollars and human suffering (and in the case of pesticides, in environmental degradation)."[15]

The drug addiction metaphor fits well. Like drug abusers, industrial farmers "go to higher and more frequent dosages, and they are not reluctant to use more persistent and more toxic materials," wrote S. E. McGregor, an expert on bee pollination at the USDA. "There is great pressure upon the grower by the chemical companies to use insecticides to excess, and even upon State officials not to discourage such usage. Insecticides are like the dope drugs. The more they are used the more powerful the next one must be to give satisfaction— and therein develops the spiraling effect, the pesticide treadmill. The chemical salesman, in pressuring the grower to use his product, prac- tically assumes the role of the 'dope pusher.' Once the victim, the grower, is 'hooked' he becomes a steady and an ever-increasing user."[16]

In the 1970s, one place you could find an "agribusiness jungle" was Hawaii, a state where three large corporations were able to exempt themselves from one of the EPA's rare regulatory successes. In the 1970s the EPA got rid of heptachlor, a DDT-like pesticide that had caused enormous ecological harm and had possibly caused cancer in humans. But the Velsicol Corporation, which produced the spray, and the Dole and Del Monte companies, which owned the sprawling pine- apple farms of Hawaii and used heptachlor liberally, convinced the EPA that banning this poison would hurt their business, and the EPA allowed them to continue selling and spraying heptachlor for years.

The results were predictable. By 1982, heptachlor was turning up in unexpected places, such as milk. Why? Because pineapple growers had chopped up the heptachlor-loaded leaves of the pineapple plant and fed them to the island's dairy cows. This so angered Senator Daniel K. Inouye that he sent a letter to John Tolan, vice president of the Pineapple Growers Association of Hawaii, excoriating both the industry and the EPA, which was supposedly in charge of monitoring it.

"The pesticide contamination problem in Hawaii is much bigger than most of the public currently imagines," Inouye wrote. "The EPA has been ineffective in enforcing its regulations governing the use of pesticides in Hawaii, and widespread abuse of pesticides continues— both in use and application."

Pineapple growers were notorious for ignoring the state law that required they wait a full year before selling fruit sprayed with heptachlor. But it wasn't just the pineapple industry, Inouye said. The sugar industry was using heptachlor in its cane fields, and workers were regularly seen spraying pesticides from the back of trucks without wearing any of the required protective gear. "State enforcement and testing procedures are notoriously lax, and if people really started looking for pesticides in Hawaii's environment, they would find them in alarming quantities," Inouye said.

I don't know how the pineapple farmers of Hawaii responded to Inouye's criticism, but the EPA ignored it. The agency's own researchers in Hawaii had been documenting the terrible ecological and health effects of plantation agriculture for decades, and nothing Inouye said surprised them. If anything, Inouye barely scratched the surface of pesticide abuse in Hawaii—or throughout the rest of the country.

As cogs in this system, farmers are often too close to the pesticide merchants to see them for what they are. They rely on them, and they find it difficult to acknowledge that pesticides might be damaging their crops. In 1974, an EPA study found that when farmers needed information about sprays or pest problems, as many as half rushed to their chemical dealers, who give them expensive and plentiful prescriptions, disregarding other, less harmful alternatives. The result? Chemical sprays reduced the yield of crops.

A decade later, farmers were still putting themselves at the mercy of the chemical salesmen to answer their questions and solve their technical problems. Chemical salesmen rewarded farmers with food, taking them out to dine at least three times a year to keep the taste of wine and prime rib fresh in their mind for the next growing season. In Iowa, farmers came to love these feasts, and more than 75 percent of them relied on their neighborhood chemical merchants for agricultural advice. In Georgia, where, as of 1980, only 33 percent of the farmers were more than fifty-five years old, 75 percent of the farmers rushed to their USDA county agent with their questions about agricultural practice.[17]

Although they were public employees, county extension agents were even more docile than the EPA in doing the bidding of the chemical industry; county agents resented the little that the EPA occasionally did to guide farmers to protect the environment. About half of the farmers of Georgia were small farmers, though they spent a fortune, in aggregate, for the chemicals they put on and in the land.

Robert Metcalf was another scientist all too aware of the cozy relations between government, academia, pesticide companies, and the industrial-sized plantations of corn or soybeans. A University of Illinois professor, Metcalf was a genius of his times: he had been active in the 1940s and 1950s when the country accelerated its attempt to control nature. And his knowledge of the pesticide industry was personal: he had invented the compounds known as carbamates, which were less toxic than the widely distributed organophosphates. When the University of California, Riverside, refused to patent his invention, American Cyanamid made a fortune on it.

Metcalf also had a hand in the development of pesticide synergists like piperonyl butoxide, which increased the toxicity of pesticides. But after witnessing the abuse of his discoveries—and seeing the general misuse of pesticides—Metcalf became a fierce critic of the agribusiness-pesticide complex. He developed methods for detecting pesticide residues in food, and he began advocating for biological control of insects. Metcalf could see the dangers of monoculture farming that requires farmers, for instance, to spend a billion dollars a year just to spray for corn rootworms. Those farmers probably knew—and should have known—that rootworm damage can be prevented simply by rotating crops, but with the urging of the marketers of chemical sprays, they adopted this dangerous practice.[18]

In the late 1960s, Metcalf assisted in the government's greatest assessment of the risks of pesticides, a somber study that claimed that pesticides, like other chemicals, had become so intertwined in American agriculture that "we must learn to live with them." However, the report also warned about the potential dangers of these sprays and recommended regulating them promptly to safeguard future generations. Even though science is constantly evolving—each generation may prove a previous generation's conclusions incomplete or even wrong—scientists should always come to the aid of policymakers trying to make the right decisions about pesticides.

"Safety evaluation is an edifice whose construction is never completed; nor does it remain functional without periodic reconstruction," the study reported. "All that the public has a right to expect is that regulatory decisions should be the products of scientific competence and experience, mature judgment and full possession of all existing data."[19]

As clear and sensible as these sentiments were, the truth from the very beginning was that good science about the dangers of pesticides was being ignored and even scorned. In 1969, the same year this report was released, Robert van den Bosch testified in a California court that the pesticide industry was out of control. Speaking on behalf of farmworkers, who were at grave risk of chemical contamination, Van den Bosch said that pest control in the United States "is essentially not an ecological matter. It is largely a matter of merchandising." "In essence," Bosch said, "we are using the wrong kind of materials in the wrong places at the wrong times in excessive amounts."[20]

In 1987, Robert Metcalf issued his own warning about pesticides, taking an open and public position that challenged his own colleagues in the scientific establishment. By this time he had witnessed the abandonment of ethical science, and he was fed up with the corruption pervading the agricultural-industrial complex. He had also lived to see the unraveling of his own contribution to the farmers' weapons against pests. "The short-sighted and irresponsible use of pesticides and antibiotics is producing strains of monster-bugs that are resistant to our chemical weapons," Metcalf wrote. "The outlook is dismal—and getting worse."[21]

And so it had. As chemical abuse continued to spread, more and more toxic compounds were required to do the same work. By the early 1980s, some 432 insects and related organisms were immune to one or more bug sprays. Fungicides were also becoming useless to a significant degree. Agricultural pesticides "have often been used unnecessarily, excessively, and otherwise abused such as to shorten their useful life," two University of California scientists, Boysie E. Day and George P. Georghiou, testified before a congressional committee on July 12, 1981.

A foundational myth of industrialized agriculture is that sprays have something to do with increasing the yields of crops. But we have known since for at least forty years that pesticides actually *stifle* the yield of growing crops, as you would expect from poisons that indiscriminately kill insects, plants, and countless other forms of life. In 1970, J. Sedivy, a European scientist, published a study showing that after dusting the pollen of alfalfa with melipax, a toxaphene-like spray, no more than 10.5 percent of the grains would germinate, compared to 62.1 percent of the pollen left clear of the deadly dust. With only 0.3 percent of fribal emulsion, another poison similar to toxaphene, only 28.2 percent of grains germinated, compared to 81.5 percent of the grains sprouting in the absence of the toxin.[22]

In 1971, three other scientists, A. G. Gentile, K. J. Gallagher, and Z. Santner, found that as little as 100 parts per million of a spray called naled would completely destroy the germination of both tomato and petunia pollen. They also discovered that other pesticides—DDT, dicofol, azinphos-methyl, dichlorvos, Gardona, and endosulfan—made it impossible for *all* pollen to germinate. No less important, those poisons blocked the pollen tubes from reaching their full length. So these chlorine-based toxins and nerve-poisonous pesticides made tomato and petunia and other plants not more but less productive.[23]

Other studies proved that the less a farm was sprayed with chlorine-based insecticides (primarily aldrin), the higher the corn yields.[24]

The scientific results are powerful, and clearly counter to the prevailing mythology of agricultural pesticides. But this brand of science has been hard to come by for one simple reason: most academic scientists, when they examine America's agricultural system, don't ask the right questions. Their work is funded largely by agribusiness, so—naturally—scientists tend to believe this system is the best in the world, and that pesticides make that system possible. Such delusions become intransigent beliefs, both within and without the government.

And all along, nature continues to take its course. By 2003, there were 520 insects and mites, 273 weeds, 150 plant diseases, and 10 rodents that were resistant to at least one fungicide or pesticide.[25]

In 2005, Cornell's David Pimentel reported that the use of pesticides had come to cost the public about $10 billion per year: more than $1 billion for damage to public health, $1.5 billion for the increasing resistance of pests due to the overuse of pesticides, $1.4 billion for the loss of crops, $2.2 billion for losses in wild bird populations, and $2.0 billion for groundwater contamination.[26]

Some of the chemicals causing all this trouble are known as pyrethroids, part of a new class of extremely toxic insecticides that in fantastically small amounts also kill fish and other water animals.[27] Despite their names, the pyrethroids are not closely related to the naturally occurring compound pyrethrum. Popular variations like permethrin, pydrin, and cypermethrin are actually similar to the chlorine-like chemicals toxaphene and DDT. They make organophosphates (nerve gases) even more acutely toxic. Pyrethroids also resemble DDT-like compounds because they are fat-soluble—meaning that they accumulate in fat tissue—and they resemble parathion-like nerve toxins because they poison the nervous system.[28]

Pyrethroids bind themselves so tightly to soil particles that they can be extremely difficult to detect. They may stay in the sediment of rivers and lakes for more than a year, continuously killing or incapacitating small fish.

Pyrethroids are so toxic they are sprayed in just ounces per acre. Yet even in such small quantities, the poison has is "acutely toxic" to zooplankton at all concentration levels, eliminating it almost completely. Zooplankton is linked with phytoplankton (microscopic plants) and the fish that consume them, so the toxin's destructive powers amplify as it spreads through an ecosystem and moves up the food chain. Cypermethrin, more toxic to life than permethrin, is deadly to some water animals in the low parts per trillion[29].

Despite the acutely deleterious nature of pyrethroids, EPA nonetheless "registered" them for use. In 1990, a number of states asked EPA for an "emergency exemption" to use a pyrethroid called esfenvalerate (or asana) to battle grasshoppers. The request would allow spraying this extremely powerful poison on an additional 20 million acres of land in North and South Dakota, Minnesota, Kansas, Montana, Oklahoma, Colorado, and Wyoming.

When this request reached the desk of James Ackerman, chief of the EPA's ecological effects branch, he was stunned. Asana was "extremely toxic to aquatic organisms," Ackerman formally pointed out on April 11, 1990. The lethal concentration for the freshwater animal *Daphnia magna* was as minute as 0.032 parts per billion; for the estuarine animal *Mysidopsis bahia*, it was 0.008 parts per billion. Given the way poisons bioaccumulate—several contaminated smaller fish being eaten by single larger fish, who are in turn eaten by larger fish, or birds, or mammals—these numbers—especially given the 400 percent increase in the acreage for the spraying of asana—would be dangerous for countless species, including our own.

Worse still, over half of this land would be in the "prairie pothole" region of the Midwest, "which has been well documented as the most important production grounds for our national waterfowl treasure," Ackerman wrote.[30]

Despite its founding mandate as an agency devoted to protecting the environment, the EPA routinely does just about everything based not on health risks but on the basis of dollars and cents. It nearly always weighs the costs of protecting people and the natural world from pollution against the benefits that unregulated pollution brings to businessmen and manufacturers. Allowing nerve poisons and cancer-causing sprays on America's farms and vineyards may kill or injure farmworkers, but it will benefit industrial grape growers and chemical merchants. Since farm workers, particularly those who migrate throughout the country, have little social support in the United States, EPA finds it easy to side with the owners and users of poisons.[31]

EPA does not advertise its bias. It tests and pushes its unethical policies under the cover of science, but it does not reveal just how compromised this science actually is. For example, farmworkers are on the front line of pesticide danger, yet the agency marshals its considerable regulatory authority to "prove" that migrant farmworkers face "no unreasonable adverse risk" in grape fields drenched with nerve pesticides and carcinogens. Meanwhile, its economists and biologists largely ignore the "costs" of pesticides (such as their chances of causing cancer) and instead collect data on their "benefits," that is, their potential to make money for the companies that produce them.

It goes without saying, of course, that if farmworkers are at risk from these poisons, so, too, are the people who eat what they grow.

Should a case ever be made that the EPA should remove a certain chemical from the market, scientists responsible for the "benefits assessment" of pesticides typically exaggerate the economic "loss" to farmers. Take a toxin off the market, and farmers might have to spray a more expensive chemical, and consumers would pay higher prices for food. Rarely is the cost of illness included in these economic "assessments."

When the EPA banned DDT in 1972, the chemical industry and large farmers made loud and dire predictions about food shortages and hunger. Yet ever since, organic farmers have continued to produce crops without DDT or any other synthetic chemicals. Still, EPA economists refuse to cite any evidence on the benefits of nonchemical pest control methods. The only thing that interests them is keeping the pesticide system intact; should there be a serious problem with one pesticide, they simply strive to replace one chemical with another.[32]

The "benefits analysis" process is simply another device, in other words, for the perpetuation of the pesticide regime demanded by the country's industrial farmers. In truth, the only "benefits" of this process have been flowing to the manufacturers of these toxins who hold seventeen-year patent-monopolies. Over their lives, some of the registered, EPA-approved pesticides can earn $50 to $100 million. Such phenomenal earnings come from the almost astronomical amounts of pesticides farmers and others use. In 1983, the Department of Food and Agriculture of California calculated that 743,186,620 pounds of pesticide active ingredients were sold in that state alone.[33]

In 1990, a group of EPA scientists working out of Dallas reported on the ecological and human impacts of pesticide the country's huge south central region. "Man depends upon a predictable global ecology for air quality, water, food, shelter, and medicines," the scientists concluded. "Ecological problems such as loss of terrestrial and wetland habitats result in species extinction and overall loss of biological diversity. Humans depend upon a diverse plant and animal gene pool for food production. If genetic diversity is diminished, adaption to changing environments will decrease as will resistance to diseases, pests, and the elements. The end result will be fewer and less productive varieties of food and fiber crops. The net effect of decreasing diversity in ecosystems is an unstable system."

Ecological problems in the middle of the country would have dire consequences for the huge water supply found in the Ogallala Aquifer; the elimination of wetlands in Louisiana; and the additive discharges of chemicals to surface water from agriculture (nitrogen, phosphates, pesticides, and animal waste), industrial discharges (organic and inorganic), and urban runoff (organics, sewage, pesticides).

"Although humans are one species among thousands, they are the only species that can chemically and biologically alter the planet," the scientists wrote. "Human activity has changed the course of evolution through agricultural and industrial technology; we must begin to understand that, ecologically, humans have a responsibility to preserve the earth's life if but to protect human life. We have not demonstrated the knowledge, wisdom, or compassion to accept this role."[34]

The concern of my colleagues for some kind of balance between humans and nature is an ancient philosophical concern. Aristotle acknowledged the mystery and majesty of animals; for Plato, earth was not merely alive, but was itself the oldest of the gods. The value of a healthy—if not divine—natural world continues to be at the core of civilization.

In the modern United States, we have allowed industry to utterly disregard these traditions in the service of their own self-interest. In 1974, an EPA contractor, Rosmarie von Rumker, expressed astonishment and anxiety over the habit of the farmers to keep drenching the same land with poisons. The incessant growing of corn and soybeans means "heavy applications of chemical pesticides and fertilizers are made to the same land year after year."

"Most of the chemicals remain in the upper 1–3 inches of topsoil, and their routes and rates of degradation under field conditions are often not known," she said. "It is surprising and somewhat alarming how little information is available on the individual or collective effects of these chemicals on the soil microflora and -fauna [soil microplants and animals] and on the long-term fertility of the topsoil, one of our most important resources."[35]

Distinguished scientists including A. D. Pickett, Rachel Carson, Robert Metcalf, Paul Ehrlich, Robert van den Bosch, and David Pimentel have made similar statements. They have spoken out, protesting the violence we legalize in the "registration" of barely tested petrochemicals. Van den Bosch especially spoke in stark and graphic terms about agribusiness and the destructive practices of the chemical industries, which he dubbed the "pesticide mafia."

CHAPTER 3

The Dioxin Molecule of Death

I N 1978, eight women from the small western Oregon town of Alsea sent a letter to the EPA documenting a frightening series of miscarriages—all of which had occurred shortly after the spring herbicide spraying season. The women wanted to know if there was a connection between their spontaneous abortions and the weed killers that timber companies had been spraying in the forests surrounding their homes.[1]

The EPA administrator, Douglas Costle, found the letter disquieting. He sent it to Steven Jellinek, the agency's top toxics official, who asked staff scientists to look into the connection between the spraying of these herbicides and the incidence of women giving birth to children without brains or with fatal brain defects.

The results of the study were damning. EPA investigators found highly toxic compounds known as dioxins in the sediment of a local creek in Alsea, and they discovered that these poisons were seeping into the bodies of the people of Alsea, with devastating results: women living near a highway that had been sprayed with herbicides were having miscarriages at nearly triple the normal rate.[1]

Over the next few years, what started as a local health scare would turn into a seismic environmental moment that indelibly revealed the troubling relationship between the EPA and the chemical industry. It would show just how vulnerable the American public can be when its environmental watchdogs are compromised by powerful businesses. And it would shine a strong light on a chemical compound that by the late 1970s the American public was becoming all too familiar with: Agent Orange.

Agent Orange is best known as the acutely toxic defoliant used by the United States as a chemical weapon during the Vietnam War. The compound was a fifty-fifty mixture of two widely used herbicides: 2,4,5-trichlorophenoxyacetic acid (known as 2,4,5-T) and 2,4-dichlorophenoxyacetic acid (or 2,4-D). Both of these compounds had been used domestically for years as agricultural weed killers.

The trouble with these chemicals had to do with unintended consequences—in this case, the inadvertent creation of dangerous chemical by-products. The term "dioxin" is actually a generic word for a group of more than two hundred powerful contaminants: 75 are chlorinated dibenzo-p-dioxins (CDDs) and 135 are chlorinated dibenzofurans (CDFs). It's important to understand that no company intentionally manufactures dioxins. They are an industrial by-product arising during the production of compounds like pesticides. When you make 2,4,5-T, for example, you also get a lethal compound called 2,3,7,8-tetrachlorodibenzo-p-dioxin (or 2378-TCDD).

Although these sprays were certified as harmless to humans both by their American manufacturers (Dow Chemical, Monsanto, Diamond Shamrock, and Hooker Chemicals) and by the U.S. Department of Agriculture, they were nonetheless contaminated by TCDD-dioxin, which turned out to be one of the most acutely toxic molecules known to man. Its widespread effects in the Vietnam War—not only on the Vietnamese but also on our own soldiers—vividly illustrate what might be called "dioxin's revenge."[2]

The United States, ignoring the international 1925 accords against chemical warfare, had sprayed the forests of Vietnam with dioxin-contaminated Agent Orange in order to destroy the jungles that gave cover to the movements of the Viet Cong and the North Vietnamese army. But using these dangerous compounds also meant that America was waging war on nature itself.

The United States sprayed millions of gallons of herbicides over the forests and rice fields of Vietnam. The result: a huge swath of forest and countryside, 4.5 million acres, became a wasteland of barren and deadly soil and poisonous water. No one knows exactly how much Agent Orange the U.S. Air Force dumped over Vietnam and Laos between 1962 and 1971, but in 1987 the Air Force estimated it had sprayed 17.4 million gallons. Close to 5 million Vietnamese were exposed to this horror; four hundred thousand died or were maimed, and half a million children were born with birth defects. Death would remain lurking in the land for decades to come.[3]

There was no secret about the horrendous effects of this chemical on man and nature. Only months after this weaponized toxin was introduced, both Vietnamese and American soldiers showed signs of dioxin's insults to the body: fluid-filled cysts on the skin, and particularly on the face. But time would bring far worse problems: soldiers and airmen who had sprayed Agent Orange from aircraft or been exposed to it on the ground began to exhibit symptoms of everything from persistent numbness, dizziness, and memory loss to depression, violent rages, and suicidal tendencies. Many of these soldiers ultimately died of cancer. After the war, thousands of veterans would testify that they suffered neurological problems, impotence, miscarriages, and deformed babies.[4]

Yet it would take years for the U.S. government to acknowledge that our veterans had experienced debilitating symptoms of dioxin poisoning. Congressman Bob Eckhardt, Democrat of Texas, accused the Department of Health, Education and Welfare (now the Department of Health and Human Services) of dragging its feet in researching and studying the problems of veterans. And Senator Charles Percy, Republican of Illinois, scolded the Department of

Veterans Affairs for failing to take up the veterans' Agent Orange complaints.[5]

After years of denial, the government was finally forced to respond to mounting clinical evidence of the impact of this chemical time bomb, even in those who had been exposed to only trace amounts of the compound. There were no Purple Hearts awarded to those gravely injured by dioxin, but their wounds were real—and they never healed. The suffering inflicted on the people of Vietnam, North and South, combatant and noncombatant alike, was, for many years, an unacknowledged legacy of shame inherited by our country.

What the women in Alsea, Oregon, were learning, to their horror, was that the same chemicals that were causing such trouble among Vietnam vets were now entering their own bodies as well.

In March 1979, after the Alsea study revealed a link between the herbicides and miscarriages, the EPA published "an emergency suspension" restricting most of the uses of 2,4,5-T (a major constituent of Agent Orange) and Silvex, an herbicide similar to 2,4,5-T. Two months later, despite industry pressure to do nothing, the agency canceled most uses of both 2,4,5-T and Silvex.[6]

This should have been a fairly straightforward decision. After all, the EPA was simply moving to ban a chemical that had been shown to have terrible effects on soldiers abroad and pregnant women at home. Yet the effort to ban 2,4,5-T had dramatic consequences for EPA employees trying to do their job. Sales of 2,4,5-T and other dioxin-laced pesticides were in the hundreds of millions of dollars, and the EPA's discovery of the dangers of these compounds threatened some very big businesses. The chemical companies that made these pesticides wanted payback.

Dow Chemical tried to "silence us," Hale Vandermer, an EPA investigator, explained to me. "It immediately launched a campaign of disinformation to discredit our epidemiological study, ridiculing us in the scientific community."

Inside the EPA, the scientists responsible for the Oregon study were "dead," Vandermer said. Senior EPA officials began "demolition right in our branch." Scientists involved in the Alsea investigation saw their careers, or at least their effectiveness, come to a premature end. They were relegated to administrative positions in which, the EPA reckoned, they would never again do work that might harm the interests of the chemical industry.[7]

The Oregon study taught EPA staffers like Vandermer a bitter lesson about the ruthlessness of industry executives and their apologists and enablers inside the EPA. The dioxin study "destroyed our epidemiological program," Vandermer said.

The agency's epidemiology team was a network of physicians and toxicologists in some of the country's leading medical schools doing original research on pesticides and public health. In the early 1970s we had been spending some $15 million per year, and at this time, in 1983, "we barely had the program doing anything, with a little more than $1 million a year," Vandermer said.

According to Vandermer, "The beauty of that network was that for a modest sum we had the field capability for both monitoring and investigation of a problem. Immediately after an accident, for instance, our medical advisers would be on the scene asking questions, collecting data, offering aid. But more than that, our epidemiological program built a tradition of training, research and education in agricultural medicine and public health. Our investigators published hundreds of articles in a number of scientific journals. They solved many problems, and, fundamentally, they forced the medical and scientific establishments to wake up to the real public health dangers of pesticides."

Hale Vandermer was right. The discovery that one of mankind's most toxic substances had been used in the very backyards of pregnant women did not become a shining example of the kind of public health protection the EPA had been founded to provide. It became, for the agency, a kiss of death.

And that was just the beginning.

On March 22, 1980, a woman named Lorraine Carter from the town of Mineral, Washington, sent a handwritten letter to Edwin Johnson, essentially repeating the plea of the Alsea women of Oregon.

"The communities of Elbe, Mineral, and Ashford, Washington are experiencing some unexplained health problems, and we would like the E.P.A. to undertake an epidemiological study of the area," Carter wrote. "We first became concerned because of an unusually high miscarriage rate in the town of Ashford (population 450). Ten women became pregnant from late July to early October. Eight of these women miscarried from late October to March."

A month later, April 22, 1980, Carter and ten other women from Mineral, Elbe, and Ashford sent a more detailed letter to Doug Costle, the EPA administrator. They said that from January 1979 to March 11, 1980, thirteen pregnancies ended with ten miscarriages, "with a cluster of nine miscarriages within a 6 month span." And it wasn't just people who were suffering: "[T]here are numerous reports of goats, cattle, and sheep that have become barren; rabbits, cats and dogs giving birth to deformed young, or having persistent recent histories of miscarriages, dead tropical fish, dead bee hives, etc., and reports of deformed wildlife, and a notable decrease of birds and squirrels, and gardens that have mysteriously withered and died."

The story had a familiar ring. This time the culprit wasn't 2,4,5-T, but its twin, the other half of Agent Orange—a compound known as 2,4-D. Lorraine Carter reported that her community had been sprayed by 2,4-D and "a variety of other herbicides." She told Costle she knew from the experience of those in other communities that these chemicals could cause miscarriages.

Indeed, inside the EPA, the dangers of 2,4-D were becoming increasingly worrisome. "Private citizens and environmental organizations from numerous locations throughout the country are expressing their thoughts and fears that miscarriages (spontaneous abortions) and birth defects in their communities are occurring in alarming numbers because of 2,4-D exposure," an internal EPA memo noted. An EPA response officer cited examples of 2,4-D tragedies in the Swan Valley, Montana; Broken Bow, Oklahoma; Trego, Wisconsin; Ashford, Washington; and several locations in Oregon. He also made a case for undertaking a variety of studies for a better understanding of the impact of 2,4-D.

But nothing happened, largely because by this time the EPA was ensnared in yet another battle with Dow Chemical. And as had been the case with the battle over 2,4,5-T, there were both lives and hundreds of millions of dollars at stake.[8]

THE FIVE RIVERS DECEPTION

In July 1979, just two months after the banning of 2,4,5-T and just before the women from Mineral voiced their own worries about 2,4-D, three more Oregon women began complaining of spontaneous miscarriages and other medical effects from being contaminated by toxic herbicides.[9]

In July 1979, the EPA received a letter from five women, including Melyce Connelly, who lived in the Five Rivers village, not far from Alsea, in Oregon's Siuslaw National Forest. The women begged the EPA administrator to ensure that two herbicides, 2,4-D and picloram, "cease to be sprayed until their safety has been unequivocally established, and that the miscarriages and the health of the population be studied immediately."[10]

The women had a right to expect prompt and trustworthy answers to their questions. What they got was years of bungling and ineptitude.

In essence, Edwin Johnson, the director of EPA's pesticide programs, asked his staff to repeat in Five Rivers what it had done in Alsea: test for dioxin contamination in samples taken from water and sediment as well as from humans and animals. Johnson's assistants asked the Epidemiological Studies Program of Colorado State

University—which was funded by EPA—to carry out the Five Rivers study.

On November 2, 1979, Johnson wrote a letter to Melyce Connelly assuring her that the water and sediment samples from the Five Rivers area "are being analyzed for 2,4-D, picloram, 2,4,5-T, Silvex, and dioxin." In addition, he promised Connelly that she would "receive the results of these analyses directly, as soon as they are available."

The EPA, however, did no such thing. Connelly received nothing from him or his staff. In fact, the investigation seemed designed to fail. Jim Weaver, the congressman from Oregon representing the women of Five Rivers, would later describe the Five Rivers study as "a morass of misinformation."

The EPA "assured the residents of the Five Rivers area that they would 'receive the results of these analyses,'" Weaver's letter said. "Nearly four years later, not one resident has been notified, and the study remains unfinished."[11]

Weaver told William Ruckelshaus, the former Nixon appointee who had returned from industry to run EPA again under Reagan, that he shared the Oregon women's "frustration and anger," and he demanded that the EPA hand over all documents related to the Five Rivers study. "Many Americans feel they can no longer trust the agency's credibility or forthrightness," Weaver said.

What happened next would hardly reassure Weaver, his constituents, or anyone else.

As promised, experts from Colorado State University collected their samples from the environment, the animals, and the women in the Five Rivers region and sent them to an EPA laboratory at Bay St. Louis, Mississippi. The samples included drinking water sediment and tissues from a mouse, cat, shrew, bird, and a "baby born without a brain."[12]

The samples then traveled from Mississippi to Professor Michael Gross at the University of Nebraska–Lincoln. But Gross analyzed the samples only for dioxin, because no one from EPA asked him to also examine the samples for 2,4,5-T, 2,4-D, Silvex, and picloram, as the EPA had promised the women of Five Rivers. Still, he reported, some of the samples had dioxin levels ranging from 160 to 5,800 parts per trillion.

Dr. Gross then sent the results of his work to the EPA's dioxin coordinator in Washington, D.C., but it apparently went no further. This was an extraordinary lapse, considering the toxicity of dioxin and what was at stake for these women and their families. Meanwhile, Dr. Gross had to answer questions about dioxins in a lawsuit brought against EPA, so he released the results of his analyses.[13]

Then something strange happened. An ABC News investigation discovered that some samples contaminated with dioxin, which had been sent to the EPA lab in Mississippi, had somehow become mixed up with samples from another site in Michigan. How could this have happened? How had the samples been misidentified?

One version of how the samples reached their destination comes from a senior EPA official. According to Homer Hall, deputy director, Benefits and Use Division, Office of Pesticide Programs, EPA, Colorado State University scientists sent sediment samples from Oregon and sludge samples from Region V to Dr. Mike Gross at the University of Nebraska for analysis. The attorney for the plaintiff alleged that "this was all a part of an EPA coverup."[14]

If the mix-up was frightening for citizens and embarrassing to the EPA, it could hardly be seen as an isolated example of bureaucratic mismanagement. The truth was, the EPA had made its mind up about 2,4-D before the Five Rivers disaster study had even been concluded. The EPA had evidence showing dioxin contamination in Oregon for three years, but they refused to release it because of the study's certain effects on the regulatory fate of 2,4,5-T. With 2,4-D, there was too much at stake. Not because of threats to human health, but—once again—because of threats to industry profits.[15]

In episodes of finger pointing, recrimination, or blundering, bureaucracies always resort to official inquiries, and in this case the

EPA conducted two in-house investigations. The Office of Pesticide Programs produced a report declaring itself innocent of all error and blaming the confusion over the samples on no one in particular. "The confusion of the samples from Five Rivers with those from Region V seems to have been a clerical error committed by the Nebraska laboratory," an EPA report said. "While there was no actual mix-up in the identity of the samples themselves but only in the reporting of the results, this error is another lapse [in the investigation by the EPA.]"[16]

The Office of the Inspector General, drawing on an early version of the report of the Office of Pesticide Programs, also somehow found very little wrong with the way the Five Rivers study had been done. "It appears that (a) the samples were never analyzed for herbicides; (b) the TCDD [dioxin] analysis of the samples was incomplete; and (c) the people of Five Rivers had never been advised of the available results" despite repeated legal efforts to get them, an EPA report said. The regional office apparently never received the results of the analysis of its samples, and the mislabeling of the Region V samples as samples from Oregon "seemed to be a clerical error in an EPA cooperative laboratory; there was no actual mixup of the samples."[17]

Once again, the constant shuffling of the EPA bureaucracy appeared to be at the root of the problem. John C. Martin, the EPA's inspector general, pointed out that the reorganization upheaval of 1976–1980 contributed to EPA's "failure" to adequately complete the Alsea Study or respond to the Five Rivers incident. But in a way, those reorganizations were not a failure, but a success: they succeeded in demoralizing, demoting, and removing the very people trying to carry out the EPA's mission.

Once again, it seemed that every time someone outside the EPA warned about the dangerous effects of an enormously popular pesticide, EPA regulators would rush to defend it. Bad data was coming to the EPA not merely from the Five Rivers case, but also from the battle with Dow over 2,4,5-T and, almost simultaneously, from the Colorado organophosphate study. In a furious move, senior managers responded precisely the way industry would have wanted them to: they broke up the Health Effects Branch. It was a classic case of shooting the messenger: the Health Effects Branch was "reorganized" out of existence, replaced by an ineffective alternative, the Field Studies and Special Projects Section, designed to pacify industry (and especially Dow Chemical). By the time the Health Effects Branch was abolished, around 1982, it had twenty-five staff members. By 1986, its replacement had six staff members. The same decline struck another effective organization, the Special Pesticides Review Division, which investigated hazardous pesticides. In 1981, when Reagan came to power, it had one hundred scientists and support staff, and by late 1986, its staff numbered twelve. The Reagan administration knew how to demolish the effective parts of the EPA.

"Reorganization" is usually a messy process. Some win and others lose. But the Reagan administration made reorganization a weapon. Those who had the misfortune to report on the Five Rivers case were, in the logic of EPA politicians, losers. The EPA simply could not handle such drama. Key scientists were exiled to greener pastures, far from the centers of power where real decisions get made. Vandermer learned the price of bringing senior managers bad news: retribution is swift and severe. He was sent to the U.S. Agency for International Development, which shipped him to Egypt, where for two years he evaluated pesticides in an AID-funded project. Jack Griffith, the chief of the Alsea investigation, found himself moved to the University of Miami, where the EPA was funding an epidemiology program.

"I suggested that, if we ignore the findings of the Colorado farmworker study [see chapter 6], which showed the brain damage effects of neurotoxic pesticides, we are likely to have more and more people with less and less intelligence," Vandermer said. "For that they stripped me of my duties for two years. They also gave me an unsatisfactory rating for my job, which is the closest thing to being fired."

Vandermer was furious. He was about to file a formal grievance when one day he was offered a deal: if he dropped his grievance, the EPA would pay his salary at another government agency or university of his choice.[18] Vandermer accepted the deal.

Despite industry's claims, the truth about 2,4-D's toxicity is well known, and it has been for a long time. On September 26, 1983, S. M. Jalal, a professor of biology at the University of North Dakota, wrote a note to Edwin Johnson, the director of the EPA's pesticides office. Jalal said he was "surprised" to learn that 2,4-D, an unusually common lawn care product, did in fact contain TCDD dioxins. An EPA study released a couple of years before Jalal's note had concluded that the TCDD dioxin is a "likely" human carcinogen and may be "the most toxic chemical ever known to man," with awesome degenerative power that could cripple, cause cancer, and kill experimental animals at "exceedingly low doses."[19]

Yet as always, relentless industry pressure took place behind closed doors—or through congressional phone calls. Once again, the EPA began parroting industry, claiming (without citing proof) that there was no evidence that 2,4-D had *any* dioxin contaminant. Chemical companies began releasing reports claiming that 2,4-D was not only harmless, it helped reduce hunger; they cited USDA studies claiming that banning 2,4-D would drive up costs to growers and would thus make food more expensive for consumers.[20]

Invoking the USDA to defend industrial pesticides was hardly a surprising move. The USDA has a long history of releasing studies favorable to the industrial status quo. By the late 1990s, after the chemical industry's sustained rhetorical exaggeration in defense of 2,4-D, the EPA had managed to restrict only some of its uses. Today, 2,4-D remains one of the most common herbicides in the United States. It is still in the farmer's shed and the suburban homeowner's garage.[21]

By the time of the Alsea Creek and Five Rivers fiascoes, the EPA was reeling from its mismanagement of toxic pesticides. It wasn't just the miscarriages in Oregon or the effects of Agent Orange

on Vietnam soldiers; it wasn't just the results of a Colorado neurological study that revealed that organophosphate pesticides were
very bad for people's health; nor was it the poisoned drinking water
discovered on Long Island or the shocking revelations of fake science
for hire (both of which I will discuss later). But in combination, these
overlapping crises caused tremendous unrest within EPA, especially
as the Carter era evolved into the far more disruptive administration
of Ronald Reagan following the election of 1980. The news from the
Five Rivers neighborhood, coming to the EPA in 1979 while the
agency was still in disarray because of the Alsea study, almost broke
the camel's back.[22]

Both the Alsea and Five Rivers studies became environmental
battlefields, especially because the Reagan administration had just
arrived in Washington, and Reagan's political appointees at the EPA
wanted nothing to do with the suffering women of Oregon. The
mission of Reagan's EPA was the protection of the industry, including
Dow Chemical. This was hardly surprising, since the chemical industry had its fingerprints all over Reagan's election and (later) his
appointments to the EPA. Reagan came to power with a commitment
to silence or abolish any government activity that might cause trouble
for business. His primary environmental goal came straight from
industry: relieve companies of all "regulatory restraint."

PURGING TROUBLING SCIENCE AND SCIENTISTS

Reagan's choice to run the EPA, Anne Gorsuch, was—from this point
of view—the perfect choice. Her first action was to decimate the
EPA's law enforcement attorneys. Gorsuch's deputy, John W.
Hernandez, soon compromised the EPA's own scientists studying
dioxins. Hernandez arrived at the EPA after a stint as dean of civil
engineering at New Mexico State University. For most of 1981, 1982,
and early 1983, when Hernandez was finally asked to resign, he put
the power and prestige of his office at the service of Dow Chemical,

the manufacturer of napalm and 2,4,5-T and a company that was used to getting its way inside the EPA.

In 1979, before Hernandez arrived in Washington, the EPA had concluded that the heavy dioxin contamination of the Tittabawassee River and Saginaw Bay in Michigan was the direct result of an influx of wastewater from Dow Chemical's Midland works, a 1,900-acre manufacturing plant. EPA charged that Dow was the most significant source, if not the only source, for that dioxin pollution.[23]

As others at the EPA had done before him, Hernandez was interested in making Dow look good. He took the highly unusual step of giving the company a copy of an internal dioxin report prepared by Dr. J. Milton Clark, a scientist working for the agency's Region V out of Chicago. This report explained the risks that dioxins and furans (highly toxic dioxin-like chemicals) posed to wildlife and humans in the Great Lakes region, including Michigan, where the Dow plant was located. The report emphasized the extraordinary low levels of TCDD, in parts per trillion, that killed or caused cancer in wildlife. Clark later said it was "entirely inappropriate for Hernandez to let Dow comment directly on the draft report."[24]

More than anybody else on the EPA's staff in Chicago, Valdas V. Adamkus, the acting regional administrator, was responsible for the dioxin report. He staked his reputation and political survival on its findings. "The toxicological calculations indicated a substantial cancer risk from the consumption of contaminated fish," Adamkus reported to David Kee, director of the Air and Hazardous Materials Division at EPA headquarters in Washington. Yet amazingly, Washington's EPA staff, while not disputing the study's conclusions, suggested his conclusions be removed "in order not to alarm an overly sensitive public."[25]

Hernandez was clearly aware of the findings of the dioxin report, and his decision to hand an internal EPA report to Dow was both inappropriate and irresponsible. Adamkus would later testify under oath that he was "disturbed, almost destroyed" that Hernandez would give the report to Dow Chemical—which, of course, was quite pleased with Hernandez's decision. Dow now had a chance to censor the report, and it did—demanding in telephone conversations with senior EPA officials, including David Kee, that the EPA delete from the report all references to Agent Orange and the dioxin pollution of the Tittabawassee River and Saginaw Bay. It also demanded that nothing be said about the EPA's Alsea study, or that dioxins cause cancer and birth defects, or that it was hazardous to eat fish from the Great Lakes.[26]

Hernandez clearly agreed with Dow. Under his watchful eye, the scientists of Region V had no option but to delete the offending information from the report.

News about Hernandez's political interference—fighting for Dow Chemical as if he worked for the company, which in effect he did—became too embarrassing even for the Reagan administration, and a mass exodus from a humiliated EPA ensued. Hernandez (and others) were asked to resign because of pressure from powerful Democratic congressmen and senators. Reporters noted that Hernandez was accused of "ordering EPA regional staffers to cooperate with Dow Chemical in revising the report, which in its final version dropped a section concluding that Dow's Midland plant was the major source of dioxin contamination in the area."[27]

Anne Gorsuch—by then known as Anne Burford, after a recent marriage—was forced to resign after Congress cited her for contempt for refusing to turn over Superfund records. In her 1986 book *Are You Tough Enough?* Ms. Burford said she was only "following orders."

"When congressional criticism about the EPA began to touch the presidency, Mr. Reagan solved his problem by jettisoning me and my people, people whose only 'crime' was loyal service, following orders," Burford wrote. "I was not the first to receive his special brand of benevolent neglect, a form of conveniently looking the other way, while his staff continues to do some very dirty work."

Rita Lavelle, the person in charge of the EPA's hazardous waste program, meanwhile, was sentenced to six months in prison and fined

$10,000 for lying to Congress about what and when she knew about her former employer, the Aerojet General Corporation, dumping toxic waste near Riverside, California. Reagan had dismissed Lavelle during congressional investigations into allegations of favoritism to industry and the failure to use a $1.6 billion federal cleanup fund for toxic waste sites. Although Lavelle was the only one charged with a crime, some twenty other high-level administrators resigned under pressure. "You have indeed violated the public trust," the federal district judge told Lavelle. "The perjury offense strikes at the very core of the trust that had been conferred [upon] you."[28]

Of course, while all of this was going on, the work of EPA scientists on critical issues like TCDD was forced to take a back seat. The political appointees either showed no interest in continuing EPA's dioxin studies or diverted resources from the dioxin work to less hazardous and less controversial projects.

Yet even by the time Reagan came to power in 1981, news about the extreme toxicity of dioxins—especially given the damage done by the spraying of Agent Orange over the jungles of Vietnam—was already out. Veterans had kept up their pressure for government assistance, and in 1979, Congress passed legislation mandating federal studies of Agent Orange.

But the Centers for Disease Control and the Department of Veterans Affairs and the Air Force continued their deception, working on "validation studies" without even measuring the amount of dioxin in the suffering veterans. (Harvard's Matthew Meselson, who had studied the effects of Agent Orange in humans, rightfully accused the government of wasting money on meaningless studies.)

The reason these studies were meaningless is hard to miss: government agencies, from the Department of Veterans Affairs to the Centers for Disease Control and the Air Force, knew that if a connection was made between dioxin and miscarriages in women in Oregon, the American victims of Agent Orange would have to be compensated. By the late 1980s, despite the convincing evidence the EPA had accumulated on the dangerous toxicity of dioxin, the federal government—especially the Pentagon, the Department of Veterans Affairs, USDA, and even the EPA itself—was still trying to downplay its own research. USDA and EPA suppressed information that might have threatened the marketability of 2,4-D, and the Pentagon and the Department of Veterans Affairs did their best not to compensate the thousands of veterans of the Vietnam War who claimed that dioxin exposure had caused their cancer or other crippling afflictions.

Product liability lawsuits over asbestos had bankrupted the Johns Manville Corporation, and the big chemical companies and their fixers in government were well aware of the risks such claims would pose to Dow Chemical, Monsanto, Uniroyal, and Diamond Shamrock, all of which had manufactured Agent Orange for decades.

In the end, Vietnam veterans finally lost their hope that the federal government would come to their aid. But in 1979, some of them filed a class action suit against seven companies manufacturing Agent Orange, and five years later, the companies settled out of court for $180 million. Very little information about the dangers of dioxins ever became public.[29]

The more that scientists inside and outside the EPA learned about the dangers of dioxins, it seemed, the more chemical companies learned how to convince policymakers that these compounds were harmless. These worlds continued to chart their absurdly parallel paths throughout the Reagan era.

On August 15, 1983, Reagan's EPA issued its draft "Dioxin Strategy," confirming what Hale Vandermer had said years before about the critical role of dioxins in Alsea, Oregon. The EPA stated clearly that TCDD came into the world during the production of 2,4,5-trichlorophenol (2,4,5-TCP), a basic chemical feedstock used to make several pesticides and herbicides, including 2,4,5-trichlorophenoxyacetic acid (2,4,5-T), Silvex, hexachlorophene, ronnel, and erbon.[30]

Now, though, the EPA went further, noting that TCDD's acute toxicity kills animals at "lower levels than any other man-made chemical." In addition, TCDD initiates and promotes cancer at a potency 17 million times greater than that of benzene, 5 million times greater than carbon tetrachloride, and a hundred thousand times greater than PCBs. TCDD also bioaccumulates in animals at dramatic rates: twenty thousand times greater than benzene, six thousand times greater than carbon tetrachloride, and four times greater than PCBs.[31]

Given that dioxin-laced weed killers had been used all over America for decades, in other words, the prospect for dioxin-induced cancer or other diseases had become too big a worry for the EPA to ignore. The agency warned its regional cleanup crews to be exceptionally cautious whenever they detected dioxin contamination above one part per billion. This may sound like a small amount, but consider this: one part TCDD per *trillion*—which is a thousand times smaller than 1 part per billion—is still toxic enough to mutate living entities such as chicken embryos.

Yet despite the mounting evidence, chemical giants continued to deny the problems associated with their products and continued to harass and demonize anyone at the EPA who suggested these compounds be regulated. If Dow Chemical set the pace for this performance, another chemical behemoth, Monsanto, was not far behind.

Monsanto had produced 2,4,5-T in Nitro, West Virginia, for about twenty years, ending in 1971. The company also used its Nitro plant for more than fifty years to make rubber, herbicides, and numerous other chemicals. In 1949, an explosion in the factory had contaminated workers with dioxin. Thirty years later, in 1979, a train derailed in Sturgeon, Missouri, and spilled 19,000 gallons of chlorophenol, a dioxin compound that Monsanto used in making wood preservatives. In the 1980s, Monsanto would use these incidents for two company-sponsored studies purporting to show that dioxin exposure did not cause cancer in workers.

The workers were not so sure. Frances Kemner and other Monsanto employees exposed to chlorophenol in 1979 sued the company in a Missouri court in 1980. Their lawyers accused Monsanto of (among other things) lying to the EPA about the dioxin in its wastes and lying to workers about the existence of dioxin in its chlorophenol factory. Monsanto had had the technology for making chlorophenol with less dioxin but did not do so until after the 1979 Missouri accident; from 1970 to 1977, the company dumped 30 to 40 pounds of dioxin a day into the Mississippi River, and they sold products (including Lysol and Weed-B-Gon), all contaminated by dioxin, for more than thirty years.

During the trial, which lasted four years, the paucity of research on the links between dioxin and cancer in humans persuaded the jury to absolve Monsanto of responsibility for causing workers' cancer. But it did find the company guilty of arrogance and willful negligence, fining it more than $16 million in punitive damages.

News of the Missouri trial of Monsanto eventually got to Cate Jenkins, an EPA scientist with a doctorate in chemistry who joined the EPA in 1979, the same year I arrived. A few years later she became a whistle-blower for the first time: in 1988, she wrote letters to congressional leaders about corruption in the relationship between EPA and the wood-preserving industry.[32]

The wastes of that industry are laced with dioxin, Jenkins had learned, and when she came across the Monsanto case, she became suspicious about the company's dioxin studies. She went over the Monsanto studies with a fine-tooth comb and found significant deficiencies in both their design and their conclusions. She immediately concluded that the studies had been tampered with.

She had reason to worry. The EPA's own studies, remember, had showed that dioxin was "the most toxic chemical ever known to man."[33]

On February 23, 1990, she sent a memo to Raymond C. Loehr, chairman of the executive committee of the Science Advisory Board of the EPA, suggesting that the Monsanto studies were fraudulent.[34] The Kemner Brief, she said, alleged that Monsanto deliberately cooked its data, altering research to "prove to the world that the only health consequence of dioxins was the relatively harmless, reversible [skin] condition of chloracne."

Jenkins hoped that EPA scientists would audit the Monsanto studies—and other dioxin research—for fraud. She urged the advisory board to focus on studies done by the industry in order to "determine whether misclassification of medical records or other errors has resulted in similarly flawed conclusions." Jenkins suspected that companies doing research on their own workers "would be particularly prone to bias," for the obvious reason that any evidence that a company product caused an employee cancer could mean hefty, asbestos-sized lawsuits.

Jenkins's memo set off alarm bells inside EPA, and someone in the agency inevitably leaked the memo to Monsanto. On October 1, 1990, James H. Senger, Monsanto's vice president, sent a letter to Donald Clay, EPA assistant administrator for solid waste and emergency response, furious at what he termed "baseless charges." The Monsanto studies, he said, had a "science-based focus." Senger also complained that the "untrue allegations" repeated in the EPA memo cause "extreme prejudice" against Monsanto. "I wish to stress," Senger said to Clay, "that Monsanto believes the charges against the two [Monsanto] studies [by Cate Jenkins] are utterly without merit." Finally, Senger urged Clay to have the EPA audit those two studies and publish the results of the audit in a scientific journal.

While Monsanto was trying to convince the EPA of Jenkins's misdeeds, the EPA started a criminal investigation of Monsanto, led by EPA agents John West and Kevin Guarino from EPA's National Enforcement Investigations Center in Denver. On November 15, 1990, Cate Jenkins explained her conclusions in a memo to the investigators.[35]

First of all, she said, the EPA relied on Monsanto's dioxin studies in everything it did. The result, naturally, was that the EPA failed to acknowledge that dioxins cause cancers or any other serious health effects other than chloracne. This meant the EPA utterly underestimated the danger of dioxin-contaminated products such as the wood preservative pentachlorophenol and the weed killer 2,4-D.

Second, Monsanto alone was responsible for the falsification of the dioxin studies. Given that the National Institute of Environmental Health Sciences had partially funded one of the Monsanto studies, EPA investigators could charge Monsanto with "fraudulent use of government funds," Jenkins said. Third, internal Monsanto documents that came to light during employee testimony revealed that Monsanto had known since the 1960s that some of its products (including the Agent Orange weed killers, 2,4,5-T and 2,4-D, pentachlorophenol, and the disinfectant Lysol) were contaminated by dioxin.

Moreover, Monsanto subverted its own dioxin studies by covering up the neurological diseases suffered by workers exposed to the compound; excluding workers with cancer from its studies; and even adding dioxin-exposed workers to the "control" group of its studies.

On January 24, 1991, Jenkins sent another memo to West and Guarino, again stressing Monsanto's overwhelming influence on weakening the EPA's regulation of dioxins in air, water, pesticides, and waste programs.[36]

The implications of these findings were far-reaching. Perhaps most obviously, the EPA's Monsanto-influenced dioxin policy effectively discouraged litigation against Monsanto. But the Department of Veterans Affairs had also used the EPA's compromised dioxin findings to deny compensation to veterans exposed to dioxin during the Vietnam War. (Australia and New Zealand did the same thing to their own war veterans.) The White House had ordered the Centers for Disease Control to reject veterans' claims that their cancers had anything to do with their exposure to dioxin during the war.

There was, of course, a great deal of money at stake in these maneuvers. Monsanto (and the White House, apparently) did not want Americans making the connection between the poisons that had caused cancer in soldiers sickened in the jungles of Vietnam and the dioxin-laced pesticides citizens used in their homes or on their suburban lawns.

EPA's criminal investigation of Monsanto lasted for two years without reaching a conclusion about the studies. One result that was not in doubt: the EPA apologized to Monsanto for suggesting its studies were fraudulent, and then, in a vindictive fury, launched a harassing investigation into Jenkins herself.

"I don't think Cate [Jenkins] should be involved with anything that puts her in direct contact with the regulated community or the general public," an EPA manager said. "If we insist on retaining her, place her in some administrative or staff position (like Bill Sanjour) and not worry about whether she is happy."[37] Jenkins was made a nonperson. She was relieved of official duties, and for close to two years she was left without an assignment. On April 8, 1992, she was ordered to a clerical position.

But Jenkins fought back, filing a harassment complaint with the Department of Labor, and in May 1992, an examiner from the Department of Labor investigated Jenkins's grievance. He interviewed EPA managers who had worked with Jenkins. "Cate [Jenkins] appears to be on a mission to eliminate dioxins," an EPA official told the examiner. "Management has been too soft in the past in dealing with Cate's activities."[38]

The examiner, however, sided with Jenkins. He ruled that the EPA had discriminated against her for doing things allowed by the whistle-blower law. He rejected the agency's arguments for giving Jenkins a clerical job and recommended that she be given her official job back and be reimbursed for any legal fees and costs she had incurred defending herself.

The EPA rejected the examiner's recommendations and appealed his ruling to the Labor District Director, who agreed with the decision of the examiner. The EPA again appealed the decision to an administrative law judge.

At this stage of the conflict, Jenkins's lawyers questioned EPA officials under oath and brought their own witnesses to testify about the character and achievements of Cate Jenkins. Out of this "trial" there emerged another picture of Jenkins: a dedicated and skillful scientist who had decided that regulating dioxins was worth fighting for and who had been ostracized by her own agency for the offense of carrying out its stated mission.

Jenkins, the court learned, had earned several cash awards for a performance that "exceeded expectations"; she had never been disciplined or criticized for her behavior in dealing with the public or the industry. Beyond this, her supervisor testified that he had spoken to Monsanto about her; another manager said he would not give Jenkins any assignment that involved Monsanto; another reported that had Jenkins not been on a "crusade on dioxins," he would consider her a valuable member of his team.

One of the witnesses who praised Jenkins, John Thomas Burch Jr., was a lawyer and a Vietnam War veteran who headed the National Vietnam Veterans Coalition. Jenkins had made a real difference in the veterans' struggle for justice, Burch said; she was the only government official who always assisted the veterans. Burch emphasized that Jenkins's memos on the Monsanto dioxin studies "broke a roadblock," triggering legislation that made it possible for thousands of veterans to receive medical care. The veterans had honored Jenkins with a plaque for exemplary service.

The administrative law judge also ruled in Jenkins's favor, but once again the EPA appealed, this time to the Secretary of Labor, who also ruled for Jenkins. Finally, after wasting two years in useless litigation, EPA was forced to restore Jenkins to her official duties.[39] "Although she had committed no crime, Jenkins had been vilified and harassed for the sin of wanting to protect the public from dioxin," wrote William Sanjour, a colleague of Jenkins who chronicled the EPA's dishonorable vendetta against her.

> Many wrongs, including violations of EPA's own regulations, were committed by those who illegally harassed her, but no one has suggested punishment for them. And while many EPA officials

were willing, even anxious, to apologize to Monsanto, none has
come forward to apologize to Dr. Jenkins.

When Jenkins made her allegations, and when the veterans
groups made known the full implication of those allegations, a
government with a decent respect for the welfare of its armed
forces would have publicly ordered a full and impartial investigation with all the resources and support necessary and let the chips
fall where they may. Instead, our top government officials were
silent or even worse, they let it be known that they despised the
messenger and had nothing but friendly feelings for the accused.
The United States government gave no support or encouragement
to a scientific, civil, or criminal investigation of Monsanto. No
mere office director in EPA is big enough or strong enough to take
on an influential giant like Monsanto without that support and
encouragement.

The EPA "should stop running a KGB-type operation that tries to
control anyone who calls attention to waste, fraud, and abuse by high-
ranking officials and powerful private interests," Sanjour went on.
"The agency should pay attention instead to the message of these
whistle-blowers. Failed attempts at suppression only increase the
public's distrust of its government."[40]

Sanjour was right. Without a thorough government investigation
of the Monsanto dioxin studies, we cannot say for sure that Cate
Jenkins's allegations were accurate. Yet the EPA was not about to challenge Monsanto. Even before Sanjour denounced the government's
complicity with Monsanto, another critic emerged—this one a central
figure in the Vietnam War itself—and accused the federal government
of covering up the connection between dioxins and cancer.

Admiral Elmo R. Zumwalt was the commander of U.S. Naval
Forces in Vietnam from 1968 to 1970. From 1970 to 1974 he served
as the chief of naval operations and as a member of the Joint Chiefs of
Staff. On October 6, 1989, he was appointed special assistant to the

Secretary of the Department of Veterans Affairs, and it was in that capacity that he reviewed all evidence regarding the health effects of Agent Orange on American soldiers in the Vietnam War. This meant looking over the studies carried out by the Department of Veterans Affairs, the Air Force, the Centers for Disease Control, and the Department of Health and Human Services.

For Admiral Zumwalt, Agent Orange was more than an abstract policy question. His son, Elmo Zumwalt III, who also served in Vietnam, was exposed to the defoliant and became (like many other Vietnam veterans) dangerously ill with lymphoma (a cancer of the lymph system) and Hodgkin's disease. He eventually died of the diseases. Zumwalt's grandson, Elmo IV, was born with a congenital dysfunction that hinders his ability to concentrate.[41]

Admiral Zumwalt accused the Centers of Disease Control of fraud, manipulation, and interference in carrying out valid dioxin studies. "The major federal government health studies on the effects of Agent Orange on Vietnam veterans have significantly understated those effects as a result of deliberate political manipulation of scientific data and methodology," he said. Zumwalt became particularly angry with a physician and manager at the Centers for Disease Control who, he asserted, "has made it his mission to manipulate scientific data and procedures so as to prevent the true facts about dioxin from being determined." Zumwalt was certain that the CDC manager was "politically motivated," covering up the effects of dioxin exactly as the companies that produced them had done; the CDC valued "profits above other concerns."[42]

The antidote to these misleading studies had to be research done by scientists funded neither by the government nor the chemical industry, Zumwalt said. He had reviewed enough unbiased studies to know that sufficient evidence existed on the harmful human effects of Agent Orange and dioxin—not least a 150-page summary report (done by Cate Jenkins herself) called "Diseases Significantly Associated with Agent Orange and Dioxin."

A month after Admiral Zumwalt's searing critique, Jenkins sent her dioxin report to Robert M. Hager, a public interest lawyer in Washington, D.C. In her September 5, 1991, letter, Jenkins assured Hager that recent studies showed clearly that "humans are probably a more sensitive species to the effects of dioxin than animals." This was in direct contradiction to the conclusions reached by the CDC and the EPA, who continued to work to convince the American people that dioxin's dangerous reputation was overblown, especially when confronted with a number of litigation cases and toxic waste cleanup decisions.

The companies, and their allies in government, had reason to worry: in 2004, the residents of Nitro, West Virginia, sued Monsanto for the harm they had suffered as a result of the company's manufacture of the Agent Orange chemical 2,4,5-T. The class action suit focused only on the dioxin by-product, accusing Monsanto of burning dioxin wastes in their community, spreading contaminated soot and polluting homes with unsafe levels of dioxin. In February 2012, Monsanto agreed to settle the case for $93 million.[43]

Meanwhile, Monsanto, Dow Chemical, and other companies continued to manufacture dioxins and dump them into the environment. By 2007—some twenty-eight years after EPA had sounded the alarm, and more than a century after the company began dumping dioxins into Michigan's Tittabawassee River—Dow Chemical had already spent some $40 million to "study" its mess, but not much to actually clean it up. And there was a lot to clean up: one hot spot had the highest levels of dioxin ever recorded in the Great Lakes region. "We're talking a huge area of contamination here," said Robert McCann, a spokesman for the Michigan Department of Environmental Quality. "It can no longer be argued that there isn't a serious dioxin problem here," said Ralph Dollhopf, associate director of the EPA's regional Superfund office in Chicago. "There is no question about Dow's culpability. It's past time for this work to be done."

Mary A. Gade, administrator for EPA Region V, assured the American people that the July 13, 2007, settlement would force Dow to clean up three "dioxin contaminated hot spots." Gade spoke too soon. Just six months later, the EPA "cut off cleanup talks with Dow Chemical."[44]

Although you'd think that four decades of battles over dioxins would have moved us toward a consensus on the cleanup of this poison, the truth is not so simple. And as bad as the Reagan administration was during the 1980s, when it comes to dioxins, the Obama administration has done little better. On May 26, 2009, Obama's EPA administrator, Lisa Jackson, wrote that dioxin threatened both Michigan's public health and its environment and promised that the EPA would release an official reassessment of the compound by the end of 2010, and during public meetings in Michigan, senior EPA officials explained agency plans to clean up Dow's decades-old dioxin mess. But as usual, nothing substantive happened. Dow and the American Chemical Council, a public relations front for the chemical industry, asked the EPA to extend the comment period, and the agency obliged, telling anxious citizens to wait for a report from their Science Advisory. Meanwhile, Dow did what it has been doing for decades: lobbying Congress and the White House (to the tune of $12 million).[45]

Michigan residents were understandably disheartened. "It is completely useless to expect any government agency to reign in corporate polluters because the debate is endless, centering around the apparently controversial position that poison is bad for people," a woman named Barbara Rubin wrote to her local newspaper. Another Michigan resident, Mike Lily, wondered who would ever be able to fight "Dow's 12 million dollars in influence." The result? "Another generation of children will be raised on a highly contaminated flood-plain while EPA plays footloose and fancy free allowing Dow to steer the path forward."[46]

And so it goes at the EPA. Two decades after she first blew the whistle on dioxins, Cate Jenkins is still fighting the good fight at EPA and still running into trouble with administrators. She was fired from the agency in 2010 after accusing the EPA of underestimating the health consequences of the toxic dust created by the attacks of September 11. Jenkins sued the agency under the federal Whistle-Blower Protection Act, and she was (again) eventually reinstated. "I think it shows to us that the agency was trying to get rid of her and silence her by making this allegation, and to go to the length of even a constitutional violation to get her out of there," Jenkins's lawyer said.[47]

To say the least, the suppression of honest voices like that of Cate Jenkins is demoralizing inside an agency that is supposed to be doing exactly her kind of work.

CHAPTER 4

DDT: A New Principle of Toxicology

A PRIL 29, 1982, was a hot day in Washington. By six in the afternoon I was exhausted, looking forward to my walk to the Pentagon, from where I would take Metro bus number 8 to my home in Alexandria.

On my way to the water fountain just before leaving the EPA office, I noticed, over near the Xerox machine, a pile of papers meant to be thrown in the trash. Curious, I looked over the small hill of documents, and in an instant I knew I had stumbled upon a little treasure. What I'd found was a stack of correspondence from the Hazard Evaluation Division, the group of EPA scientists who deal with the technical issues of pesticides. I grabbed as many documents as I could, put them in a box, and carried them to my workspace.

The next morning, an EPA official asked me to get rid of the papers; apparently his secretary had learned that I had taken them from the trash pile. "In any future litigation, we don't want any of these papers to rise from the grave," he said, looking at me. "The office of the general counsel does not think it would be a good idea for anyone to have copies of these documents. Please throw them away."

Of course I did no such thing. And it was in that pile of dumped papers that a little gem came to light: a letter documenting the contamination of birds and fish in Texas's fecund river valleys with DDT and toxaphene.

For the past fourteen years, federal Fish and Wildlife scientists had "consistently" discovered DDT in Rio Grande fish, the letter said, "even after the Environmental Protection Agency cancelled the registration of DDT for general use on June 30, 1972."

When researchers expanded their monitoring for DDT, they also discovered high levels of toxaphene, a DDT-like spray, and DDE, the carcinogenic metabolite of DDT. Both were dangerous chemicals in their own right.

"Our past monitoring studies clearly indicate that a significant pesticide contamination problem exists in the Lower Rio Grande Valley with respect to fish and wildlife resources," the letter said. "We feel our data is significant in that our residue values have been triplicated, and pesticide residues have been confirmed by the best analytical procedures in use today. We sincerely hope that some regulatory action will be forthcoming concerning the contamination of the lower valley, before these contaminants pose a threat to human health."[1]

Despite this powerful evidence of high amounts of DDT and toxaphene in the fish of Texas, the EPA and the government of Texas did nothing. Strangely, researchers at the medical school of Texas Tech University actually tried to "prove" that there was no toxaphene in the fish in the Rio Grande—an effort that seemed counterproductive at best. And when the federal Interior Department appealed directly to the EPA's regional administrator, that official apparently decided that avoiding confronting politicians and industry representatives in Texas and Washington was more important than warning Texans to stop eating local fish. The truth was, of course, that had the EPA's Texas official revealed the DDT contamination of fish, it would have raised a storm with Texas politicians, industry, and EPA political appointees in Washington, and no doubt would have cost that person's job. In that sense, the official's behavior—his refusal to take on industry power—was typical of senior administration officials: causing waves has its effects, and those effects are mostly nasty.

And so it has gone with toxic chemicals over and over and across the decades: scientists collect data and issue warnings, and people in charge of making political decisions—many of them intimidated by (or beholden to) large corporations—ignore them.

Nearly a decade before Rachel Carson published *Silent Spring* in 1962, Morton Biskind, a physician from Westport, Connecticut, documented the willful blindness of scientists working with agricultural poisons. Since the end of World War II, he wrote, he had observed "curious changes" in the incidence of certain ailments in both men and domestic animals. Strangely, with the exception of hoof and mouth disease, not one of these conditions was mentioned in the comprehensive U.S. Department of Agriculture handbook titled *Keeping Livestock Healthy*.

Not a word about the manifest dangers of pesticides. How could this be? In Biskind's mind, this glaring omission alone should have been sufficient to raise a suspicion that a new threat had arrived. By the time DDT was first made available for the general public in 1945, scientific research "had already shown beyond doubt that this compound was dangerous for all animal life from insects to mammals," Biskind wrote. Cats, dogs, sheep, cattle, horses, monkeys—when they were exposed to DDT, these animals and many more developed degenerative problems with their organs, their muscles, their brains.

The compound was equally dangerous to birds, fish, crustaceans, lizards, frogs, toads, and snakes. Tragically, many beneficial predator insects—dragonflies, ladybugs, and praying mantises—were even more susceptible to DDT than were the crop-eating "nuisance" insects the compound had been designed to kill. By 1945 it was also well known that once mammals or people were exposed to DDT, the compound became stored in their body fat and could be found in their milk. DDT had a way of hanging around, even inside people's bodies.

All of this foreknowledge made DDT's catastrophic impact on our national landscape—Biskind called it "the most intensive campaign of mass poisoning in known human history"—that much more insidious. We knew it was dangerous, yet we kept on using it— for three decades. Only when Carson's book appeared, and our national symbol, the bald eagle, was on the verge of extinction because of DDT contamination, did we finally acknowledge what scientists had been saying for years.

"Virtually the entire apparatus of communication, lay and scientific alike, has been devoted to denying, concealing, suppressing, [and] distorting the overwhelming evidence," Biskind wrote. "A new principle of toxicology has, it seems, become firmly entrenched in the literature: no matter how lethal a poison may be for all other forms of animal life, if it doesn't kill human beings instantly, it is safe. When nevertheless it unmistakably does kill a human, this was the victim's own fault—either he was 'allergic' to it (the uncompensable sin!) or he didn't use it properly."[2]

Biskind was both perceptive and courageous. His message went against the stream well before Carson made the dangers of DDT a national scandal. It's possible that the timing of his essay—it appeared in 1953, at the height of the Cold War—was less than ideal. The explosion of the atomic bomb gave enormous power to physicists, who design and build nuclear weapons. Suddenly, a kind of "physics envy" descended on the sciences, and the rest of society reorganized its thinking to accommodate the existential questions of death the physicists (and their bombs) opened up. Ironically, such broad anxiety seemed to shift attention away from chemists and their own dangerous concoctions, which also fundamentally altered life. The government's military imperatives, including the aboveground testing of nuclear weapons and the rapid growth of agribusiness, pushed aside any voices that questioned the wisdom of industrial chemicals. So enamored was the Nobel Prize committee with DDT's effect on malaria that it awarded Paul Miller of Geigy Chemicals the Nobel Prize in Medicine in 1948.

A decade and a half later, Carson would denounce the hegemony of chemicals as "the sinister and little-recognized partners of radiation in changing the very nature of the world—the very nature of its life." America's industrial monoculture farming was already clashing with natural systems of pest control.

"We allow the chemical death rain to fall," Carson wrote. "The crusade to create a chemically sterile world seems to have engendered a fanatic zeal on the part of many specialists and most of the so-called control agencies. On every hand there is evidence that those engaged in spraying operations exercise a ruthless power."[3]

Like Biskind, Carson was astonished at the silence of federal regulators at the USDA. She could already see that political and economic forces were at work, adopting and spreading this new (and profitable) skepticism about toxicology that largely reigns supreme today. "These [pesticide] sprays, dusts, and aerosols," she wrote, "are now applied almost universally to farms, gardens, forests, and homes— nonselective chemicals that have the power to kill every insect, the 'good' and the 'bad,' to still the song of birds and the leaping of fish in the streams, to coat the leaves with a deadly film, and to linger on in soil—all this though the intended target may be only a few weeds or insects. Can anyone believe it is possible to lay down such a barrage of poisons on the surface of the earth without making it unfit for all life?"[4]

Few people since Carson died in 1964 have spoken so openly about that tragic inevitability. Carson was thorough in her absorption of the published scientific literature on pesticides. She looked at the industrialized agriculture of her time and rightly blamed America's "single-crop farming" as the source of trouble. She said monoculture farming had more in common with engineering than with natural systems. And since engineers were redesigning and plumbing the country to water the developing giant farms, she thought of pesticides as crude weapons like "a cave man's club . . . hurled against the fabric of life." She connected this violence with the still-fashionable ambition of modern industry to "control nature."

That idea—that modern people could dream of controlling the natural world—made Carson very angry. She lambasted such thinking as hubris. This kind of thinking and ambition, Carson said, mirrored a "Neanderthal age of biology and philosophy, when it was supposed nature exists for the convenience of man," she wrote. "It is our alarming misfortune that so primitive a science has armed itself with the most modern and terrible weapons, and that in turning them against the insects it has also turned them against the earth."[5]

Here's how the DDT story unfolded. In its early days, pesticides seemed to represent a triumph of Western science and technology: both a proven weapon to subdue the "undesirable" aspects of nature and an elixir of cleanliness and even health. "The great expectations held for DDT have been realized," ran an advertisement in *Time* magazine in 1947. "Exhaustive scientific tests have shown that, when properly used, DDT kills a host of destructive pests, and is a benefactor of all humanity. Today, everyone can enjoy added comfort, health and safety through the insect-killing powers of DDT products. [DDT] helps to make healthier, more comfortable homes [and] protects your family from dangerous pests. Use DDT powders and spray—then watch the bugs 'bite the dust.'"[6]

The scientific community, such as it was, mostly lauded the chemical—and issued dire warnings of life without it. "To abandon the use of DDT and other valuable insecticides would subject people to an inadequate and unbalanced diet due to crop loss and disease epidemic far more serious than any we now know," two Illinois scientists, Rolland K. Cross, state health director, and Harlow R. Mills, chief of the Natural History Survey, wrote in 1951. "We should not be concerned so much with whether DDT or other insecticides should be used, but should concentrate upon using the right insecticide at the right time, in the right place and in the right way."[7]

DDT did indeed kill insects—at least for a while. But its damaging effects on the environment and on human health would persist for generations. As Biskind pointed out, DDT did not discriminate. It doomed birds by making the shells of their fertilized eggs so brittle that they cracked under their parents' weight. Because DDT bioaccumulates as it moves up the food chain, the compound became particularly deleterious to predatory birds, bringing peregrine falcons, ospreys, brown pelicans, and bald eagles to the brink of extinction.

DDT also killed countless insects it had not been designed to target and thus also killed fish and small animals that ate DDT-poisoned fish and bugs. The compound's legacy is doubly pernicious because it lasts for decades in nature and continues to accumulate in the fat of the animals—and people—at the upper reaches of the food chain.[8]

By the time the EPA finally banned DDT in 1972, the compound had already widely contaminated staple human foods, especially meat and milk. A year after the ban, a federal judge wrote that he did not know what to do with DDT that had contaminated nearly everything Americans ate.[9] "Although the cancer aspects of DDT are frightening, the obvious solution to that problem, that is, a total ban on foods containing DDT, is not available," he wrote. "Virtually every food contains some DDT. DDT has presented, and apparently will continue to present, a massive dilemma both for EPA and for society."[10] In 1979, two Wildlife Society scientists, Steven G. Herman and John B. Bulger, reported that DDT was still "the most widespread and pernicious of global pollutants."[11] A few years later, Richard Balcomb, an EPA ecologist, wrote that DDT remained toxic to many terrestrial and aquatic animals. "It has been shown to cause acute mortality of birds, bats, fish and invertebrates as well as have profound chronic effects in many species at low exposure levels."[12]

What was going on? Why, years after DDT was officially taken off the market, was so much DDT showing up in the bodies of birds and animals?

Part of the story had to do with the chemical industry, which had never forgotten how DDT lost public and legal favor. Even in the 1950s, the industry's rhetoric was already full of half-truths, lies, and fear, and it would only become more sophisticated and vitriolic over time. And this growing (not to say ignorant) love affair with chemicals could not help but shape both science and public policy.

Immediately after EPA banned DDT in 1972, Dick Beeler, the editor of *Agricultural Age*, an industry magazine, accused EPA of mishandling the compound's cancellation. "The entire process smells badly of farce and fraud," he said. "The [cancellation] fraud, however, is no worse than the original one perpetrated by the environmental mystics and pseudo scientists who hoodwinked the public and its political medicine men on DDT. Perhaps the greatest fraud of all is the one those same cultists and politicians have pulled on themselves, for the big losers in the DDT battle are the very object of their oft professed affection: the consumer, the common man, the underprivileged and the oppressed."

Beeler criticized EPA administrator William Ruckelshaus (a Republican appointee) for ignoring "the facts and scientific opinion"; EPA policy, he said, seemed as if it had been written by Rachel Carson, Barry Commoner, and Paul Ehrlich, three influential environmental thinkers.[13]

Plainly, the chemical industry had already become rife with cunning and contempt: cunning in its pretense of respect for science, and contempt in its attitude toward actual scientific evidence, the rule of law, and the tide of democracy, including the influence of the rising environmental movement. Beeler called environmentalists "mystics," probably wishing to somehow divorce their argument from science. From Beeler's funhouse-mirror perspective, an establishment Republican like Ruckelshaus is indistinguishable from a reformer like Rachel Carson, and DDT is the friend of the consumer and the oppressed. It was this sort of colorful (and ludicrous) rhetoric that had shaped the chemical industry's agenda for years—and scared Carson's colleagues from taking it on.

Carson herself, of course, was practically burned in effigy by the chemical industry. "Rachel Carson's candor and innocence brought

on her the fury reserved for those who neither connive nor concili-
ate," wrote Paul Shepard and Daniel McKinley, professors at Williams
College and the State University of New York–Albany. "Her brother
biologists, almost to a man, did excellent imitations of people frightened by big money and authority and deserted her before the
Establishment which controls the funds that keep scientists fat."[14]

Yet even in the face of this rhetoric, some scientists continued to
do their work, and they continued to turn up worrisome trends. In
May 1983, Robert A. Jantzen, director of the U.S. Fish and Wildlife
Service, became worried that many of the EPA-approved pesticides
were pushing rare insects, birds, fish, and other animals toward
extinction. Many of these poisons were being sprayed on corn.

"It is my biological opinion that the use of certain pesticides on
corn is likely to jeopardize the continued existence of the following
species and result in the destruction or adverse modification of the
critical habitat of the Everglade kite, slackwater darter, valley elder-
berry longhorn beetle, and Delta green ground beetle," Jantzen wrote.

The problem, Jantzen said, was that DDT was still showing up in
insecticides. One compound, Kelthane, contains as much as 9 percent
DDT, Jantzen wrote—an exceedingly dangerous problem given
that DDT and its principle metabolites "cause reproductive failure in
raptors and certain fish-eating birds."

Already the peregrine falcon, a beautiful bird and a symbol of
predatory grace and freedom, had become extinct in the southwestern United States during the first reign of DDT, and now, nearly a
decade after DDT had been banned, the lives of new birds imported
to this region were in jeopardy. Jantzen urged the EPA to demand
that Kelthane "be manufactured to eliminate the DDT component or
a substitute for Kelthane should be used."

Jantzen also insisted that the EPA prohibit the use of the offending chemical. To avoid jeopardizing the Aleutian Canada goose, he
said, the EPA should prohibit the use on corn of nongranular chemicals that are toxic to birds, between the end of August and the middle

of May, especially in California's Central Valley and in Oregon's Coos, Curry, and Tillamook Counties.

"The widespread use of this chemical was responsible for the total elimination of the peregrine falcon from the eastern half of the United States," Jantzen wrote. "Since the use of DDT was cancelled in 1972, this situation has improved, and reintroduced peregrines are once again breeding in limited numbers in the East. However, there are strong indications that DDT is currently being introduced into the environment in the southwestern United States."

Falcon nests that had produced nearly two dozen young in the late 1970s had produced none since; most had been abandoned. Eggs from one nest were found to contain 30 to 51 ppm (parts per million) of DDE (the carcinogenic metabolite of DDT). Eggshells removed from the nests were more than 20 percent thinner than shells from the pre-DDT era.

In 1982, researchers examined the birds typically fed upon by peregrines and found high levels of DDE in everything from mourning doves and red-winged blackbirds to grackles and killdeer. Since the killdeer, red-winged blackbird, and great-tailed grackle are year-round residents of Texas, the scientists concluded the pesticide burdens "were obtained locally." Because Kelthane was applied not just to corn but a variety of crops, it was clearly accumulating in animals throughout the food chain, Jantzen wrote. More frustrating, even though DDT had been banned for ten years in the United States, American companies were still selling it in Mexico, and "both the peregrine falcon and many of its prey species are known to migrate south of the United States."

"The most severe problem," Jantzen continued, "appears to be along the Rio Grande and Pecos river systems in southern New Mexico and western Texas; however, DDT contamination is still present in the American peregrine falcon throughout the West. Therefore we must conclude that the use of Kelthane, or any other pesticide containing high levels (in excess of 1 percent) of a DDT compound, is likely to jeopardize the continued existence of the peregrine falcon."[15]

To Jantzen, this was unacceptable, and not merely for the peregrine falcons. The blunt-nosed leopard lizard, for instance, may range over some 640 acres of land for insects. It would be a highly vulnerable victim of DDT. Gray bats travel long distances over land and water hunting insects for feeding their young; they can eat three thousand bugs in a single night. When these insects are contaminated with pesticides, they become poisonous themselves, and Jantzen warned that gray bat "maternity colonies" were especially at risk. By the 1980s, American newspapers were reporting an alarming and unexplained collapse of bat populations, one more result of ignored warnings about pesticides.

Plainly, DDT-contaminated chemicals like Kelthane were extending the poisonous reign of DDT, especially during the Reagan years. In 1983, my colleague Padma Datta asked me a penetrating question: Why, given the EPA's banning of DDT, had the Reagan EPA registered a dozen products with DDT contamination of up to 20 percent, and why were these products still on the market? Had Rohm and Hass, the main manufacturer of Kelthane and other pesticides contaminated by DDT, managed to influence EPA policy? (A Rohm and Hass representative had also asked Padma to lunch, but Padma had declined.)

For their part, EPA officials must have been aware of the Kelthane-DDE products decimating birds like peregrine falcons. Certainly those same officials knew the chemistry of the related organochlorines, DDT and Kelthane: under certain manufacturing and environmental conditions, Kelthane would become DDE, the carcinogenic isomer of DDT. Thus Kelthane was also used as an inert. And under such deceptive classification, one did not have to worry about the effects.[16]

On Reagan's watch, more than a hundred new pesticides had been registered to "protect" corn, which grows across immense swaths of the country (and which forms the centerpiece of a global agricultural empire). The fate of the insects and birds and other animals that understand neither human toxicology nor corporate profit models was left unaddressed.

Over at Fish and Wildlife, Robert Jantzen built his case about the peregrine falcons with meticulous care. The peregrine was living on borrowed time, given the deadly metamorphoses of DDT into other chemicals (Kelthane becoming DDE, the carcinogenic form of DDT), and given that Mexico—right across a national border that was invisible to falcons—continued to use DDT in large quantities.

EPA officials, of course, knew that Kelthane and other pesticides contained DDT. At the very least, Jantzen said, "the EPA should not tolerate farmers spraying toxins all over the home of an endangered species. Ditto for corn insecticides, which harm a wide variety of protected species, from the whooping crane to the Indiana bat."

In recent decades, we have been told that DDT and DDT-like pesticides have been removed from the arsenal of the American farmer. But since DDT lasts a long time, this infamous poison can still be found in the food birds eat. And new, equally hazardous materials have replaced DDT. They kill life even when present in fantastically small amounts.

Fifty years after its publication, *Silent Spring* remains a popular book—and a popular target. Pesticide apologists continue to attack the book, and some global health experts praise DDT for being "the cheapest and most effective long-term malaria fighter we have."[17]

Sadly, most Americans remain silent and oblivious to the dangers of industrial pesticides. Carson's book had a great impact in the 1960s, but our collective memory of her warning is fading fast. Dangerous pesticides are still being sprayed on American crops today, while the EPA, as usual, stands silently by.

CHAPTER 5

Why Are the Honeybees Disappearing?

O N January 19, 2011, I received a troubling note from Harriett Crosby, a Maryland farmer. The bees she was raising on Fox Haven Farm were dying.

"All the bees in all hives have died," Ms. Crosby wrote. "Silently, billions of bees are dying off all over the country and our entire food chain is in danger."[1]

What Ms. Crosby had witnessed on her own farm, a calamity repeated all over the country, was tragic. In the United States alone, bees produce more than 200 million pounds of honey a year, but this is only the most visible thing they contribute to human livelihood.

Bees live at the very heart of our food system: they pollinate millions of acres of fruits, vegetables, and nuts, including blackberries, blueberries, cashews, pumpkins, and sunflowers; tens of millions of acres of beans, cotton, flax, peanuts, peas, and soybeans; and tens of millions of acres of hay crops such as alfalfa, clover, and lespedeza. In 2005, the benefits of honeybees to agriculture were estimated to be about $40 billion.[2]

Yet consider this: In 2008, there were 680,000 acres of almond groves in California alone that produced 1.6 billion pounds of almond meat, valued at $2.3 billion. In a three-hundred-mile stretch in California's Central Valley, millions of almond trees are regularly sprayed with a deadly soup of poisons, including parathion neurotoxins. The result? The premature death rate for pollinating bees in California and the rest of the West Coast is about 30 to 60 percent. A beekeeper I invited to my environmental policy class at northern California's Humboldt State University once described how he would drive a truckload of beehives south, where he would "rent" his bees to pollinate some corporate farmer's crops. "I would return home, always with a third of my bees dead," he said, his voice trembling. "That's the price I paid for making some extra money. The farmer's pesticides would kill my bees."

In October 2006, the U.S. National Research Council reported that America's bee populations were moving "demonstrably downward." For the first time since 1922, American farmers were being forced to "rent" bees imported from other states, trucking billions of bees all over the country and even buying bees from Australia.[3]

What has happened?

Writing in the eighth century BCE, the Greek epic poet Hesiod, a near contemporary of Homer, considered honeybees a reward that the gods bestowed on honorable farmers.[4]

Ancient Greece reserved a special place for this useful insect. Bees were protected by Aristaios, the immortal son of the nymph Kyrene and Apollo, the Olympian god of light, prophecy, and healing. Like his father, Aristaios was gifted with prophecy and healing. But above all he was a rural god: he invented and promoted beekeeping, the growing of olives, and the care of flocks and the preparation of wool. Under the protection of Aristaios, honeybees flourished in Greece.

The Greeks' greatest natural philosopher, Aristotle, studied the life of honeybees, noting their remarkable organization as societies of extremely useful insects, each honeybee devoted to a specialized function, most gathering nectar and pollen from flowering plants and trees for making honey, some caring for the grubs, and others guarding the hive. Aristotle was impressed by the cleanliness and purpose of honeybees coexisting with humans.[5]

In the late third century of our era, about seven hundred years after Aristotle, Pappos, a Greek mathematician in Alexandria, Egypt, admired honeybees for their·"instinctive wisdom" in designing hexagonal cells, the most efficient shape for containing honey. Somehow honeybees figured out that the hexagon was greater than the square and the triangle for holding more honey. Pappos, too, admired the cleanliness of the honeybees and their labor in collecting "the sweets from the most beautiful flowers which grow on the earth" for making their honey, a kind of ambrosia, which the divinely blessed honeybees give us all.[6]

Nearly three thousand years later, honeybees continue to bring us prosperity, creating honey and pollinating many of the most beautiful and useful plants on earth.

You would think that farmers would be able to recognize the importance—not to say grandeur—of bees. For countless generations, they did. In this country, B. N. Gates warned in 1917 (in the first volume of *Transactions of the Massachusetts Horticultural Society*) that the farmer "may fertilize, and cultivate the soil, prune, thin and spray the trees, in a word, he may do all of those things which modern practice advocates. Yet without honeybees to transfer the pollen from the stamens to the pistil of the blooms, his crop may fail."[7]

In our time, factory farming and our national obsession with pesticides have driven pollinating insects—honeybees in particular—to the brink of extinction. And although headlines about "bee colony collapse" have recently begun appearing in our daily newspapers, the origins of this tragedy go back decades and are not hard to trace.

As early as 1947, scientists were noticing that bees contaminated by pesticides acted as if they had been exposed to severe cold. The poisoned bees land "on leaves, twigs, or lumps of soil, selecting warm spots, and generally sitting motionless unless disturbed," the researchers wrote. "Sometimes they fell from these perches, then revived and departed slowly, as a cold bee does, or in erratic flight to alight again a few yards away. In crawling they were much slower than arsenic poisoned bees. After becoming unable to crawl they would be helpless, sometimes for hours if protected from direct sun. They often lay on their backs or sides making feeble movement with legs and antennae."[8]

In other words, farm sprays caused brain damage in bees. Poisons disoriented them, making it often impossible for them to find their way home. This is the main reason millions of bees disappear, leaving behind hives full of pollen, honey, and larvae. This is no "syndrome" or "colony collapse disorder." This is the deadly result of decades of agribusiness warfare.

Until the 1960s, bees died primarily because of the incredible variety of poisons farmers sprayed on their land, even when fruits and seeds were about to set. As they searched for nectar and pollen, bees would become saturated by these invisible—and deadly—mists and dusts. Even if they somehow survived the toxic clouds and made it back to their hives, they would behave in strange ways: some would stay near the hive and freeze to death; others would be utterly confused, stupefied, even paralyzed. Still others would enter their hives carrying cargoes of poison-laced pollen and nectar, which would devastate the colony in very short time.

In the 1970s, the USDA apiculturist S. E. McGregor warned farmers that no amount of technology could replace the critical role of bees in pollinating the nation's crops. There are more than three thousand plants giving food to humans, McGregor wrote, but only three hundred are grown widely. Of these, no more than a dozen (grains such as rice, wheat, corn, sorghum, millet, rye, and barley) are responsible for 90 percent of the world's food. All of these are pollinated by the wind and by insects. Oilseeds (coconuts, cotton, oil palms, olives, peanuts, rape, soybeans, and sunflowers) give humans more than 50 percent of the fats and oils in their diets. Insects pollinate many of these useful crops. All told, a third of our diet is directly or indirectly dependent upon insect-pollinated plants, McGregor wrote. Farmers, he said, should never forget that "no cultural practice will cause fruit or seed to set if its pollination is neglected."[9]

This precarious condition worsened sharply in 1974 when EPA licensed the nerve gas parathion, a dark, garlic-smelling poison in a class of nerve toxins known as organophosphates. Parathion was synthesized at the end of World War II in the same industrial German cauldron that cooked up the chemical weapons tabun, sarin, and soman. Parathion was first licensed as an insecticide in the United States in 1948, and for several decades, millions of pounds of this war gas were sprayed throughout the American countryside.[10]

Once inside a man or a bee, an organophosphate can destroy an enzyme, cholinesterase, which is responsible for the normal functioning of the central nervous system; the victim develops severe convulsions and can die. This may not happen quickly: parathion poisoning first causes headaches, nausea, muscle spasms, and drooling or frothing at the mouth.[11]

One undiluted drop is lethal to an adult human being; the compound can cripple and kill farmworkers. Some workers die from acute parathion poisoning; others will suffer for decades with intellectual and behavioral disabilities, retinal degeneration (resulting in blindness), paralysis, and cancer.[12]

Among animals, it takes extraordinarily minute amounts of parathion—40 parts per trillion to 5 parts per billion—to kill freshwater invertebrates. Something like 1 part per billion of parathion is fatal to oysters, and 17 parts per billion kill striped bass. Parathion also causes cancer and blindness and has been shown to rot the sciatic nerve in experimental animals.

Parathion is also more dangerous to young and female animals than it is to male animals, and it threatens dozens of endangered species throughout the country, including prairie chickens in Texas, geese in California, and a species of freshwater mussel in the Tennessee River. And it's not just parathion in its original form that causes problems. Once it is sprayed on a field, strange things rapidly begin to happen. The toxin's molecules rearrange themselves; in the skin and flesh of crops and vegetables or in the land, the compound transforms into not one but several poisons known as metabolites, which can be ten to sixty times more devastating to life than parathion itself.[13]

And if these chemicals can contaminate farmers and animals, they also can get into our food. In August 1985, Barbara Britton, an EPA scientist, said she was "astonished" to discover parathion levels in food more than five thousand times the level considered safe for nursing infants. Five months later, Britton pointed out what (to her) had become obvious: parathion was "acutely toxic to humans, domestic animals and wildlife," and jeopardized the "continued existence of 33 endangered species."[14]

Parathion's widespread use and acute toxicity could only mean tragedy for bees, especially when engineers figured out how to increase its effectiveness by making it "time released." Pennwalt Corporation's gas, known as Penncap-M, was designed with parathion wrapped in tiny nylon bubbles just 5 to 50 microns in size—just about the size of pollen grains. Now, with the poison remaining inactivated on the surface of a flower for several days, bees would carry these invisible spheres of asphyxiating gas—again, exactly the shape and size of pollen—straight back to the hive, where it would spread death from one season to the next.[15]

So-called microencapsulated methyl parathion is "the most destructive bee poisoning insecticide ever developed," according to Carl Johansen, a professor of entomology at Washington State University.[16] Johansen's home state once had some hundred thousand acres of apple trees that depended on bees for pollination. In late 1970s, the state earned $400 million per year from bee-pollinated crops alone. So Washington absolutely required a healthy population of bees. The slightest misuse of Penncap-M was "extremely hazardous to bees" and was certain to cause disaster to pollinating insects, Johansen wrote. Even hobbyist and small-time beekeepers were in danger of being "wiped out by Penncap-M sprays in eastern Washington."[17]

A year before Johansen's dire assessment, the president of the Washington Beekeepers Association warned that the viability of the honeybee industry hangs by a tenuous thread. "Past experience has shown that honey bees cannot survive within foraging distance of blossoming crops or blossoming cover crops or weeds that are subject to treatment, settling or drift of encapsulated insecticides," Elwood Sires wrote to the director of the Washington State Department of Agriculture. "All insecticides are harmful to honey bees and costly to honey beekeepers, but micro-encapsulated insecticides are deadly to the bee colonies because they are carried back to and stored in the hives."[18]

Even if farmers use Penncap-M according to the label directions, they would still cause "serious adverse effects on honey bee populations," wrote the EPA biologist Norman Cook in the late 1970s. The toxin starts a deadly chain of events: honeybees forage among treated crops, collecting pollen and capsules of poison, which they take to their hives. The capsules contaminate the pollen and honey. It then takes about eight hours for the poison to severely damage or kill the entire colony.

And it does not end there: beekeepers often reuse the destroyed colonies' combs in new hives, which, within 24 to 48 hours, causes "severe adult mortality" among honeybees of the new hive. Even contaminated combs stored for a year or more remain capable of bringing swift death to honeybees, Cook wrote.

"The most startling aspect is that honey, pollen, and wax from decimated colonies are not destroyed by the beekeepers," Cook reported. "The wax is remelted and used in new combs. The honey is sold to the public and depending upon honey-extraction processes, contains capsules of Penncap-M. The pollen stored in combs is used in new hives, but can result in adverse effects to new hives. The pollen collected from 'pollen trap" (and this pollen also contains capsules) is sold in health food stores."[19]

By the early 1980s, Frank Robinson, secretary-treasurer of the American Beekeeping Federation, admitted that the country's beekeepers were suffering "extensive losses each year from the widespread and sometimes indiscriminate use of toxic chemicals." Vernon W. Miller, a beekeeper from Cutler, Illinois, lost all of his sixty-nine colonies of bees to "the beekeeper's famous special, Penncap-M." Miller had been forced to surrender ten years of beekeeping, "as I have neither political clout nor money enough to fight a big corporation [Pennwalt, the owner of Penncap-M]. As the victim, I have no rights."[20]

Beekeepers also feared that parathion in honey and pollen could be causing serious harm to public health. Todd D. Hardie, a pollen broker from Franklin, Vermont, told the EPA he was "deeply concerned about pesticides appearing in bee pollen that is used for human consumption."

"As a broker of North American pollen, primarily from California and Colorado, I feel a great responsibility to consumers who eat the tons of pollen that we sell," Hardie wrote. "Some of our pollen comes from high mountains, where there is supposedly no possible link with pesticides, but most of the pollen is coming from agricultural areas where pesticides are used. Would it be possible to get bee pollen tested in [an] EPA laboratory?"[21] An EPA official wrote back that the FDA, not EPA, would take care of his problem. Not a word about Hardie's legitimate fears.

Why the silence? The late 1970s were a time when honey was still a favored food for infants. But then scientists discovered that some babies dying of the so-called sudden infant death syndrome or crib death had eaten honey contaminated with lethal botulinum toxin. In 1978, the Sioux Honey Association, the world's largest honey producer, urged parents not to give honey to children less than a year old.

Could there be a connection between crib death and pesticides? Botulinum toxin occurs in nature, but like the man-made parathion, it is an asphyxiating nerve poison that can choke a human being just as it can choke an insect. Organophosphate sprays, like parathion, combine with other toxic chemicals to form synergistic super-poisons. Even minute amounts of parathion could become monstrously toxic in the presence of minute amounts of botulinum toxin. There may be something in some infants' intestines that triggers the lethal reaction. Tiny capsules of parathion in the honey and other foods infants eat could be that trigger. Parathion alone could also do the job.

Botulinum spores are everywhere in the environment, and in most cases they are harmless. But they have also been connected to sudden infant death syndrome (SIDS), which kills as many as ten thousand American infants every year. Botulinum spores create toxin-producing bacteria in the intestines of infants, and these bacteria give off the deadly clostridium that kills the infant by respiratory arrest. In other words, botulism acts like parathion or other nerve poisons.[22] Thus an infant with any nerve pesticide in his stomach might face death not merely because of the toxic power of parathion alone but from the botulinum spores lying dormant in the stomach as well. The two poisons interact with deadly effects. It may be that the parathion molecules activate the botulinum spores.[23]

The widespread use of deadly Penncap-M slow-release bubbles worried and angered three ecologists at the EPA, particularly Norman Cook. They knew that in addition to killing bees and other beneficial insects, the encapsulated parathion causes various degrees of neurological damage and, quite possibly, death for small and large mammals, terrestrial and water invertebrates, and birds—even at rates of just a pound of poison per acre. The gizzards of most birds would grind down and rupture the nerve poison microcapsules, causing crippling disease or death.

The EPA ecologists also knew that bees would continue to die from the encapsulated parathion because Pennwalt Corporation had persuaded the EPA to approve the spraying of the company's product during the spring bloom, when all pollinating insects would be out foraging for nectar and pollen. They told their bosses that Pennwalt's parathion was showing up in both honey and pollen. The least

Pennwalt ought to do—according to the law—was to notify EPA about such serious public health hazards. (The Federal Insecticide, Fungicide and Rodenticide Act [FIFRA] allows the EPA to punish companies not reporting the hazardous effects of its products.) But Pennwalt did nothing, and the EPA—as it had done so many times before—simply turned away.

In February 1980, Pennwalt tried to convince the EPA that its nerve capsules were safe. But the ecologists who reviewed Pennwalt's data concluded that such information was "a parody of scientific research." They also said they had yet to come across any other spray that was "as uniquely hazardous to bees as Penncap-M."[24]

Clayton Bushong, the senior EPA manager heading the group of ecologists concerned about the farmers' toxins killing bees, was caught in a political vortex, with worried scientists on one side and a powerful corporation on the other. Bushong did what responsible bureaucrats do: he sent memos up the food chain. Having digested Johansen's warnings and the findings of scientific research about the dangers of Penncap-M, Bushong advised his superiors that pesticides in "time release" capsules cause "extreme hazards to nontarget pollinating insect populations," the consequences of which "would not only be environmentally disastrous but also would be disastrous to the production of food crops which require pollination by insects."[25]

Bushong wanted to protect bees, but he also shared McGregor's larger concerns: he understood that farmers, the land, and pollinating insects were inseparable. He knew that the time had come to declare a moratorium on encapsulated parathion sprays and to ban farming practices responsible for causing damage to bees and other pollinating insects.

Senior EPA managers in the Carter administration ignored him. Instead, they permitted Pennwalt to sell its time-release gas for use on an even wider array of produce, from artichokes, cabbages, and potatoes to wheat, soybeans, apples, and pears. The move dramatically raised the chemical exposure of both bees and the American people.

The evidence could not have been clearer. In 1979 an EPA scientist named Richard M. Lee discovered how to stain parathion microcapsules so they could be identified in honey and pollen. Sure enough, on testing on a bee colony on the field, he "found microcapsules in the queen bee's gut and honey."[26]

Sadly, and predictably, Lee's discovery and talent went nowhere. He neither published his research nor continued with his honeybee investigations. Instead, he was forced to become a paper pusher at EPA headquarters while the agency's top pesticide managers made sure that Lee's laboratory would no longer be used for research threatening to industry. As with so many EPA moves, this was done to keep bad news about nerve gas pesticides secret.

This was not the first time Lee had rocked the boat at the agency. Just a few months earlier, he had warned managers that bees were also becoming threatened by another parathion-like toxin called EPN. In addition to being powerful in its own right, EPN made other agrochemicals even more virulent. Even nonlethal dosages of EPN decimated worker bees, Lee told EPA's pesticide boss, Edwin Johnson.

Three years earlier—the year the EPA had nearly approved the marketing of an extremely powerful nerve poison, leptophos—both an EPA chemist, Gunter Zweig, and a Duke University expert on poisons, Mohamed Abou-Donia, had warned him that EPN was far more potent a neurotoxin than leptophos, which the EPA had already restricted.

The evidence against these poisons mounted. The University of Illinois's Robert Metcalf said he had absolutely no doubt that EPN was a highly hazardous insecticide that could produce irreversible and life-threatening neurological damage in animals and human beings. Metcalf advised Johnson to severely restrict the exposure of people to nerve poisons like EPN, which are known to cause delayed crippling disabilities and subtle neurological disorders.[27]

Richard Lee and Robert Metcalf were wasting their time. They soon saw all too clearly that the EPA's business was to protect pesticide makers—neurotoxins or no neurotoxins. For nearly four decades, millions of pounds of EPN were sold every year, especially in areas that grow cotton. Only in 1987, after years of reported mass bee kills, did EPN begin to disappear from the farmers' armory.

Forty years after EPA first began approving neurotoxins enclosed in microscopic spheres, the same lethal tradition remains in place. And bees continue pay the price. Clothianidin, for example, is a bee killer belonging to a chemical group known as neonicotinoids—neurotoxins that disrupt the immune system of animals. Farmers have been buying clothianidin and other neonicotinoids since 2003 to "treat" corn and other major crop seeds. Plants (such as corn) grown from these soaked seeds become toxic at fantastically small amounts to any insect touching or eating them.

Neonicotinoids differ from conventional spray products in that they can be used as either seed dressings or soil treatments. When used as seed dressings, the insecticide will migrate from the stem to the leaf tips and eventually into flowers and pollen, writes Henk Tennekes, a Dutch toxicologist, who has warned that these systemic poisons have caused a drastic decline of insect-eating birds in Holland, the UK, Germany, Ireland, France, and Switzerland.

Neonicotinoid insecticides act by blocking receptors in an insect's central nervous system. "Any insect that feeds on the crop dies, but bees and butterflies that collect pollen or nectar from the crop are also poisoned," Tennekes writes. "The damage is cumulative, and with every exposure more receptors are blocked. In fact, there may not be a safe level of exposure." Worker bees neglect to provide food for eggs and larvae. A bee's navigational abilities break down. Exposed to very small quantities of the insecticides, entire colonies can collapse.

Neonicotinoids are also lethal to birds, as well as to the aquatic systems on which they depend. "A single corn kernel coated with a neonicotinoid can kill a songbird," according to a March 2013 report by the American Bird Conservancy. "Even a tiny grain of wheat or canola treated with the oldest neonicotinoid, imidacloprid, can poison a bird. As little as 1/10th of a corn seed per day during egg-laying season is all that is needed to affect reproduction with any of the neonicotinoids registered to date."

The bird conservancy accuses the EPA of ignoring the poisoning of the surface and groundwater by neonicotinoids. "Neonicotinoid contamination levels in surface and groundwater in the US and around the world are strikingly high, already beyond the threshold found to kill many aquatic invertebrates. EPA risk assessments have greatly underestimated this risk, using scientifically unsound, outdated methodology that has more to do with a game of chance than with a rigorous scientific process."

"It is astonishing," the report continues, "that EPA would allow a pesticide to be used in hundreds of products without ever requiring the registrant [chemical company] to develop the tools needed to diagnose poisoned wildlife." The report concludes that the EPA remains in a state of "enforced ignorance" and "in the dark."[28]

Some scientists have associated the rise of infectious disease in honeybees, birds, fish, bats, and amphibians to the widespread use of neonicotinoids. These chemicals cause immune suppression in honeybees and fish, resulting in the death of the affected organisms from disease. In January 2012, Steve Ellis, a beekeeper for thirty-five years and the secretary of the U.S. National Honeybee Advisory Board, worried openly about the possible end of his ancient profession.

Equally worrisome, the fact that ground and surface water contaminated by these poisons "cause irreversible and cumulative damage to aquatic and terrestrial (non-target) insects must lead to an environmental catastrophe," Tennekes writes. "The data presented show that it is actually taking place before our eyes, and that it must be stopped."[29]

Tellingly, though neonicotinoids are made by Bayer, the German giant chemical and pharmaceutical company, Germany (along with

Italy, France, and Slovenia) have banned this insidious compound. Other European regulators "seem to have turned a blind eye to data on the danger that one of the world's biggest selling pesticides [the neonicotinoid imidacloprid] could pose to bees and other pollinators," said Joan Walley, Member of Parliament in the UK.[30]

In a leaked EPA memo dated November 2, 2010, EPA scientists admitted that a 2003 Bayer study supporting the use of clothianidin was flawed. EPA scientists revealed that this insecticide "poses an acute and chronic risk to freshwater and estuarine/marine free-swimming invertebrates" and was "highly toxic" to honeybees.[31]

So, given all this evidence and all this concern, why has so little been done to protect bees? As always, the answer comes down to politics and money. For several decades, honey producers in the United States have worried that protesting the death of their bees would bring down the wrath of industrial farmers, who will either wipe them out with sprays or ruin them by suggesting that honey and pollen may be full of tiny capsules of nerve gas and numerous other poisons. This explains a depressing catch-22: even as their bees continue to die, honey producers have been largely silent; they are willing to lose some of their hives as a price for the social contract they have with the farmers whose insecticides kill their bees.

The Beekeepers Association of Texas, for instance, opposed state regulations creating a buffer zone between sprayed fields and other property. Beekeepers keep their mouths shut in order to survive, and farmers want to believe their crops are not harming people. No consumer would buy honey with pesticides in it.

Eduardo Gutierrez, the farmworker coordinator of the Texas Department of Agriculture, told me on December 27, 1984, that a beekeeper in Corpus Christi, Texas, who supported buffer regulations was nearly "wiped out"—by farmers who sprayed his hives directly. The farmers wanted to teach him a lesson about whistle-blowing.[32]

By the late 1980s, cities and various local and state governments had already spent decades using "vast quantities of insecticides with no concern for the havoc they bring on beekeepers by the destruction of their colonies and loss of their crops," wrote Dee A. Lusby, president, Arizona Beekeepers' Association. The number of bee colonies in Arizona had declined from over 150,000 to less than 63,000, Lusby wrote. "Some say the Environmental Protection Agency is required by law to 'Protect the Environment.' If this is so, why are not bees given the same consideration bestowed to other farm-domesticated livestock? Why are beekeepers treated like second-hand citizens in this state and several others without right of due process by law? Our beekeeping industry is being and has been systematically destroyed in this state due to a lackadaisical administration within our state's own Commission of Agriculture and Horticulture and the Environmental Protection Agency."[33]

Dee Lusby's concerns apparently touched no one. Her letters were long, replete with historical references and full of useful technical details about the lives of bees: why we need them, why we must protect them, especially from killer pesticides. For several years, especially in the 1980s and early 1990s, Lusby sent her letters to several state and federal agricultural and environmental administrators and key members of Congress. They all ignored her.

I talked to Lusby in July 1989. She told me that beekeepers who complain about pesticide poisoning paid a price. Farmers would "spray bomb" their hives, sometimes killing all the bees. Such was the cost of this war that few beekeepers dared go public with their grief and loss. This remains true today.

Lusby did not back down. EPA regulators are "like monkeys acting with rubber stamps and there are never any no's," she wrote on August 31, 1990, in a letter to dozens of state and federal officials— including chairmen of major congressional committees.

"The chemicals that kill and damage honeybees have been known for years," Lusby wrote. "So why doesn't the EPA, Congress, USDA, APHIS [Animal and Plant Health Inspection Service], States, and farm users listen? Well, it's because they never have had to, and because a veil of conspiracy-of-silent approval by looking the other way and seeing nothing exists. It's like seeing a clean house neat and proper looking on the outside, but on the inside and the closets there is filth that hasn't been cleaned up in many, many years. This is shameful!"

Lusby knew all about encapsulated insecticides. She was well read, and sophisticated about the technical and political aspects of beekeeping and farming. She warned that "beekeepers are told to accept the loss [of their honeybees to pesticide poisonings] and shut up or be blown out of business."[34]

Dee Lusby was unusual in her intimate knowledge of beekeeping and in her courage to speak out. In reading her long letters I felt the same outrage I experienced at the EPA. The problem is not that we don't know, but that government and industry refuse to do what is best for all of us, and for the natural world. The environment, science, and public health be damned.

Certainly now, in 2014, honeybees are facing an existential crisis, especially in America. In the late 1970s, when my EPA colleague Norman Cook was documenting honeybee death in the asphyxiating embrace of microencapsulated nerve gas pesticides, the situation was bad. But now nerve poison syndrome has become a holocaust for honeybees. Neonicotinoids take over the crop or plant; no matter where the honeybees are, nearly all crops are toxic to them, from their roots to their leaves and sweet nectars. The crops themselves become living pesticides. So now honeybees (and, by extension, honeybee keepers) are once again on the verge of extinction.

Since silence is clearly no longer an option, beekeepers are at last beginning to speak up.

When the EPA approved yet another neonicotinoid insecticide (sulfoxaflor, manufactured by Dow Chemical), beekeeping groups sued the agency in 2013.[35] Earthjustice, a public interest law firm, represented the honeybee organizations. "Our country is facing widespread bee colony collapse, and scientists are pointing to pesticides like sulfoxaflar as the cause," an Earthjustice lawyer, Janette Brimmer, said. "The effects will be devastating to our nation's food supply and also to the beekeeping industry, which is struggling because of toxic pesticides. This lawsuit against the EPA is an attempt by the beekeepers to save their suffering industry. The EPA has failed them. And the EPA's failure to adequately consider impacts to pollinators from these new pesticides is wreaking havoc on an important agricultural industry and gives short shrift to the requirements of the law."

Jeff Anderson, a beekeeper, said that the EPA's approval of sulfoxaflor "will speed our industry's demise" and that the EPA's claim that the product's label includes robust terms for protecting pollinators "is a bald-faced lie! There is absolutely no mandatory language on the label that protects pollinators. Further, the label's advisory language leads spray applicators to believe that notifying a beekeeper of a planned application absolves them of their legal responsibility in FIFRA to not kill pollinators."

The testimony against neonicotinoids was fast and furious. "The honeybee industry is very concerned since the EPA has failed to adequately address our comments about realistic risk to pollinators posed by sulfoxaflor," said George Hansen, president of the board of the American Beekeeping Federation. "The EPA continues to use flawed and outdated assessments of long-term and sublethal damage to honey bees."

"The sun is now rising on a day where pollinators are no longer plentiful," said Rick Smith, beekeeper and farmer. "They require protection three hundred sixty-five days a year in order to be abundant at the critical moment their pollination service is required by the plant. EPA's assessment process has chosen not to use long-established and accepted published information concerning pollinator foraging habits in the Environment Hazards Section of the sulfoxaflor label."[36]

Europeans, too, have begun taking on their corporations and government regulators over the bee crisis. The neonicotinoids are just another version of DDT, except more insidious and toxic, writes the British environmental author George Monbiot. Neonicotinoids are "ripping the natural world apart." Just as the producers of DDT claimed innocence for their golden spray, the manufacturers of neonicotinoids claim their products are harmless to all life save the target insects. "[W]e have gone into it blind," Monbiot writes. "Our governments have approved their use without the faintest idea of what the consequences are likely to be. The UK is collaborating in peddling the corporate line that neonicotinoid pesticides are safe to use—they are anything but." Governments that "should be defending the natural world have conspired with the manufacturers of wide-spectrum biocides to permit levels of destruction which we can only guess. In doing so they appear to be engineering another silent spring."[37]

CHAPTER 6

Agricultural Warfare

D R. MOHAMED Abou-Donia was waiting for me at the Raleigh-Durham airport. It was an early September morning in 1983, and I had taken the day off from Washington to visit Dr. Abou-Donia at Duke University, where he was a professor of pharmacology. An Egyptian-born American expert in neuropharmacology, Dr. Abou-Donia gave me a tour of his laboratory, where for several years he had doggedly investigated the impact of pesticides on the nerves and brains of animals and people.

I wanted to meet Dr. Abou-Donia because I knew from his research papers that he was not a typical scientist; indeed, his research had caused tremendous concern and anger among EPA staff. And I had a hunch that the research Dr. Abou-Donia had published would offer insight into something much larger: the structure, behavior, and effects of organophosphate chemicals used both in chemical warfare and on the American farm.

Dr. Abou-Donia is one of eight children, the son of a textile merchant in the cosmopolitan city of Alexandria, Egypt. In the 1950s, he remembers, his childhood neighborhood was full of Greeks who were forced to flee Gamal Abdel Nasser's fervent nationalism. Dr. Abou-Donia received an undergraduate degree in the chemistry of pesticides in Alexandria in 1961, then went to the University of

California, Berkeley, where he earned his doctorate in pharmacology, specializing in the chemistry of drugs and poisons.

His training complete, and newly married to an American wife, Dr. Abou-Donia returned to Alexandria, where he took a position in the department of plant protection in the college of agriculture of Alexandria University. Soon, however, he began to feel oppressed by the stifling educational and social conditions of his country. He was not merely a good scientist, but an honest man. This proved to be his undoing.

In the summer of 1971, some thirteen hundred water buffaloes dropped dead near cotton fields in the Nile delta that had been sprayed by leptophos, a highly profitable compound manufactured by Velsicol.

When the Egyptian government asked Dr. Abou-Donia and several other scientists to look into the tragedy, the scientists began by feeding experimental buffaloes crops contaminated with small amounts of the suspected poisons.

It quickly became clear that for the experimental buffaloes, leptophos caused paralysis and death. Yet—in a scene that has become all too familiar in the United States—the scientists working with Dr. Abou-Donia tried to sabotage the findings. Then the Egyptian minister of agriculture interrupted the experiment and sequestered the results. Because the university where he worked would not fund research that had been banned by the agriculture minister, Dr. Abou-Donia suddenly found himself on his own—all because he had done honest science.

The political strong-arming of his research made a deep impression on the young Dr. Abou-Donia. Outside his own circle of colleagues, he began noticing a strange parade of scientists and government bureaucrats arriving at Alexandria's luxurious Hilton Hotel to break bread with the multinational corporations selling pesticides to Egypt and the rest of the world.

His research on water buffaloes stymied, Abou-Donia decided to look into the effect of leptophos on chickens instead.

Once again, he found that the nerve agent caused irreversible (and lethal) damage to the experimental animals. Less than two weeks after the experiment began, young chickens rapidly began to lose weight and feathers and had great difficulty standing upright. A loss of muscular coordination (known as ataxia) caused swift paralysis and death from respiratory failure. Like the buffaloes before them, the birds were suffocating because their lungs failed.

Even before Dr. Abou-Donia published his warning about leptophos, news of the spray's destructive power had crossed the desks of EPA staff. Agency chemists Gunter Zweig and Donna Kuroda were particularly alarmed by what they had heard from Wendell Kilgore, a University of California professor who had been in Alexandria in 1972 and had learned about the plight of the water buffaloes and the obstruction of Dr. Abou-Donia's work.

Kuroda had also spoken to Robert Metcalf, an internationally renowned entomologist from the University of Illinois, who told her to do everything she could to keep leptophos off America's dinner table. Zweig then urged his senior colleagues to reject Velsicol's application for spraying leptophos on lettuce and tomato crops.

Not long afterward, Ronald Baron, an EPA scientist working out of the primate and pesticide effects laboratory in Perrine, Florida, found leptophos "capable of inducing a delayed neurotoxic response," a somewhat diplomatic way of saying leptophos kills after a few days of exposure.[1]

Despite the growing evidence being compiled by the world's scientists, EPA's political bosses were determined that Velsicol would get the chance to sell enough leptophos in the United States to cover the bulk of the country's supply of lettuce and tomatoes. EPA regulators dismissed Baron's discovery; injecting poison under the skin of chickens, as Baron had done, was not the same thing as feeding the poison to the birds. It was the dose that mattered, they reasoned, not the poison itself: senior EPA scientists were convinced the poison could be applied to food at low enough levels that it would not harm those who ate it.

And of course EPA scientists deferred to the authority of the Velsicol company itself, which naturally claimed that leptophos had been given a clean bill of health by the company's researchers.

In fact, leptophos had not been tested by Velsicol scientists; the work had been contracted out to a company called Industrial Bio-Test, which, as I will discuss in detail in the next chapter, did the dirty work for chemical and pharmaceutical industries so they could get their products approved by the government.

So even though evidence was mounting that leptophos would likely do to people exactly what it had done to water buffaloes and chickens in Egypt, Velsicol insisted to the end that the EPA should approve leptophos, and the EPA agreed. By 1974, the agency was prepared to look on while millions of Americans ate lettuce sprayed with 10 parts per million of this neurotoxin, and tomatoes with 2 parts per million.

In fact, the dangers leptophos posed to people were evident in Velsicol's own manufacturing plant at the Bayport industrial park, just thirty-five miles from downtown Houston. More than sixty workers making leptophos from 1973 to 1976 suffered horrible effects. Within only a few months of working with the solid, waxy substance, workers became confused; at least two were paralyzed.[2]

The evidence against leptophos was becoming irrefutable. Zweig and Kuroda, the EPA chemists who first sounded the alarm about the compound, sought the support of another EPA colleague, Howard Richardson, a medical doctor and noted government pathologist. Richardson examined the slides IBT had used in its experiments with chickens treated with leptophos, and he found the results "highly questionable and unreadable."

That was August 27, 1974. Just a few days later, Richardson and his wife Mary, also a physician with the EPA, left for a month in Europe, where they learned that the European chemical industry and European governments had reached an understanding that under no circumstances would they allow an insecticide like leptophos to get into food.

When the Richardsons returned to the United States convinced that leptophos was too dangerous to use safely, their stance added pressure within the EPA to revoke Velsicol's license. When news of the suffering of the Houston workers finally leaked in early 1976, the compound's toxic career in the United States was abruptly brought to an end.

When Velsicol appealed to keep leptophos on the market, a committee appointed by the EPA administrator declared that the compound "can lead to a progression of neurotoxic effects including central and peripheral neuropathy, ataxia, weakness, paralysis, and ultimately death."[3] This was, of course, music to the ears of Mohamed Abou-Donia, whose findings on the poisoned water buffaloes in Egypt had started the ball rolling. But as was true for the EPA's Zweig, Kuroda, and Richardson, Dr. Abou-Donia did not make many friends in the chemical bureaucracy of Washington.

"Leptophos pushed me out of Egypt," Dr. Abou-Donia told me. "I said to my American wife that if we stayed at the University of Alexandria, we would have to go on the take. So we left for the United States because I treasured my integrity, and because I really wanted to do good science. At Duke University I have done that. You can imagine my surprise, therefore, when I discovered that the United States and Egypt have this in common—both countries have the same chemical bosses. The people that did the bribing in Cairo and Alexandria are also the people that create all this terrible mess with the regulation of pesticides in Washington, D.C."

When the Reagan administration came to power in 1981, things only got worse, he said. "All the doors of EPA were shut on my face. EPA regulators said they no longer were interested in the delayed effects of nerve poisons. We desperately need to know more about these agricultural chemicals because they are used in such large quantities by so many people all over the world. You hear that a farmworker was poisoned by this or that organophosphate toxin—and that's it. At Duke University we are completely cut off from farmworkers and the entire agriculture of North Carolina. The state university has its extension agents, but they don't talk to us and we don't talk to them. And you know that the only people who want me to get back on pesticides research are the chemical warfare people of the U.S. Army."

Clearly, the fate of poisoned farmworkers has been considered far less urgent than guaranteeing profits for chemical companies; farmworkers, especially migrant workers, being at the very bottom of the socioeconomic ladder, carry little ammunition to counter the powerful voices of industry lobbyists. There are few stories more illustrative of this power imbalance than the tale of the work carried out by the Owens brothers.

In the early 1970s, the National Science Foundation and EPA awarded a grant of $600,000 to study pesticide exposure among migrant farmworkers to Clarence B. Owens, a professor of agronomy at the Florida Agricultural and Mechanical University. Owens was an ideal scientist for the study: an academic who did not mind working with his hands or mingling with workers at the very lowest strata of society. An African American scholar with compassion for migrant workers, Owens decided in 1976 to become a migrant farmworker himself. He would join America's untouchables, the ever-replaceable appendices to America's giant chemical farms, who were little better off than serfs in nineteenth-century Russia.

"The people perish. They are accustomed to the process of perishing," Leo Tolstoy wrote in his 1899 novel, *Resurrection*. "Customs and attitudes to life have appeared which accord with the process—the way children are allowed to die and women made to overwork, and the widespread undernourishment, especially of the aged. And this state of affairs has come about so gradually that the peasants themselves do not see the full horror of it, and do not raise their voices in complaint. For this reason, we, too, regard the situation as natural and proper."

I don't know if Owens knew Tolstoy's work, but he clearly had similar concerns: he wanted to see with his own eyes how migrant farmworkers in America are also accustomed to the process of perishing as they work our land and harvest our food. He worked alongside the workers of the Lawrence and Adams crews (two small groups of migrants named after their crew leaders) as they moved from fields in central Florida to coastal and then central North Carolina, central Pennsylvania, and New York's upper Hudson River Valley.

Owens joined these workers so he could experience their exhaustion, hunger, and humiliation and observe what was happening to them as they worked in the midst of plants loaded with pesticides. As part of the research, Owens and his brother, Emiel, a professor of finance at the University of Houston, took blood samples from the workers. They also recorded what the workers ate, carefully watched their health, and studied their physiological and social behavior day and night for the entire 1976 harvest season as the Owens brothers and their fellow farmhands gathered corn, tomatoes, peaches, squash, cucumbers, gladiola flowers, potatoes, tobacco, and apples.

The resemblance of a picker's day to that of an American slave could hardly have been lost on the African-American Owens. "When I arrived at the crew chief's home at about four a.m., they were already up and the wife was making chicken sandwiches to sell in the fields," he wrote. "At four-thirty, we loaded on the bus and headed toward the 'ramp.' The ramp is a place about a block square where workers assemble in the morning and growers and crew chiefs come to select work crews for the day's harvest. We drove on and dust began to rise from the muck soils as we headed down the lane toward the cornfield. I looked out the window of the bus, as the sun was coming up, and could see nothing but sweet corn, miles and miles of it."

As Owens and his crew unloaded from the bus, they noticed workers mounting "an awkward-looking machine." This was the mule train, from which "pullers" must harvest a minimum of fifty-six ears of corn per minute—almost an ear per second. The puller walks between two rows, pulling three ears of corn in each hand and simultaneously pitching the six ears into a bin just above his head. For this they were paid about three dollars a day.

The pullers are usually wet within the first thirty minutes in the field, a result of heavy dew on the plants caused by the soil's high water table. Combined with the almost colloidal dust particles, the dew leaves the worker's clothing as wet and black as the soil. The wet particles penetrate the worker's outer clothing and also make it difficult to clean undergarments after a day's work as a puller.

Owens jumped right in, taking a position first as a lead puller, then—when the pace proved too fast—as a wing puller. The rows were six hundred feet long, but they seemed endless. "I began to understand the reason for beginning work so early in the morning," Owens wrote. "The workers cannot tolerate the intense heat generated by the sun and the corn later in the day. Fine muck particles rise as the train moves along, covering workers with particles resembling coal dust. As we approached the end of the row some fifteen minutes was required for the train to turn around and get started again."

Out on the wing, the fumes from the train's engine added to the misery. It was then that Owens, looking off some 500 yards to the left, noticed the planes, "descending to the tassel level of the corn, spraying pesticides, protecting the corn against the earworm . . . I realized that at the pace we were moving we would be pulling the newly sprayed corn before nightfall," he wrote.

By the end of the day, Owens crew had hand-packed some four thousand crates of corn. Each puller got 12 cents a crate, the packer 10 cents, the box maker 3 cents; the tractor driver, the rickrack worker, and the loader split up the balance. Pullers earned about $30 a day, the packers $25, and on down the line. "Usually about one-fourth of the daily wages were spent at the store for drinks, food, and other items for relaxation."[4]

To Owens, the workers' hardships seemed appalling. The labor camps were infested with crawling insects, mosquitoes, and flies. There was one toilet for every eight workers, and only two-thirds of them were indoors. More than half the labor camps were located within fifty yards of crops sprayed with parathion, guthion, lanate, and sevin.

Owens also knew that most of the migrant farmworkers were hungry most of the time. He found their diet was "grossly inadequate," since the food they ate "approached the critical level of 50 percent of the recommended minimum daily caloric intake level."

A man with the teeth of hunger in his belly at the same time he is harvesting crops sprayed with toxins is playing with fire, perhaps even death. The key human enzyme affected by exposure to nerve poisons is known as acetylcholinesterase. Neurotoxic pesticides inhibit the production of this neurotransmitter—and the levels of acetylcholinesterase in the man were taking dangerous dives, Owens noticed, especially when the worker was not eating well. Some 80 percent of the workers developed severe skin rashes; two dozen required medical attention. A worker caught tuberculosis. A child died. A man died. At the Pennsylvania farm where the man died, a helicopter had applied three gallons of the nerve toxins parathion and guthion per acre, 12 times the recommended rate.

The early warning signs of acute or chronic pesticide poisoning are no more distinctive than a headache or dizziness. Unless farmworkers are "down and out," they are not likely to pay attention to a headache or a "wheezy stomach." Poor working people don't stop working "unless they are taken out of a field desperately ill."

The implication of this finding alone is frightening. Pesticides cripple and kill. They are also responsible for subtle and not so subtle changes in human behavior. A migrant farmworker at the end of a harvest season is not the same person he was when he started his migration. He has been subjected to a variety of "body insults" such as spray poisoning, a bad diet, and very bad living conditions.

Fifty-six percent of the farmworkers had "abnormal kidney and liver functions: 78 percent had severe chronic skin rash; and 54 percent abnormalities in chest cavities," Owens reported. "Migrant workers are young workers, i.e., mean age of 25 years, but their health statistics resemble those of middle-aged Americans."[5]

Owens's research has broad implications. Hundreds of thousands of American- and foreign-born laborers suffer the rigors of working on pesticide-laden farms. The Owens brothers must have known their findings would be considered adversarial by the very government that was funding them. Indeed, they spent considerable time between 1974 and 1982 begging the EPA and the National Science Foundation for further research support. But the National Science Foundation dropped the Owenses in 1977, and the next year, the EPA granted them less than $10,000. That would be their last check from the EPA.[6]

The EPA was apparently uninterested in the Owenses' concern that farm sprays caused debilitating sickness to the migrants laboring in the midst of poison-drenched vegetables and other crops. A senior EPA scientist and manager told the Owens brothers that more EPA money might become available as long as they offered "no attempt to draw 'cause-effect' correlations" between pesticides and health effects.

"I then told the 'Bros.' that once EPA had this report, we would seriously review . . . any proposal they put together for the support of further analytical work (not that we would fund it, but that we would consider it)," the EPA official wrote.[7]

Yet the Owenses' study, "The Extent of Exposure of Migrant Workers to Pesticides and Pesticide Residues," submitted both under the Carter administration in May 1978 and under the Reagan administration in May 1982, clearly showed the connection between toxic sprays and sickness among farmhands.

There were other reasons why the EPA dismissed the work of the Owens brothers. In the late 1970s, the agency was agonizing over another study done at Colorado State University, in which scientists studied the long-term effects of acute poisoning by the same nerve poisons that had so damaged the migrants in the Owens study. In this case, researchers examined not just farmers and nursery workers but people who worked in pesticide-formulating plants, aircraft spray pilots, even an agricultural chemicals salesman.

In their May 1980 report to the EPA, the scientists concluded that people exposed to acute poisoning with organophosphate pesticides—even just once in their entire lives—had experienced neurological problems, damage to fine motor and language functioning, and reduced memory and cognitive, intellectual, and perceptual function. Fully a quarter of the one hundred subjects suffered brain damage.[8]

The chemicals responsible for these life-threatening effects were primarily parathion, methyl parathion, and malathion—all nerve poisons. Methyl parathion caused 54 of the acute poisonings in Texas, while ethyl parathion was responsible for 42 acute poisonings, 24 of which took place in Colorado and 18 in Texas. In Colorado, malathion had poisoned six of the study subjects.

Hale Vandermer, an EPA scientist, warned his bosses about the implication of the Colorado study. What if additional studies confirmed these findings? Could people exposed to nerve pesticides end up with shattered nervous systems or brain damage? If these results held up, Vandermer reasoned, the country would face "a health problem of epidemic proportions." After all, he noted, beyond America's farmers, more than 56 percent of American families use organophosphate pesticides to kill insects *inside their homes.* Vandermer prepared a memo for EPA's top policy official, assistant administrator Steve Jellinek, but his warning never reached him.[9]

The Owens brothers' work and the Colorado study had clearly unsettled senior EPA officials. Credible science was telling them the agrochemical nerve gases used by millions of farmers and urban residents were making people sick, even killing them outright. Their moral and legal obligation to protect public health ought to have convinced them to ban all those dangerous organophosphate toxins.

But instead, they elected to look the other way, prolonging the profit-able lives of these neurotoxins.

Immediately after learning of the preliminary results of the Colorado study, EPA managers did two things. First, they put together a kind of Potemkin "farmworker program" right in the office of the top pesticides boss, Edwin Johnson.

As I've already described, the late 1970s and early 1980s were an especially trying time for the EPA. The Agent Orange crisis, espe-cially when 2,4,5-T and dioxin were found to have caused injury to women in Oregon, had forced the EPA to restrict (and finally ban) 2,4,5-T in 1983. Now organophosphates, which are central nervous system poisons, were being shown to cause brain damage in humans. The EPA's political bosses decided that something had to be done: not to ban more chemicals, but to deflect public opinion from these find-ings. The "farmworker program" filled the bill.

I spent a year working for this program, writing a series of memos about the harsh working conditions of farmworkers. But as admirable as the project may have seemed from the outside, in reality it was a pure public relations ploy: we put out press releases touting how much the government was doing to protect farmworkers who suffered the worst effects from organophosphates exposure. By the end of 1980, the EPA scientist James Boland had two thousand copies of the Colorado study. Yet few (if any) of those copies ever saw the light of day. Boland told me that the copies were warehoused in a government facility until the order came to trash them.[10]

Next, EPA senior managers canceled a special study of malathion, a parathion-like nerve toxin, being conducted by the Medical University of South Carolina. In Charleston, both people and mosqui-toes were being fogged with malathion nine months out of every year, so it was almost inevitable that people would react to the toxin, suffer-ing from symptoms including nasal and lung congestion, skin diseases, migraine headaches, gastroenteritis and gastrointestinal bleeding, and cardiovascular disorders.[11]

Malathion was hardly a new worry. In 1976, the U.S. Army Environmental Hygiene Agency had reported that one could disrupt a rat's behavior with low dosages of malathion while leaving its blood and brain cholinesterase pretty much intact. This meant, the army agency said, "that it may be misleading to assume that behavior is normal following malathion exposure simply because blood ChE activity is within normal ranges."[12]

In Saku, a Japanese community of about thirty thousand people raising apples, peaches, grapes, and rice, farmers used helicopters to spray parathion, malathion, EPN, and sumithion (all nerve toxins) on their crops. The result? People got sick. In 1971, Satoshi Ishikawa and three other professors from the School of Medicine of the University of Tokyo published a study of the effects of these poisons on children from four to sixteen years old. They found that after lengthy exposure to the nerve poisons, 98 percent of the children suffered a reduction in their vision and 95 percent had a narrowing of peripheral visual fields. Three-quarters had neurological and brain abnormalities; many had atrophied optic nerve and liver dysfunction.[13]

A pair of pathologists named Harvey L. Bank and Diane Melendez had been testing the effects of malathion on Charleston's people, and despite the EPA's decision to cancel their study, they sent their results to the agency anyway. Their conclusions were clear: malathion hypersensitivity was a widespread disease among the people of Charleston, and people's immunological and allergic reactions took place at minute amounts of exposure to pesticides—far lower than the amounts EPA managers and risk assessors had certified as "safe."[14]

I don't know whether the EPA managers were looking only at the alarming implications of the South Carolina study when they cut it short by pulling their support and funding, or if they had done their homework and knew that malathion was not the harmless stuff they claimed it to be. But I guess that by the time they decided to do away with the South Carolina study, they knew the USDA was going to spray malathion in the orange groves of Northern California to "eradicate" the Mediterranean fruit fly. Suppressing unpleasant facts about malathion cleared the way for the USDA to indiscriminately endanger hundreds of thousands of people in the San Francisco Bay Area.[15]

In 1976, the EPA was under pressure from Congress to plug the regulatory holes it had inherited from the USDA. This translated into fifty thousand pesticide products with dubious safety records. The EPA also had to deal with more than four thousand compound "tolerances"; that is, it had to evaluate the maximum amount of pesticides to be allowed in food. This also happened to be the time when news of the massive IBT fraud (which I will discuss in the next chapter) had begun to challenge all past assumptions of scientific integrity in the regulation of pesticides.

This was all too much for Senator Edward Kennedy, who chaired the Senate Judiciary Subcommittee on Administrative Practice and Procedure. He launched an investigation that concluded that "pesticides regulation in the United States is fundamentally deficient."

The EPA has "largely failed in its responsibility to assure the safe use of pesticides," Kennedy wrote in the report. "EPA has failed the consumer and the farmer, as well as the pesticide industry. I find it incredible that a regulatory agency charged with safeguarding the public health and the environment would be so sluggish to recognize and react to so many warnings over the past 5 years . . . The EPA was warned and certainly should have known that testing data, submitted by industry as long ago as 25 years ago, should not be accepted at face value in the reregistration of thousands of pesticide products presently used in our farms and in our homes. But EPA by and large ignored these warnings. Even more alarming is that apparently EPA made a conscious policy decision sometime in 1973 or 1974 not to evaluate the safety testing data submitted by pesticide manufacturers. The record behind this decision is not entirely clear. What is clear, however, is that EPA had no sound basis upon which to assume that data 15, 20, or 25 years old was generally good and reliable . . . In my view, EPA's decision in the 1970's not to evaluate safety testing data submitted in the 1950's and 1960's was irresponsible."[16]

The South Carolina study merely confirmed what other scientists were beginning to suspect about the dangers toxins posed to the body's intricate systems. EPA had funded another study in the mid-1970s at the University of Arkansas for Medical Sciences in which the main investigator, Joan Spyker Cranmer, discovered that exposing mice before birth to pesticides had "profound" behavioral effects on the newborn animals. Cranmer was a pioneer in the examination of chemicals known as endocrine disruptors—chemicals that don't fit the accepted maxim that "the dose makes the poison."

Here's the problem. Given the infinitely subtle chemical dance that goes on inside the human body, even the tiniest exposure to some toxins can throw the body's music off key. And people who spend a lot of time in the home—notably women and children—suffer disproportionately from chemical burdens, because poisons trapped in the home can reach levels up to one hundred times higher than in the outdoor air.

Equally troubling, many chemicals, including chlorine-based poisons (DDT, toxaphene, PCBs, dioxins, and eleven thousand other organochlorines) mimic the female hormone estrogen, so they are particularly dangerous to women. Organochlorines are known to disrupt human developmental and reproductive mechanisms, causing breast cancer in women and feminization in men. Furthermore, these and other toxins can also pass from mother to fetus across the blood-placenta barrier and have deleterious effects on undeveloped organ and immune systems.

"Large numbers and large quantities of endocrine-disrupting chemicals have been released into the environment since World War II," the eminent scientist Theo Colborn has written. "Many of these chemicals can disturb development of the endocrine system and of the organs that respond to endocrine signals in organisms indirectly exposed during prenatal and or early postnatal life; effects of exposure during development are permanent and irreversible. The risk to the developing organism can also stem from direct exposure of the offspring after birth or hatching."[17]

Endocrine disruptors mimic or block hormones, and at nearly infinitesimal amounts, these chemicals cause harm to the system responsible for the development and healthy functioning of animals and human beings. The endocrine system regulates the body by sending signaling molecules and hormones into the bloodstream. Interfere with that process, as endocrine-disrupting chemicals do, and you get deadly diseases and birth defects. Large amounts of dioxin will be fatal, for example, but tiny amounts like those people get from eating contaminated foods "increases women's risk of reproductive abnormalities," according to Laura Vandenberg of Tufts University. "There truly are no safe doses for these hormone-altering chemicals. Hundreds of studies have examined people from the general population and found associations between low levels of hormone-altering compounds and infertility, cardiovascular disease, obesity, abnormal bone health, cancer and other diseases."[18]

Among the endocrine-disrupting chemicals, the most deadly and ubiquitous include pesticides, plastic components and plasticizers, phytoestrogens, preservatives, industrial chemicals, flame retardants, sunblock, and fragrances. The result of poisoning life by tiny amounts of toxins is "neurological diseases, reproductive disorders, thyroid dysfunction, immune and metabolic disorders and more," Theo Colborn writes.[19]

Warren Porter, a professor of zoology at the University of Wisconsin, has found that rats and mice exposed to toxin levels similar to those found in groundwater all over the United States suffer measurable damage to their immune, endocrine, and neurological systems. Among other impacts, he found, this damage has made the animals more aggressive. Other studies complement these findings, revealing that children exposed to pesticides in utero or at preschool age turn out to be highly aggressive, with diminished intelligence and decreased stamina.[20]

For a time, the EPA supported the innovative and original work of scientists such as Joan Spyker Cranmer, even buying equipment for her laboratory. But after the late 1970s, when agency administrators read Cranmer's report, the EPA tried to neutralize her laboratory and work, demanding that the University of Arkansas for Medical Sciences transfer the EPA equipment from Dr. Cranmer's laboratory to the Government Services Administration. The reason? Cranmer had found that low-level exposure of the women to three farm sprays (carbofuran, diazinon, and chlordane) pose "significant danger to the developing fetus."[21]

In an August 17, 1979, letter to the EPA administrator, Douglas M. Costle, Dr. Cranmer accused the EPA of destroying a laboratory that had received national and international recognition and honors for its pioneering studies of the subtle and delayed effects of environmental chemicals on living organisms. "I feel that for EPA to destroy my laboratory by recalling equipment being used to generate data needed by the Agency would be the height of administrative folly," Cranmer wrote. The letter had its intended consequence—EPA stopped demanding the return of its equipment—but the effort to disrupt the promising and timely work of Dr. Cranmer showed all too clearly how thoroughly the EPA was still beholden to agribusiness.

Cranmer is now a professor of pediatrics and pharmacology at the University of Arkansas School of Medicine and a respected member of Children's Environmental Health Network. As it has done to so many other skilled scientists, the EPA damaged Cranmer's career. Instead of encouraging her innovative and extremely useful work, the agency tried to bury her discovery and her spirit with crude managerial moves. But this behavior was also a setback for all researchers bent on investigating the origins of what (decades later) we know to be the endocrine-disrupting effect of petrochemicals on living beings.

As I explained above, the endocrine system controls the growth and development of organisms. The phenomenon that Cranmer discovered in 1979—that minuscule quantities of farm sprays have deadly effects on mice—has now been shown to be far more widespread than anyone could have imagined. So when it got rid of Cranmer, the EPA derailed a scientific advance that was not only prescient but lifesaving.

CHAPTER 7

The Swamp: The Big Business
of Fraudulent Science

I N the fight against corruption in the chemical industry and within the EPA, there have been few more courageous soldiers than Adrian Gross.

In the early 1980s, Gross was in his late fifties, five feet eight inches tall, round and muscular, with a small, nearly bald head, wire-rimmed glasses, and blue eyes. He walked bent slightly forward, usually holding a filterless Pall Mall cigarette. He often wore a tie, but he always wore a black leather jacket, carrying with him the rest of the protective gear that goes with driving a huge motorbike. He looked like an army corporal ready to do battle against a fierce enemy.

Gross was not a man for small talk, though he enjoyed telling jokes and stories. He spoke clearly, with the distinct accent of a highly educated Romanian Jew. At the age of sixteen, Gross had fled Romania for Palestine, where he joined the British army and fought in World War II. During the creation of the Jewish state, Gross fought against the British in Palestine. He then left for Canada, where he did advanced studies in veterinary pathology, before coming to the United States for more advanced education, earning a doctorate in statistics and biometry at Michigan State University.

It was this cosmopolitan background and scientific rigor that Gross brought to his work, first at the FDA and later at the EPA. His speech was characterized by ruthless logic, arrogance, and crushing contempt for the failings of less intelligent, less courageous human beings. But Gross was also unpretentious, with both a European's erudition and a peasant's forthrightness. He made difficult scientific issues easy to understand, but when he found fault with the science of others, he became angry. And if he smelled unethical behavior—and he smelled a lot of unethical behavior at the EPA—he became enraged. "Once you begin to ask questions, the entire fabric of gangsterism begins to fall apart, because some people are honest and resent having to fabricate things for too long for money," Gross told me. "People are jealous and they are ready to spill the beans once the opportunity knocks at their door."

"How do you deal with the crooks we have here at EPA?" Gross asked me. "After all, these are managers and scientists who work for the government. They are paid high salaries. Why do you think I have spent at least twenty years of my life in this struggle— fighting constant battles against those who want to feed the American people carcinogens? I'm also at war with these government scientists and administrators and chemical company men. They are destroying science in this country while they are poisoning its people, all of them."

Gross had the toughness of a military veteran who had served with the British paratroopers fighting the Germans in Europe. And no sooner did he join the bureaucracy of the U.S. government than his outstanding scientific training (as a pathologist and statistician) and cunning slowly made him one of the foremost scientific investigators in the United States.

"You only master toxicology with experience. You need fifteen to twenty years on the job to know what things to look for when you review an animal study," Gross told me. "There are more than a hundred different kinds of cancer you must be able to detect when you look at a pathology slide. We are here to see that people don't eat carcinogens. So the first thing they should do at the toxicology branch is to ask their reviewers *to read the studies we get from the chemical companies.*"

When the EPA first approached Gross, they told him they wanted him to fix a "terrible mess" in the pesticides program: staff scientists were openly using industry's own in-house (and therefore inherently biased) science in the formal approval process of dangerous chemicals. This was not oversight, it was rubber-stamping.

"The cut-and-paste business was what really broke the camel's back," Gross said. "Every Friday afternoon I used to get all my scientists together and discuss how you handle a review of an animal study. And if I had been left alone, I think, I could have made a difference, guiding those toxicologists in the right direction. But careful reading of what the chemical companies send to EPA in support of their sprays takes time. They pushed me out of that position, and the cut-and-paste reviews got into the routine of EPA's business. Now I walk through the corridors where these cut-and-paste scientists work and, once they see me, they cease their discussion and look at the ceiling. Need I say these are also dangerous people who threaten public health as much as pesticide companies do?"

Congress could easily demolish the toxic alliance between EPA's senior managers and the chemical industry, Gross says, but the truth is that congressmen and senators "don't care especially when the agribusiness contributes money for their reelection."

"You need to fire EPA's senior managers and start all over again with a small and dedicated scientific staff to do the critical job of safeguarding our people from the deleterious effects of farm sprays," Gross told me. "In this business you cannot cover up for too long, especially when you have so many people involved with simple operations like cleaning the shit out of the animal cages while scientists carry out complex experiments, each of which may involve hundreds of animals."

I knew Adrian Gross for several years. I listened to his stories for many hours over a long period of time, and I admired his courage to expose fraud in the chemical industry and the government. And when it came to fraud, there were not many bigger cases than the scientific cesspool called IBT Laboratories.

Industrial Bio-Test Laboratories was a biological research and testing organization created in 1952 to test all kinds of chemicals for human safety and environmental effects. Joseph Calandra, the man who founded IBT, was a professor and scientist with advanced degrees in biochemistry and medicine. Calandra taught at the medical and dental schools of Northwestern University in Evanston, Illinois, just outside Chicago. He built his lab in Northbrook, a suburb close to Northwestern, and when his business picked up, he expanded his testing facilities to Wedge Creek, Wisconsin, and Decatur, Illinois.

At its peak, in 1976, IBT had 230,000 square feet of space, a research farm of more than two hundred acres, and laboratories in three cities. Calandra was also in charge of some three hundred fifty people doing as many as two thousand new studies a year. In 1966, Calandra sold IBT to Nalco, a large chemical company. But he remained president of IBT until IBT went bankrupt in the late 1970s.

IBT went bankrupt because of Adrian Gross.

One of the most significant documents in any laboratory testing on live subjects is the log a technician keeps in order to record observations of what is happening to each animal throughout the course of the experiment. The animals eat food that has been poisoned, so if the poison causes serious toxic effects, a careful observer is likely to see how the toxins affect the behavior and body of the animals he has been watching. When an animal is "sacrificed" for autopsy, the visual inspection of an abnormal growth, for example, is taken a step further with a microscopic examination to determine the nature of that growth. From all that "raw data," the lab issues a report about the chemical tested and gives it to the company or organization that paid for the testing. Typically, that organization then uses the lab's findings to convince the government that its chemical product is safe for people and the environment and to "register" it for sale and general use.

Though it is far from a perfect system, and it is in many ways morally objectionable, animal testing does provide a reliable picture of what happens when toxins contaminate living organisms. Government regulators are crippled and blind without that picture. But they are far worse off if the picture they are shown is fake.

Inside IBT, scientists with advanced degrees in chemistry, toxicology, biology, pharmacology, and medicine engaged in a criminal conspiracy for close to twenty-five years. IBT executives falsified test data in order to hide the fact that their laboratory was in a shambles. Animals were escaping. Huge numbers of them were dying. Lab techs forgot to run tests on some of the animals. Researchers simply made up page after page of data and put it in the reports. They backdated documents in order to hide the scheme.

Throughout this time, IBT's services were being contracted by some of the country's largest and wealthiest chemical companies, who showed no obvious concern for rigorous, objective scientific testing. Monsanto, for example, had one of its own men in the halls of IBT faking the testing of TCC (trichlorocarbanilide), a toxic antibacterial substance that in the 1950s and 1960s began to appear widely in soaps, laundry detergents, rinse additives, and softeners. This compound was hardly benign; in 1962, a number of premature infants in California were struck with methemoglobinemia, an extremely dangerous disease originating in diapers laundered with a softener made from a mixture of quaternary ammonium and TCC.

Yet by the mid-1970s, Monsanto was still having IBT labs conduct "tests" of TCC so that it could keep using it in deodorant soaps like Dial. Scientists carried out these "studies" in the most infamous chamber of IBT—a cement cauldron of filthy water, disease, and slaughter known, appropriately enough, as "the swamp." Workers were reluctant even to step into that room because many lab animals were out of their cages. The animals in the swamp were hungry, thirsty, and mean, drowning in pools of water and excrement, rotting with disease in overcrowded quarters.

So many rats died during the study that the study should have been canceled. Instead, late-started animals were substituted into the study, and the data from the new rats was mixed in with the data for the original rats. The study lied about that data.

Monsanto's man at IBT, who was in charge of the rat toxicity studies, knew about the mixing of the data. He knew that new animals were being ordered and that they were being substituted in, and he did nothing to disclose it. After the scientist went back to Monsanto, he tried to make sure that the report was clean enough so that it could pass approval with the FDA.

And the fraud continued. Dr. Donovan Gordon, IBT's pathologist, concluded that even the lowest doses of TCC were harmful to rats' testicles. But Gordon would learn the hard way what happens when you contradict corporate "science."

Before Calandra hired him at IBT, Gordon had been a young scientist earning very little at Abbott Laboratories, a Chicago-based pharmaceutical firm. Calandra made Gordon his right-hand man in IBT's pathology lab. But he did much more than that. He helped Gordon buy a nice house in Chicago's suburb of Northbrook. He gave Gordon a car. Gordon was African American, and he was paid a good enough salary that he could, at a time of civil rights strife between blacks and whites in Chicago, put his children in private schools. That way, Calandra put Gordon in a golden cage of subservience and indebtedness. The tragedy was that Gordon was one of the first African-American pathologists to make it in the United States.

When Calandra first read Gordon's report that Monsanto's TCC caused testicular degeneration in rats even at the lowest dosage, he invited him to his office and told him that the company (and therefore Gordon) could go on doing the things they liked in life only because of the goodwill of companies like Monsanto. Why don't you look at some more TCC slides? Calandra asked. Gordon did and, the second time around, he found TCC clean and safe.

Monsanto itself then hired an independent pathologist named Dr. William Ribelin to examine rat testicle slides. But when Ribelin reached the same conclusion as in Dr. Gordon's first report, Monsanto knew this would cause problems with the FDA, so Ribelin's report was never submitted to them.

In early 1975, Calandra himself took personal control over all report writing at IBT, and he directed changes in the TCC report. Calandra conducted most of the important meetings regarding the changes, and he made the ultimate decisions on what lies were going to be included in the report.[1]

Word of this fiasco reached the EPA when Manny Reyna, an IBT technician from Latin America, told Adrian Gross how the lab was cutting corners with its testing. The entire laboratory, one of the largest in the country, was a nightmare, Reyna said.

In a corrupt place like IBT, nothing was sacred. Intimidated scientists and technicians did everything to make sure their studies found nothing that would raise questions with the government.

Here's what Gross learned: Technicians used the acronym TBDs for animals that were "too badly decomposed." When animals escaped from their cages—and they did by the dozens nearly every day—IBT men hunted them down with "little spray bottles of chloroform." IBT technicians cut tumors from the experimental animals and dumped their carcasses in the garbage. They disposed of all animals that showed any effects from the tested chemical. And if IBT researchers completed a two-year study in, say, fourteen months, they just invented all the data from the missing ten months. Meanwhile, IBT managers cut corners with lab workers; they did not train them well, and they did not pay them well. Most techs worked long hours in an unhealthy environment of brutality and alienation.[2]

IBT had been allowed to manage this swamp for twenty-four years without anybody on the outside, especially in government agencies, doing anything about it. It's not that people didn't know. On March 1, 1978, Edwin Johnson wrote a memo noting that "evidence is accumulating which suggests prior knowledge of those practices by the sponsor(s) of the [fraudulent spray] studies . . . I know that you share my deep concern regarding the seriousness of the regulatory ramifications of these recent findings of falsification of data upon which national and international regulatory decisions have been made."

Adrian Gross and his government colleagues finally confronted Gordon with the fake science Calandra was purchasing from him. Government lawyers wanted to indict him, but Gross argued successfully for giving him immunity so the full depth of the corruption at IBT could be exposed. Gordon managed to tell his story, but his experience at IBT ruined him.[3]

IBT lawyers discovered that Gordon had suffered a nervous breakdown, which made it necessary for him to be treated with hypnosis by a Northwestern University psychologist. The IBT lawyers tried, unsuccessfully, to discredit Gordon's testimony and have the court declare a mistrial. Even Monsanto dumped its man at IBT the minute the trial in Chicago came to an end.

"It was easy for me to smell the filth of IBT," Gross explained to me. "Don't forget, I was dealing with crooks who were too greedy, who were not satisfied to make a buck. And when you cheat, you are bound to make a simple error like recording all the fake numbers in neat columns at the same time with the same pencil."

Throughout the years that IBT was pulling off an enormous (and dangerous) fraud on the public, only one senior EPA official thought seriously of doing something about it: Richard D. Wilson, deputy assistant administrator for general enforcement. Wilson wanted to use the case of two nerve pesticides, acephate and orthene, made by the Chevron Chemical Company, to demonstrate what the government would do to companies that benefited from the crimes of IBT. The EPA had discovered that Chevron had submitted "inaccurate" testing data, Wilson wrote, and "the inaccuracies may have been the result of a deliberate falsification of the original test results by IBT."

Wilson told the EPA's pesticide boss, Edwin Johnson, that he knew that IBT had faked the information and that Chevron had nonetheless used this data to convince the government that it would be safe for people to eat food contaminated with acephate. What was needed, Wilson wrote, was "strong legal action against those responsible."[4]

For the government to retain any credibility, the EPA should have withdrawn Chevron's license to continue contaminating our food. But the agency did no such thing. The EPA's ears were attuned to signals from the White House, and when senior officials could (and should) have followed Dick Wilson's reasonable advice, they did not.

In fact, officials in both the EPA and the Department of Justice who were responsible for investigating and prosecuting the IBT felons made a deliberate decision not to go after corporations like Monsanto and Chevron that had benefited from IBT's crimes. If they had, the IBT case could have shut down a large segment of America's chemical industry.

Instead, the Carter administration ordered the EPA to focus only on the IBT lab in Chicago and to leave the larger fish alone. The EPA told anyone asking questions about the "safety" of the IBT chemicals that the EPA had "supplementary studies" supporting the continued registration of the IBT-sanctioned chemicals.

It wasn't as if IBT was the only bad actor. In 1977, an FDA inspector had discovered that a lab in Missouri was also making things up; in the diplomatic language of the FDA, inspectors "uncovered significant deficiencies in several animal toxicology studies." Monsanto was the lab's principal client.

EPA scientists and a FDA inspector paid a visit to a lab in Northern California that they suspected was generating data that was "very incomplete." The lab, which tested pesticides for Shell Oil Company, refused to admit the federal officials into the lab. Another FDA-EPA team of auditors visited a toxicology lab in Florida and discovered "possible data fraud." The lab was "apparently falsifying results of studies" and was "suspected of fabricating data." In Chicago, meanwhile, the Velsicol Chemical Corporation was indicted in court in 1977 for refusing to notify EPA that their best-selling pesticides, heptachlor and chlordane, "induced tumors in laboratory animals."[5]

Such cases made it hard to trust in the reliability of *any* EPA studies—especially when EPA scientists themselves (or their contractors) indulge in their own IBT-like "cutting and pasting" of a company's own "scientific" information. Such studies are unreliable "because EPA toxicologists don't really review them," Adrian Gross told me. "Instead, they go straight to the company's summary and lift it word for word and give it as their own evaluation of those studies."[6] This is what makes the EPA "so rotten," Gross said. Scientists earn good money to serve the public, but instead, "they end up covering up for the chemical industry."[7]

In 1983, seven years after Adrian Gross revealed that IBT was faking results in its multimillion-dollar testing, Joseph Calandra and three other IBT officials were brought to trial in the U.S. District Court in Chicago. The criminal trial lasted for six months and filled seventeen thousand pages of transcript.

The fact the trial took place at all was remarkable. On the one hand, you had the powerful interests of the chemical industry, and on the other hand, you had a White House and federal bureaucracy bent on doing nothing contrary to the interests of the chemical industry. This was particularly obvious during the Reagan administration, when the government was so clearly siding with industrial giants. The IBT-Nalco executives knew that, so they hired one of Chicago's most prestigious lawyers, George Cotsirilos, to get them off the hook.

Cotsirilos came close to doing just that. Calandra's lab, after all, was meeting a great need in the chemical industry, so throughout his career, both his business and his personal fortunes had soared. The grand jury sent the Justice Department lawyers in Chicago a sealed indictment of Joseph Calandra, IBT's chief executive, along with indictments of three other IBT officials.[8] Calandra was a pillar in his community, his philanthropy well known.[9]

Despite Nalco's paying George Cotsirilos hundreds of thousands of dollars, the Chicago jury found all four IBT executives guilty of fraud. Three of them were given brief jail sentences. Calandra stayed out of prison, indicted but free because his lawyer argued that Calandra had had an aneurysm of the aorta that threatened his life.

In the end, the IBT trial—as dramatic as it was—was a rare moment when such corruption was actually brought to light. For pesticides alone, IBT faked the information the government used for the registration or licensing of at least 212 ingredients. This fact is deeply troubling if you realize that the thousands of products made from these 212 "pesticide active ingredients" represent many acutely toxic and widely used sprays in the United States and throughout the world.[10]

In 1981, five years after the IBT scandal became public, EPA calculated some of the damage. Nearly 65 percent of the company's studies were deemed invalid. Data from eighteen laboratories, or about 20 percent, was considered "questionable or unacceptable for regulatory purposes." The rate of invalidity of pivotal studies "was so high that reliance on the data is risky."[11]

Some time in late 1981, EPA prepared a "fact sheet" on the IBT disaster in which the agency gave credit to the FDA for the discovery of the fraud. "FDA uncovered problems so serious that, after documentation and review of the reports, they refused to accept further IBT studies and insisted that the 40 or so studies submitted to FDA be replaced," the report said.

"Raw data" (basic information on the material tested and its effects on the lab animals) was "missing" and "shredded." For some of the data that survived, it was impossible to make certain that it was authentic. It went on. Those who worked at IBT did not fit their job descriptions. The inspectors found "undocumented changes [in study protocols], [and]several protocols [were] used interchangeably." The inspectors also found very little information on what the lab animals ate, how much, when, or what the food was mixed with. Not only that, but the lab kept "extra animals for the entire test." This is because it was common in the IBT for the animals to "die twice." The lab workers used "gang caging" for the animals.

The fact sheet also summarized the frequency of invalid IBT data. For example, in June 1980, all the two-year rat studies were invalid; in December 1981, the failure rate was 95 percent. In other words, of 41 studies reviewed, 39 were invalid. In general, the percentage of invalid studies in December 1981 ranged from 29 to 95.[12]

Far more worrisome than this laundry list of tawdry revelations was this simple fact: for about a quarter of a century, thousands of farm sprays that had been "tested" by IBT ended up in the food and drinking water of hundreds of millions of people in the United States and throughout the world. It is impossible to assess the damage of this massive poisoning, but it must surely have been a considerable factor in human disease and death.

IBT's betrayal of the public trust was spectacular largely because of its magnitude, involving as it did a company carrying out roughly 40 percent of all tests for industrial agribusiness and the chemical and drug industries. But even as this fraud was going on, other, smaller laboratories were engaged in their own versions of faking data and manipulating science.

Around this time, a female scientist told me of atrocious conditions at a veterinary, toxicology, and entomology research laboratory of the U.S. Department of Agriculture in College Station, Texas. The woman referred to Dimilin "tests" that took place in a USDA lab farm experimenting to see whether Dimilin had any effect on male chickens' levels of testosterone, a hormone vital for normal reproduction.

Dimilin belongs to a group of chlorinated diphenyl poisons known as "insect growth regulators." Growth regulation is essentially biological warfare: a chemical like Dimilin poisons (and thus inhibits) an organism's growth or development, often resulting in the disfigurement or premature death of the organism. When industry (and EPA scientists) say Dimilin "decreases testosterone levels in roosters," what they really mean is "Dimilin sterilizes roosters."[13]

Dimilin, it turned out, was especially deadly during molting. The compound made it impossible for insects and arthropods such as shrimp, crayfish, lobsters, and crabs to build a new exoskeleton; young animals would die because they had no hard tissue in their bodies for walking, flying, swimming, or protection.

But Dimilin also neutered both insects and warm-blooded animals, and in very small amounts. It takes only 75 parts per trillion of Dimilin in water, for instance, to sterilize mysid shrimp, an organism at the very base of the ocean's food chain.

In the laboratory, scientists had discovered unsettling results: feeding roosters and hens food mixed with even tiny amounts of Dimilin made them different birds. The hens grew fat and huge, the roosters became thin and small with practically no secondary sex characteristics left in their combs and wattles and nearly no sex hormone left in their testes. These remarkable discoveries came out into the open thanks to another USDA man, James E. Wright, an entomologist who published the lab's findings in 1976 in volume 14 of *Environmental Health Perspectives*.

But these findings were not what industry—or its companions in government—wanted to hear. The USDA did not appreciate EPA inspectors checking up on its scientists; The USDA argued that its findings on Dimilin were in the open literature, so how could it be blamed if companies used such findings to register the chemical with the EPA?

This reasoning was disingenuous at best. The bottom line was that the Texas lab was a mess. For starters, the poultry manager had been out following a heart attack, which meant—at the very least— that the birds did not get fed regularly. "The state of malnutrition during the critical growth period, from 0–35 days, appears to have, upon re-examination, retarded the birds' growth," the report said.

Many of the birds were overcrowded in their cages, and essentially starved.[14]

Laurence Chitlik and Salvatore Biscardi, the EPA investigators who visited the USDA's chicken lab in Texas, found the studies invalid, since the chickens' starvation probably diminished the Dimilin effect.[15]

Their EPA supervisors were also unsettled. The audit revealed "numerous irregularities in laboratory practice which ranged from conditions which unduly stressed the test animals to possible sabotage."[16]

Bizarrely, none of this caused a ripple in the companies that had used the results of the chicken study to support EPA applications to sell Dimilin as an "insect growth regulator"—which now contaminates beef, eggs, goat, pork, milk, mushrooms, lamb, sheep, and soybeans.

And on it went. In January 1985, an EPA biologist named Jack McCann got wind of pesticide testing data that a defunct laboratory had abandoned in a room at the Reading, Pennsylvania, airport. The data, which the EPA depended on to determine whether a chemical was safe, had been produced in a lab run by a toxicologist named Gaston E. Cannon. The lab had gone bankrupt before August 1983, and the airport, which had rented space to the Cannon lab, was threatening to clear the room unless it got its rent. American Standard Bioscience, the company that bought Cannon, was not exactly rushing to secure these "raw data" documents.

Between 1973 and 1983, Cannon had done more than a thousand studies in support of sixty-nine pesticides, among them some of the largest-selling, and acutely toxic, sprays used by American farmers. Cannon's clients included many American, British, Swiss, and French giants in the global chemical industry, including Union Carbide, DuPont, Zoecon, Mobil Chemical, Rohm and Haas, Pennwalt, Mobay, FMC, Chemargo, Thompson-Hayward, American Hoechst, Ciba-Geigy, Rhône-Poulenc, Uniroyal Chemical, and Velsicol. Cannon also served government institutions including the U.S. Forest Service, the U.S. Department of Agriculture, the Colorado

Department of Agriculture, and the New York State Experiment Station.

Yet such was the state of affairs between EPA, the chemical industry, and the testing labs serving that industry that in January 1985, data from these studies—without which hugely profitable pesticides would not have been allowed on the market—was about to be thrown into a Pennsylvania dump.

That February, Jack McCann told Adrian Gross and me that in his opinion, the Cannon lab might be a "mini-IBT." By using that magic acronym, the humble, soft-spoken wildlife biologist expressed his fears about the enormity of what might be revealed in a rigorous investigation of the Cannon lab.[17]

For years, McCann had had a feeling that something was not right at the Cannon lab. In the early 1970s, he warned other EPA scientists that the science being conducted at that testing facility was extremely poor. In August 1983, Gross and an inspector from the FDA had gone to the Cannon lab to audit an animal study the lab had done some years before for the Pennwalt Corporation. That two-year study had examined the effects on mice of a weed killer, disodium endothall; technicians examined mice tissue to see whether endothall caused cancer in the experimental animals.

Because the inspection of this important study was done at least five years after its execution, Gross and his colleague simply sifted through what was left in the lab in the form of written records or "raw data." They discovered that the science being practiced in the Cannon lab was atrocious. Lab techs kept five mice in every cage, which caused crowding so bad that some mice ate the others. Several of the mice that survived cannibalism had their ears chewed off.[18]

Inside the lab, the magnitude and implications of the research problems were beyond anyone's guess. The Cannon lab was very small, employing at most four scientists and three technicians. Yet for ten years it "tested" numerous industrial chemicals, drugs, pesticides, food additives, and cosmetics. In 1980, for example—in pesticides

alone—the Cannon lab agreed to do 86 animal studies for 19 chemical companies and other organizations. And in 1981, Cannon lab
started 42 studies for 12 clients. How could a very modest testing
facility like the Cannon lab do all that complex and exacting work and
do it right?

The government did not see fit to dig into Cannon's past. In the
mid-1980s, the specter of unearthing another IBT was just too much
for the shell-shocked bureaucrats of the Reagan EPA. The similarity
of the Cannon case with the IBT case probably scared off any EPA
investigation, and ultimately, nothing happened. No one went to jail
or paid any fines.

In fact, in the days since IBT and Cannon, the system of testing
and licensing most pesticides and other chemicals has not changed.
For example, in 2012, about 10 million pounds of TCC per year was
used to make antibacterial soaps in the United States alone. Even the
fraudulent IBT studies that supported the legal use of this chemical
showed it to have deleterious testicular effects on rats. Today, scientific studies are raising concerns that TCC is an endocrine disruptor.
But TCC's continued existence more than half a century after the IBT
gangsters "tested" it is an indictment of not merely the EPA but also
the chemical industry, which continues to defend it.[19]

Thus, regardless of when the shoddy work took place and whether
it was just mistakes or criminal wrongdoing, the EPA knew of problems
that might well have allowed dangerous toxins into the market, did
nothing to remedy that failure, and was more concerned with protecting the reputation of companies than with exploring a public health
threat. The bigger, underlying issue, of course, is the inherent conflict
of interest in a situation in which private labs, paid by chemical companies, do testing that the government relies on to protect the public.
Even if there is no conscious bad faith, there is inescapably a powerful
incentive to deliver results agreeable to the paying customer.

Finding four IBT officials guilty of fraud was too light a remedy,
and it came too late. IBT's transgressions were committed at a time

when IBT served not just Monsanto but several other chemical giants. The EPA knew that. An audit of IBT had "uncovered practices which not only undermine the integrity of the final reports upon which [EPA] has based far-reaching regulatory decisions, but also the integrity of the raw data underlying the studies," Edwin Johnson wrote in a letter to other senior EPA officials. "In addition, evidence is accumulating which suggests prior knowledge of those practices by the sponsor(s) of the [fraudulent spray] studies. I know that you share my deep concern regarding the seriousness of the regulatory ramifications of these recent findings of falsification of data upon which national and international regulatory decisions have been made."[20] But none of these damning implications became part of the government's strategy in pursuing IBT. The Carter administration decided to let the chemical companies off the hook and focus on IBT alone.

The IBT scandal merely revealed what my EPA colleague David Smithson would call "garbage science." IBT was not a unique case of scientific fraud—it was emblematic of a dark and deviant scientific culture, a "brave new science" with deep roots throughout agribusiness, the chemical industry, universities, and the government. IBT highlighted why labs are essential to the protection of human health: they are the means by which we evaluate the toxins ending up in the food we eat. So lab integrity is essential, which makes the case of IBT and IBT-like behavior in the chemical industry so abhorrent.

And what about the true science that never got done? In the IBT fraud, nearly half of the animal studies testing the potential mutagenic effect of pesticides were tampered with. The EPA and FDA reviewers rightly concluded that those studies were invalid. But the real significance of this classification is that the makers of the pesticides discovered that their pesticides caused gene damage, so they falsified the studies.[21]

What might we have learned had these studies been conducted (and reported) properly? Hard to say. But between 1976 and 1989,

EPA banned or restricted the use of thirty-nine pesticide active ingre-dients.[22] Two criteria for those actions had to do with the possible effects of the pesticides on animal genetics. Sixteen of these very popular agricultural sprays that were either canceled or restricted were tested for mutagenic or teratogenic (deforming) effects, or were shown to have mutagenic or teratogenic effects on experimental animals. Both of these effects are related to genetic damage that, if real, could lead to cancer or other diseases.

Similarly, Parkinson's disease, a very common degenerative disease of the central nervous system in the United States, has some of its origins in genes affected and poisoned by toxic chemicals. Recent studies show that pesticides, including DDT and DDT-like chemicals, increase the risk for Parkinson's disease as well as causing Parkinson's disease. Pesticides damage the neurons, which produce the neurotransmitter dopamine essential for good health.[23]

We don't know what, if any, of this research might have been carried out had IBT been a legitimate lab. What we do know is that for more than twenty-five years, IBT and labs like it served as the chemical and pharmaceutical industries' corrupt enablers, allowing them to sell hazardous substances to the American people. Cigarette companies hid the results of their testing from the federal govern-ment. They developed a sophisticated process of deception, presenting reassuring conclusions to the government about their cigarettes even though their own research told a far darker story.

At IBT, Joseph Calandra was determined to do what the ciga-rette companies did—and much more. As it had in the cigarette industry, scientific dishonesty could protect his industry's profits. Calandra knew the pesticide and pharmaceutical industries were no less determined to protect their empire than were the executives of cigarette companies. So this former professor and chairman of the biochemistry department of Northwestern University, working closely with executives of chemical companies, developed nearly a perfect scheme to provide the government with test results that would bring their products to the market without any problem and keep them there forever.

The other outcome of the IBT case, of course, was what it revealed about the EPA. Working under the thumb of the corporate political system, the EPA could not and did not recognize or confront IBT's corruption of American science and business. The agency gave tacit approval to IBT's perversion of science, and in the process it became complicit in the unethical production of widespread poisons.

The discovery of the IBT crime exposed this practice in a shameful light. Suddenly, the public learned that major companies were involved in the IBT crime—in fact, these companies had brought IBT into being. Strangely, and apparently to avoid deepening its reputation for covering up for chemical companies, the EPA began outsourcing the evaluation of industry studies. The EPA hired consultants to review the data from industry, while EPA scientists, including some one hundred toxicologists, became merely "managers" of that pro-industry process. The unspoken understanding in this outsourcing of government functions has been the near certainty of finding industry data satisfactory—all the time. Labs for hire still dominate the testing of chemicals, and they are as prevalent now as they have ever been. Private companies, not the EPA, hire these labs to test their products. Joseph Calandra's dream has at last been realized.

CHAPTER 8

Whistle-blowers and
What They're Up Against

I N April 1984, Regine Anderson discovered that a can of Raid Flea Killer had ruptured and begun spewing insecticide under the kitchen sink in her Austin, Texas, home. When she opened the cabinet to investigate, the fumes drifted across the kitchen floor, and as they neared her oven's pilot light, they burst into flame.

"The resulting explosion and flash fire hurled me out of the kitchen, leaving second-degree burns on both feet and bruises on my arms, as well as singeing my hair," Ms. Anderson said. "The fire department and paramedics responded. Since the warning on the can said only to store away from open flames and excessive heat (120 degrees F.) and I had followed these precautions, I feel that the can was poorly labeled as to hazards in storage."[1]

When Anderson's complaint reached the ears of the EPA's Dwight Welch, he was hardly surprised. Welch is a tall, wiry man who wanted to do good science and enforce the law. In 1978, he had discovered that aerosol agents in pesticide spray cans have the potential to explode and to start fires. The sprays have propellant gases—propane, butane, isobutane, and dimethyl ether—that are highly flammable and explosive. Welch complained to his supervisors about that hazard, but for close to a decade he was consistently rebuffed.

Welch was upset. He knew that people like Regine Anderson paid dearly—and sometimes lost their lives—because of the EPA's negligence. Welch knew that in New York City, for example, explosive and flammable pesticide sprays were infuriating fire department officials, who complained to the EPA's New York branch about numerous fires and explosions caused by the aerosol pesticide firebombs.[2]

The EPA's New York staff urged the EPA senior managers in Arlington, Virginia, to close the loophole that permits the chemical industry to produce and sell—every year—some two billion cans of potentially explosive firebombs without any effective warning to consumers.[3]

About a year after the fire in Regine Anderson's home, a pair of New York City fire marshals met with EPA officials in New York. They brought with them pictures "showing the damage caused by a pesticide spray bomb" and explosion reports taken from the Bureau of Fire Investigation files. "The marshals explained that the explosion had been caused by 'King Spray Roach and Insect Killer #XXI,'" an EPA memo noted. "They hastened to add that this brand was not the only 'Culprit.' We may be seeing only the 'tip of the iceberg. To date we have been lucky—no one has been seriously injured or killed by the explosive ingredients in these spray cans. These items, apparently, explode with tremendous force." The marshals urged that spray cans be labeled FLAMMABLE or EXPLOSIVE or both.[4]

Reagan's top pesticide appointees did nothing. Incensed, Dwight Welch talked to a reporter with Cox newspapers about a pesticide can explosion in North Las Vegas that had lifted the roof off a house. However, soon thereafter, he pleaded with the reporter to kill the story because his supervisor promised she would do something about the regulation of explosive pesticide firebombs.

Of course, Welch was aware that he was in hot water now that his bosses knew he was talking to reporters. Welch, who had been seeking a promotion, was now told he was not "a team player" and that he could kiss his long-awaited promotion good-bye.

Undeterred, Welch typed up a memo to in which he complained bitterly about EPA's indifference to the explosive issue of exploding pesticide spray bombs. "So far I have only charged bureaucratic inertia and bad manners," Welch wrote. "I have not filed criminal charges with the I.G. [Inspector General]. I have not brought it to the attention of the [political] appointees. I have not written my Congressman. I have not sought out the media. This would have made a great story for 60 Minutes or 20/20. But I am not seeking publicity. I am trying to work within the program."[5]

For a time, it seemed that Welch had triumphed. He was promoted in 1986. His bosses no doubt hoped he would withdraw to his cubicle and leave them alone, but they also did something about exploding aerosol cans. In June 1987, they ordered the makers of pesticide cans using explosive propellants like propane, butane, isobutene, and dimethyl ether to put a flammability warning on the label of their products.[6]

Yet even that nominal step toward public safety did not survive the wrath of the lobbyists from the Chemical Specialties Manufacturers Association. That November, seventeen representatives of the group met in the EPA's "fishbowl" conference room with a half-dozen EPA staff, including Dwight Welch. Lawyers from DuPont, Dow Chemical, SC Johnson, A. H. Robins, Miles, Lehn & Fink, Sprayway, Zoecon, and MGK apparently so frightened the EPA managers that just a month later, EPA withdrew its short-lived policy on labeling aerosol sprays.

Welch was furious, and he openly denounced EPA's humiliating retreat. Welch knew that each 12-ounce can of flying insect spray contains 3 ounces of propellant gas—about the same potential energy as 22.5 ounces of nitroglycerine. Indeed, gram for gram, propane is far more powerful than nitroglycerine: one gram of propane creates 12,000 calories of energy at complete combustion; the same amount of nitroglycerine gives off just 1,600 calories of energy. Welch also had evidence that between 1980 and 1987, some twenty people had died in the United States because of these explosive pesticide spray bombs sold so casually throughout the country. Abandoning the spray regulations—not warning consumers of the fire potential of pesticide aerosols—was further evidence of EPA's "being in bed" with the companies that made the products, Welch wrote to one of the senior EPA officials intimidated by the chemical men. Rather than providing evidence of their products' safety, the lobbyists simply "tried to bully us into compliance, and have succeeded."[7]

Welch found himself persona non grata within his agency. He was transferred from his position as a chemist into a bureaucratic job. During 1989 and 1990, he filed a formal grievance with the U.S. Department of Labor, accusing the EPA of destroying his career. He pointed out the "system" where he worked at the EPA was "rife with cronyism." The EPA's decision to remove him from his job as a chemist "had a great detrimental effect not only on my professional life, but my personal life as well. I am quite depressed because of it." On August 1, 1989, Welch charged the managers of the Pesticide Registration Division with allowing practices by the chemical industry that led to destruction and death. "People continue to be burned and killed by this Division's lack of responsibility in dealing with the issue," he said.[8]

Welch lost his grievance struggle. He decided to get out of the Office of Pesticide Programs and spend the rest of his career in the professional employee union. But in 1990, he offered a final shot in the conflict over exploding spray cans. "Propane, butane, and other hydrocarbon propellants are extremely flammable. Not theory, not opinion, but fact," Welch wrote. Bizarrely, under current EPA regulations, even a cylinder of propane or a case of gunpowder (which is also found in pesticides) would be found to be "nonflammable and nonexplosive."

"I did my job, reporting these facts, which none of my colleagues nor supervisors dispute," Welch wrote. "However, management in the Office of Pesticide Programs and those in charge of writing regulations have done nothing to change the regulations in all these years. Writing the regulations is not my job, doing science is. I did my part, but others, who are either too incompetent and/or too arrogant, have not."

Today, aerosol cans warn consumers to keep their aerosols away from flames or heat, and they warn against incinerating or puncturing the can. They also warn that "physical hazard may cause bursting." Some even warn that the container, if heated, may explode.

Even as all this was going on, Cate Jenkins, the EPA chemist who revealed Monsanto's and EPA's cover-up of the dioxin menace (described in chapter 3), was discovering another depressing example of collusion between polluters and her supervisors. In October 1988 she wrote to an array of powerful politicians claiming that senior EPA officials "knowingly engaged in serious violations of conflict of interest statutes and other regulations governing the use of public sector consultants." The EPA Office of the Inspector General "willfully covered-up evidence to this effect."[9]

Jenkins focused her charges on what she knew best: the development of regulations governing wood preservatives, chemicals used to treat marine pilings, telephone poles, bridge structural timber, and wood for home decks. These compounds—pentachlorophenol, creosote, and inorganic arsenicals—are acutely toxic in their own right, but they are also mixed with and contaminated by even more dangerous poisons—dioxins and furans.

In Jenkins's view, EPA consultants were serving two masters—the EPA and the wood treatment industry. Under these conditions, consultants covered up the discovery of dioxins in the wastes of Weyerhauser in Arkansas and in the emissions of the pulp and paper mills of Louisiana-Pacific and Simpson Paper in Humboldt County, California. The consultants "utilized every misrepresentation possible in favor of its lucrative industrial clients," Jenkins wrote. In other words, under the Reagan administration, EPA consultants enriched themselves from polluters even as they helped create EPA policy protecting those polluters. It was a perfect scheme.

Jenkins considered the relationship between EPA and these consultants a form of "embezzling" in which public funds paid company salaries even as they let polluters off the hook. She warned elected officials overseeing environmental policy that EPA's corruption "can lead to tainted, less protective environmental regulations." Indeed, Jenkins charged EPA's regulators with granting industry a license to pollute. "This de-regulatory effort would allow industry the new authority to determine on their own whether or not their wastes contained sufficient concentrations of toxicants to be hazardous," she said. And all this deregulatory activity cost EPA money, something Jenkins found intolerable, even "criminal."[10]

As early as 1985, Jenkins told Congress, she had approached the EPA inspector general with allegations that her superiors had colluded with a prestigious Washington lobbying firm, Arnold and Porter, to reverse a determination that two hundred open railroad cars of dioxin-contaminated dirt (from a pentachlorophenol wood preserver company, Bell Lumber and Pole in New Brighton, Minnesota) were "regulated wastes." "As a result of that reversal, the State of Illinois was forced to drop felony charges against the wood preserving company," Jenkins wrote.

Jenkins then brought allegations of corruption and misconduct at the EPA directly to the appropriate congressional oversight subcommittees. In early 1988, she brought formal conflict of interest charges to the attention of the EPA inspector general. To the shock of no one, the charges were dismissed.[11]

At the same time, of course, Jenkins was also fighting a war on another front: the Monsanto dioxin scandal. In response to her whistle-blowing—to her raising so many bright red flags about the EPA's ethically compromised collusion with industry—the EPA "relieved" her of her normal duties and transferred her to a clerical job.

But it was not in Cate Jenkins's nature to back down. Instead, she filed a grievance against the EPA, and—after a torturous legal battle—she won. On December 14, 1992, a U.S. Department of Labor administrative law judge, Glenn Robert Lawrence, ordered EPA to reinstate Jenkins and pay her "exemplary" damages.[12]

AN HONORARY WHITE MAN

I met Marsha Coleman-Adebayo in 1990 in Washington, D.C. She was working for the World Wildlife Fund, an international environmental organization. Marsha was an analyst focusing on issues affecting Africa. Not long after I met her, Marsha joined the Office of International Activities of the U.S. Environmental Protection Agency. At that time, I was also working for the EPA. In fact, in 1994, my organization, the Office of Pesticides and Toxic Substances, detailed me to OIA for one year.

Marsha and I collaborated on a number of issues, especially assisting EPA in handling the important and delicate international health problem of women and the environment. Were women more sensitive to toxins and pollution than men? Did conventional environmental protection include women in its policies? These complex questions preoccupied the 1995 international women's conference in Beijing.

Working with Marsha for a year gave me the opportunity to understand that this African-American woman, who held a doctorate in political science from MIT, had the virtues of a great education and commitment to the well-being of humankind. She loved Africa. She married a Nigerian engineering professor, Segun Adebayo. She respected my Greek culture and knowledge of history and science.

Like children, women have long been getting the brunt of global pollution. EPA tested mothers' milk in the late 1970s and found the milk contaminated by DDT-like poisons and other toxins. Women's biology make them more vulnerable to hormone-like poisons now known as endocrine disruptors; their work at home exposes them to substances confined inside the house, sometimes several times more deleterious than the polluted air of the atmosphere outside their homes.

In addition to searching the scientific literature for answers, I also talked to EPA colleagues all over the country. I then wrote a memo on the unsettling results, recommending that the EPA administrator, Carol Browner, and the head of my office, Lynn Goldman, take them seriously and do something about them. But my "ecofeminist" memo caused not enlightenment but anger, especially among senior women managers.

This is what it meant to be an analyst with an environmental–public health vision at EPA—in the 1990s or at any other time. Like me, Marsha wanted to do "good": to put the EPA on the side of protecting people and nature from the toxic assault of industry.

But Marsha had also a passion for Africa. And when on March 1, 1995, the United States established the Gore-Mbeki commission, chaired by Vice President Al Gore and South African Deputy President Thabo Mbeki, promising South Africa ways and means to facilitate a transition from apartheid to democracy, Marsha thought she would become an instrument for providing South Africa with a modicum of technical assistance for health protection.

Marsha's African contacts alerted her to the dangers of mining vanadium at Brits, South Africa. Vametco, an American subsidiary of Union Carbide, was extracting vanadium, which the CIA classified as a strategic metal for the United States. Vanadium was certainly an asset to American industry and the military, but getting it out of Africa was poisoning and killing African workers.

Jacob Ngakane, a South African black man representing the ailing vanadium workers, told Marsha that South Africa has "vast reserves" of vanadium, which is mined in pits. "Open, gaping wounds are carved into the earth," he said. "The workers in the [vanadium] mines are being poisoned . . . They bleed from their eyes, their noses, their genitals, their colons. These same young men become impotent from working in the mines. Their tongues turn green."

Vanadium also wrecked Marsha's career. Marsha quoted Ngakane in her 2011 book, *NO FEAR*, in which she details her career at EPA. She believed that the United States, through the EPA, could and should help the ailing vanadium workers, perhaps make the mining process less toxic. But sadly, Marsha overestimated both what the United States and she herself (through the EPA) could do for South Africa. She learned rather quickly that the EPA, like the rest of the U.S. government, had been co-opted by the likes of Union Carbide, Vametco's parent company (whose pesticide factory in Bhopal, India, exploded in 1984, killing thousands).

In the agency's treatment of her, racial bigotry combined with resentment of those who challenged the status quo. Marsha's supervisors, all of whom were white, mocked her, hinting she had the option of being with them or against them. Her boss even baptized Marsha an "honorary white man."

EPA reneged on its promise to offer technical assistance to the vanadium mines in South Africa. Within less than two years of the establishment of the Gore-Mbeki Commission, in December 1996, Marsha received an unsatisfactory evaluation by her supervisor, the first blow on the way to being fired in the federal government. Marsha called the unsatisfactory performance review "a white phosphorus flare."

"The white flare of an unsatisfactory performance rating meant that from then on the agency's dealings with me were on autopilot," she said. "There would be no reasoning. There would be no reconsideration. There would be formulaic responses, form letters, and scripts. If there was any negotiating, it would be on agency's terms, and would be about just exactly what it would take to get rid of me."[13]

Marsha fought back. She sued the EPA for racism and retaliation—and she won. An embarrassed Congress wanted to maintain the illusion that it did not approve of the silencing of whistle-blowers like Marsha. So it passed the Notification and Federal Employee Antidiscrimination and Retaliation (NO FEAR) Act of 2002. President George W. Bush, hardly an environmental steward, signed this bill into law. Marsha's case helped trigger this law, though great numbers of federal employees had struggled for decades for just such action. Sadly, and predictably, the law remains toothless, with no money appropriated for enforcement. It was a cheap congressional trick for avoiding responsibility; Congress knows full well the roots of corruption but refuses to remedy its archaic system of patronage and corporate welfare.

Nonetheless, Marsha was proud to describe the NO FEAR legislation as the first civil rights law of the twenty-first century.[14]

Marsha's story, of course, reveals far larger national environmental and political issues. It shows in microcosm the racism in American society, our callousness and imperialism in foreign policy, and the corporate domination of the government and the world. And it shows that if Reagan's presidency was disastrous for the EPA, the Clinton presidency did little to reverse the capture of government by industry. Clinton and Gore and their appointees at the EPA and in the rest of the government handled South Africa badly, exacerbating the corporate-friendly trends among the leaders of postapartheid South Africa.

Marsha's case gives an insider's rare view of the alien universe of the federal government, in which a few politically motivated bureaucrats, beholden to money and the president, drag administration after administration along in the path of corporate power.

CHAPTER 9

When Will the Well Run Dry?

I N 1979, disaster bubbled to the surface of Long Island's sandy soil. Union Carbide discovered aldicarb, one of the most acutely toxic insect poisons used in the United States, in most of the drinking water beneath the lush potato fields on the eastern end of Long Island. No one knows for how long the people had been drinking and washing in the poisoned water. Neither the local New York government nor the EPA had done any checking for the potato neurotoxin until the harm had already been done.

Union Carbide, which manufactured aldicarb (also known as temic), broke the bad news to the EPA on the morning of August 23, 1979. The contamination, an EPA official wrote, was "extremely serious with potentially grave consequences to Long Island residents."[1]

A week later, Steven Jellinek, the EPA's highest official dealing with pesticides during the Carter administration, wrote a letter to David Axelrod, New York's health commissioner, warning of the contamination's impact, "particularly [on] infants and children." Anyone dependent on well water, Jellinek said, should find "alternative sources of water."

"The amount of aldicarb found in some wells sampled so far may present an unacceptable degree of risk to human health," Jellinek noted. "Of special concern are the exposures to small children. Aldicarb is one of the most acutely toxic pesticides currently registered for use in this country. For infants, whose diet may be 100 percent milk, dilution of milk or formula with aldicarb contaminated well water would pose a significant hazard. While the extent of the contamination of the well water on Long Island is uncertain at this point, the problem may be far reaching and is one of serious import."[2]

The poisoning of Long Island's drinking water was just the beginning of a national disaster. Soon Union Carbide "discovered" aldicarb in the drinking water supplies of Wiseonsin, Virginia, Maine, Florida, Georgia, and Oregon, raising the number of potential victims to immediate and long-term disease and death to millions.

Stanley Mazaleski, an EPA toxicologist, urged his bosses to test aldicarb for its possible impact on the nervous system. His efforts were in vain; instead of being thanked, he was hounded out of the agency. (Mazaleski also knew too much about the EPA's malathion studies, which showed that malathion and other neurotoxins affect people at minute amounts.) Yet additional water testing on Long Island revealed not only traces of aldicarb ranging up to 515 parts per billion—roughly 1,700 percent greater than the legal amount EPA allowed in food or drink—but also evidence of carbofuran, another highly toxic insect poison.

In the early 1970s, David Coppage and three other EPA scientists had exposed pinfish to lethal and sublethal seawater concentrations of malathion. They observed that even if the fish did not die from their exposure to malathion, their chances for a normal life were compromised. Even sublethal dosages of the poison "may cause physiological and behavioral modifications that reduce animal survival ability."[3]

People living among the potato farms of the East End of Long Island were facing an "unacceptable degree of risk, and decidedly most unacceptable to children," wrote Salvatore Biscardi, an EPA toxicologist.[4]

Why was aldicarb buried next to the potato seeds when it, like ethylene dibromide or parathion, can be devastating to people in minute amounts of parts per billion? These nerve poisons starve the brain and the nerves in days, or cause irreparable neurological and behavioral wounds. They kill slowly or on the spot. Some, like dibromo-chloropropane, sterilize both people and animals. Others, like toxaphene, leave behind a storm of molecules hanging in the air, moving with the wind for a few yards in a farm or for hundreds and thousands of miles around the earth. Or, like thalidomide, certain agrochemicals damage fetuses being carried by women and other female animals.

Maurie Semel, a biologist of the Long Island Horticultural Research Laboratory at Riverhead, New York, witnessed Long Island's aldicarb poisoning and was disheartened by this example of yet another toxic (and fruitless) war against insects. Ever since the potato beetle first appeared in 1874, she discovered, Long Island's potato farmers had been waging a battle as toxic as it had been futile.

Even with modern synthetic pesticides, she concluded, potato beetles from Long Island to Virginia and Colorado were "beyond the threatening stage of effective control." A far more effective (and benign) copper-based method of blight control known as the Bordeaux mixture had long since been replaced by synthetic fungicides, which not only failed to kill beetles, but harmed fungi that were themselves inherently hostile to the beetles. The farmers' new chemical weapons, in other words, were making life easier for their worst insect enemy.

In Long Island in 1972 alone, potato farmers used about thirty thousand gallons of a nerve poison known as azinphos-methyl against the Colorado potato beetle, Maurie Semel wrote. That poison left the beetles pretty much intact. So a year later, farmers sprayed their plants with 70,000 gallons of aldicarb, plus a ton of the ineffective azinphos-methyl, 80 tons of methoxychlor, 13 tons of carbaryl, 68,000 gallons of parathion, and 5 tons of endosulfan.[5]

The discovery of aldicarb in Long Island's drinking water had practically no impact on the practices of the chemical industry or those of the EPA. In other agencies, however, the poison was raising red flags. "Laboratory tests have shown aldicarb to be very toxic to birds, mammals, and aquatic organisms," F. Eugene Hester, the acting director of the U.S. Fish and Wildlife Service, wrote to EPA's chief ecologist. Four years earlier, Hester noted, aldicarb contamination had killed 830 gulls, chickens, and songbirds in England and Germany. Fearing for the survival of endangered birds such as the prairie chicken, Hester urged the EPA to ban the use of aldicarb on sorghum crops in more than a dozen Texas counties.[6]

The EPA did no such thing. Instead, the EPA struck a deal with Union Carbide under which the company added the following language to its aldicarb product label: "Under the Endangered Species Act, it is a Federal offense to use any pesticide in a manner that results in the death of a member of an endangered species. This Act protects Attwater Greater Prairie Chicken in the Texas counties of Aransas, Austin, Brazoria, Colorado, Galveston, Goliad, Harris, Refugio, and Victoria. Prior to making application in these counties, the user must determine that this species is not located in or immediately adjacent to the area to be treated."

Even with this meaningless injunction, which EPA approved on July 2, 1982, Union Carbide left off its list four counties in which Fish and Wildlife had recommended *prohibiting* aldicarb. In other words, the compromise EPA worked out with Union Carbide was probably illegal. But who was going to complain?

The EPA was thus entirely responsible for a policy dangerous to an endangered species in order to satisfy Union Carbide and Texas farmers. This story also served as an emblem of the "regulatory relief" policy sought by Vice President (and Texan) George H. W. Bush.

Like the potato farmers of Long Island, some 90 percent of rural people in the United States rely solely on groundwater for drinking. Given the broad contamination of our country's waterways, this means many of these people are in danger of being poisoned.

In 1983, for example, EPA discovered weed killers in Ohio's drinking water, including the herbicides atrazine, alachlor, metol-achlor, linuron, cyanazine, and simazine. Poisoned water moved from the Sandusky and Maumee Rivers to the finished tap water of the municipal water treatment plants of Tiffin, Fremont, and Bowling Green. These same weed killers are contaminating drinking water almost everywhere in the United States. In 1991, EPA estimated that about 50 million Americans were drinking water potentially contaminated with pesticides.

By the late 1980s, the EPA had found sixty pesticides in the groundwater of thirty states. This is not surprising, given that in 1988, America used 2.7 billion pounds of pesticides, 75 percent of which went to farms. However, this 2.7 billion pounds (of "active" ingredients alone) is but a small fraction of the total amount of toxic material that makes up pesticides; most toxic material, as noted in chapter 2, EPA classifies as "inerts."[7]

In 1984, the EPA chemist who monitored Ohio waters for pesticides, Padma Datta, spoke to me several times about one popular weed killer, alachlor. Every year between March and July, alachlor gets into the rivers of all corn-growing states, including Ohio, Iowa, Illinois, and Nebraska; between 100 and 200 million pounds of alachlor are used in the United States every year. Yet not only is the compound toxic to fish in the low parts per billion, but it degrades into some twenty metabolites, five of which are carcinogenic. It causes cancer in both rats and mice; at about 126 parts per million, it causes cancer in sites throughout the animal, especially in the brain, liver, and kidney. At just five parts per million, it is responsible for a rare form of cancer of the lining of the nose, Datta said.

Yet the EPA branch that funded the Iowa and Ohio research failed to inform the Office of Pesticide Programs that it had discovered the poison in drinking water. Why? Datta asked. Did it have anything to do with the fact that alachlor is a $1 billion molecule owned by Monsanto? "Our Hazard Evaluation Division knew about the carcinogenicity of alachlor, so these scientists-managers are embarrassed," Datta said. "They don't regulate alachlor because, as they argue, alachlor does not 'trip any trigger.'" ("Trigger" is the term

EPA scientists use to express the potential adverse effects of toxins. When a chemical is shown to cause cancer in experimental animals, it is said to "trip the cancer trigger.")

Each time Datta's supervisors met with the corporate owners of these weed killers—Ciba-Geigy or Monsanto—senior EPA officials would send Datta out of town so he never had a chance to ask the corporate polluters any question. He especially resented having to fly to Dallas, Texas, for computer courses while Monsanto representatives lobbied his colleagues in Crystal City.

Reagan's EPA administrators kept what they knew close to their chest. They never contemplated banning alachlor, which (since the government typically buys up stocks of banned substances) would have forced them to spend roughly a billion dollars to buy and destroy remaining alachlor stocks. And EPA managers knew, of course, that alachlor was hardly the only herbicide poisoning America's waters. The corn herbicides atrazine, simazine, and cyanazine are also carcinogens: all three cause mammary tumors in female rats. These toxins kill plants by disrupting photosynthesis, a critical biological process without which there would be no life. So anything disrupting photosynthesis is, by definition, a deadly biological weapon. Yet every year throughout the 1980s, farmers sprayed up to 110 million pounds of these weed killers on their crops.[8]

Throughout the 1980s, EPA managers did precious little to warn Americans about their contaminated drinking water. Nor did they take action to prevent the poisoning by banning these biological weapons. In 2009, alachlor was still being found in the drinking water of Ohio and several other states, and in 2011, atrazine was still the king of weed killers all over the country.

Tyrone Hayes, a professor of biology at the University of California, Berkeley, discovered that doing good science was not enough to convince the EPA to ban the use of highly profitable sprays. Hayes, who had been passionate about protecting wildlife since childhood, became angry when the Swiss company Syngenta, owner of the weed killer atrazine, challenged his discoveries on the deadly effects of atrazine on frogs. Though Syngenta had funded Hayes's research, they disputed his findings. Hayes stood his ground. Atrazine, like alachlor, was a menace to both wildlife and human health, he wrote. But Hayes ultimately finally understood that simply publishing data was not enough. He began to speak out, putting his articles on the Internet and openly advocating the banning of atrazine.

American corn producers have been addicted to atrazine since 1958. Europe—including Switzerland, where atrazine is manufactured—has banned it. But American farmers, including three-quarters of corn farmers, still spray more than 80 million pounds per year. Such prolific use has contaminated most water in the United States, including the drinking water of millions of people. Atrazine compromises the immune system of animals, increasing their susceptibility to disease, Hayes writes; as a potent endocrine disruptor, it also sterilizes wildlife. As little as 0.1 parts per billion of atrazine can turn tadpoles into hermaphrodites. "Atrazine induces breast and prostate cancer, retards mammary development, and induces abortion in laboratory rodents," Hayes writes. "Studies in human populations and cell and tissue studies suggest that atrazine poses similar threats to humans."

Atrazine also feminizes males to the degree, Hayes says, that male fish and amphibians produce eggs and egg yolk. "In fish, amphibians, and laboratory rodents, the decrease in testosterone results in decreased sperm counts, impaired fertility, and a reduction in masculine features," Hayes writes. "Similarly, atrazine exposure is associated with decreased sperm and reduced fertility in humans."[9]

Studies done in the United States since 2009 are confirming Hayes's discoveries and the warnings of my colleague Padma Datta. Atrazine in drinking water has been shown to cause hormonal changes and menstrual and other reproductive irregularities in women, especially in Illinois and other states in the Midwest. Hormonal changes are sure signs of added risk of illnesses including osteoporosis, diabetes, heart disease, and cancer, and a 2009 study linked atrazine in drinking water to low birth weight in children born in Indiana.[10]

In 2011, another global study of twenty-two scientists from North and South America, Europe, and Japan confirmed the deleterious and "gender-bending" effects of atrazine. "It doesn't matter if you are a fish or frog, a cat or dog, if you are exposed to atrazine, there is a problem," Hayes, the lead scientist of this study, wrote.[11]

As if fertilizers and agricultural sprays were not enough, traces of pharmaceutical drugs are also ubiquitous in America's drinking water. In 2008, an Associated Press study documented the contamination of the drinking water of 41 million Americans with prescription drugs. Studies have shown that small amounts of drugs disrupt the development of wildlife, feminizing male fish and, in many other inimical ways, damaging the natural world.[12]

One of the results of all this poisoning is its effect on the very beginnings of human life. Paul Winchester, a physician and professor of clinical pediatrics at the School of Medicine of the University of Indiana, reported on May 7, 2007, that premature births and birth defects in the United States peak at the very time (from April through July) when farmers spray and fertilize their crops and the residues of those poisons are at their greatest concentrations in the country's surface water. Another pediatrician at the University of Indiana School of Medicine, James Lemons, warned in 2007 that what we put into the environment can have "pandemic effects," harming pregnancy and even the development of the infant and child.[13]

Pesticides are especially injurious to women because women are uniquely susceptible to persistent, bioaccumulative, hazardous pollutants such as DDT, polychlorinated biphenyls, dioxins, furans, mercury, cadmium, and lead. Very low exposure of a pregnant woman to the 2,3,7,8-dioxin can cause irreversible effects on the sexual differentiation of the fetus. Other reproductive and developmental poisons such as ethylene oxide, carbon monoxide, 1,3-butadiene, and radiation exacerbate the effects of indoor poisons (including radon, tobacco smoke, asbestos, household cleaners, and pesticides) on women.

Nitrates, a component of agricultural fertilizers, are particularly dangerous to pregnant women and newborns. Yet in 1984, the U.S. Geological Survey discovered hazardous amounts of nitrates in 24 percent of 124,000 water wells. In late 1980s, about half of Iowa's eight hundred public water supplies were contaminated by pesticides and fertilizers.

DDT-like pesticides increase the likelihood for birth defects by as much as 450 percent, and they have been linked to cardiovascular disease. Some six thousand cancer cases per year may result from the pesticide residues of two hundred potential carcinogens in food. Something to ponder, given that the United States is suffering from an epidemic of cancer, and that 98 percent of the food is legally sprayed with these two hundred pesticides, many of which are carcinogens.[14]

This crisis was inevitable. The United States—and industrial farm states like Iowa, in particular—have been bingeing on farm "nutrients" for a long time; Iowa, for example, is 90 percent plowed under with industrial corn and soybeans.

Part of the issue is that no one looks at the problems from a broad perspective, such as the overall effect of all these chemicals on crops, the environment, and society at large. Instead, farmers identify a single-level problem—a pest, a fungus—and say, this poison solves *this* problem. Then, when the pest becomes immune or a new one comes along, there's always another poison to deploy. There is a tragic lack of holistic thinking in the agricultural establishment.

The consequences of the industrial scale of agriculture go beyond chemicals, of course. If farmers deplete rivers, they find ways to tap (and then deplete) water from the depths of the earth, as is now happening with the Ogallala Aquifer in the Great Plains. In such a single-minded, convoluted system, one pays attention only to the myriad technical problems of keeping crops and animals alive and multiplying. This eliminates asking complex biological and social questions, much less philosophical ones.

What happens when our insecticides kill most insects? What are birds supposed to eat? Herbicides kill the microorganisms responsible for the movement of nutrients to the growing crop. What does this do to the nutritional value of the food we eat? The practitioner of one-crop farming does not ask questions like these. The farmer who has become heavily dependent on herbicides does not see the ecological tragedy taking place in his soil. He is oblivious to the dead fish that float to the surface after rains flush his pesticides into the river. He refuses to acknowledge the danger in the poisoned crops he feeds to animals and people (including, inevitably, his own children).

In 1960, the United States used 7.5 million tons of fertilizers. Twenty-one years later, in 1981, the country's farmers applied 23.7 million tons of nitrogen, phosphate, and potash. In the years 1960 to 1976, Iowa farmers went from applying a hundred thousand tons of nitrogen fertilizer to more than a million tons. The more fertilizer Iowa farmers put on the land, the more runs off their farms and into the waters they and other Iowans drink.

The fertilizer loss in the Big Spring basin in northeastern Iowa is about 50 to 75 pounds per acre.[15] The Big Spring basin is about 103 square miles in size. Padma Datta, who reviewed the use of pesticides for growing corn or oats, found that atrazine and another product, known as lasso, were the most popular weed killers with Iowa farmers. Datta found atrazine in amounts up to 2.5 parts per billion in Big Spring groundwater; he estimated that up to 4 percent of all the pesticides sprayed over crops of the Big Spring basin were ending up in the basin's water table.[16]

Farmers pay a high price for their chemical addiction, suffering an increased frequency of cancers of the stomach, prostate, bone and connective tissue, blood, lymph tissue, and bone marrow. Compared to nonfarmers, Iowa farmers develop these cancers from 40 to 100 percent more frequently. In general, Iowa farmers, and probably all farmers using pesticides, "are subject to higher than expected mortality rates from certain types of cancer," studies show. In a study of white male Iowa residents dying from 1971 to 1978, for example, it was concluded that farmers "had statistically significant elevated mortality rates from the following six cancer types: lip cancer, stomach cancer, prostatic cancer, lymphatic cancer, leukemia, [and] multiple myeloma."

These results were consistent with an Iowa study based on the years 1964–1970 and with studies completed in other states. The more bushels of corn and soybeans the large farmers of Iowa produce, in other words, the more cancer they harvest—and sell to the rest of us.[17]

CHAPTER 10

Fallout

T HE people who run chemical companies, as well as those engaged in industrial-scale agriculture, are calculating people. Their eyes overlook downstream concerns like environmental health or human health and stay focused on the bottom line. For them, the destruction of insects is a source of profit; other consequences of their products are someone else's concern. They seem uninterested in the fact that insects not only represent 75 percent of the planet's biomass but also form the very base of the global food chain—including the human food chain. Ignorance of this fact, along with a broad indifference to the environment, has become deeply troubling, said Glenn B. Wiggins, a distinguished Canadian entomologist, in his presidential address to the entomologists of North America in November 1982.

The unprecedented prosperity of North American society "stems directly from the abundance of productive soils, fresh waters, equable climates, forests, and grasslands that are the foundation of our environment," Wiggins said. "[T]he terrestrial and freshwater parts of it, at any rate, are really an insect world. And it is scarcely an exaggeration to say that man will have to learn a great deal more about those insects and the useful as well as destructive things insects do in order to secure harmoniously his own place in that world."[1]

It remains to be seen whether people can be educated enough so that one day they may live "harmoniously" on an insect-dependent earth. George M. Woodwell, a renowned scientist with the Marine Biological Laboratory at Woods Hole, Massachusetts, is not optimistic. He speaks of the earth being "in the throes of a series of biotic changes that are unprecedented in human history" and denounces these changes for impoverishing the earth.

"One might dream that on the only green planet we know, life would have a special value of its own, just as books and works of art do in our culture," Woodwell writes. "And if the interest in life *per se* were not sufficient to protect it, one might hope that simple, selfish interest in human comfort and sustenance might confer a special status on living systems and force their conservation. Unfortunately, neither occurs. The stacks are open in the world's great library of life and we advertise to the vandals."[2]

Here are some numbers you aren't likely to hear broadcast by the pesticide industry. In 1954, insects destroyed about 10 percent of America's food crops. In 1980—more than twenty-five years and untold tons of pesticides later—insects and disease destroyed nearly four times as much food—some 37 percent, worth about $85 billion. Without even raising the harrowing questions of environmental and human health, it seems reasonable to ask a simple question:

Has it been worth it?

If farmers grew food entirely without using pesticides, they would lose about 41 percent of their crops, according to David Pimentel, Cornell's renowned professor of entomology. This would lead to a rise in the price of food of about 5 to 10 percent. Yet when we consider the significant damage done by fully armed chemical farmers, growers, and ranchers, this seems a modest price to pay. In 2003, Pimentel calculated the "environmental and societal damages" from the legal use of pesticides to be about $12 billion per year.[3]

Pimentel is one of the few scientists swimming against the agrochemical stream. For several decades, Pimentel has been asking questions about the energy, economic, and social costs of America's agriculture and the industry's ways of dealing with insects, weeds, and crop and animal diseases. Pesticides may be necessary sometimes, Pimentel says, but the costs we pay for them are far too great to justify agribusiness's increasingly unsafe practices.

Pimentel chronicles the hugely inefficient—and dangerous—consequences of chemical trespass. Only minute amounts of sprayed pesticides actually reach their target pest insects and plant pathogens. For example, about 0.003 percent of the 1 kilogram per hectare of insecticide sprayed on a field of collard greens actually hits the cabbage white butterfly caterpillar. In bean fields, no more than 0.03 percent of the sprayed insecticide hits aphids. On cotton farms, the heliothis caterpillars are hit by an absurd 0.0000001 percent of the spray; the rest ends up elsewhere—in other insects, birds, and fish, as the poisons seep into soils, wash down rivers, and blow in the wind. This is true for the vast bulk of agricultural poisons, which (as we have seen) collectively total hundreds of millions of pounds.[4]

"It is nearly impossible to control insects and mite pests on crops by applying the spray insecticide directly to the target pests," Pimentel has concluded.[5] His writing, full of numbers and results of scientific studies, raises important questions: Is industrialized agriculture as benign—or even as effective—as its industrial patrons seem to think? Or is it just a con game, a successor to the nineteenth-century patent medicine hustle? Another way of asking this question: Have we been duped?

When I came across Pimentel's early work, I became intrigued. I distributed some of his articles to my EPA colleagues and invited Pimentel to come to the EPA to present his ideas.[6] One November morning, Pimentel showed up in my office, a small corner of an immense room in the second floor of Crystal Square #4 in Crystal City, Virginia. This was eight months after the election of Ronald Reagan, and the EPA was already in critical condition.

A senior EPA official and I spent two hours with our distinguished guest. Our meeting began with the official presenting the boilerplate overview of the work he supervised, replete with the usual nonsensical claptrap about priorities, limited resources, deregulation, and so on. But the real embarrassment began when the official tried to explain the purpose of what he called the "policy analysis model," a phrase designed to trivialize research into the negative consequences of pesticides.

"There's a continuing need to relate changes in regulatory control by EPA on pesticide matters to changes in user behavior to changes in the health and the environment," the official said. EPA control options must be evaluated, ultimately, in terms of the "net benefits expected if the options are exercised."

"To do this, the options must be identified clearly and expressed in operational terms," the official continued, in typically opaque bureaucratic rhetoric. "The options must be linked to alternative user behaviors and user behaviors linked to a set of definitive changes in the health and the environment. Comprehensive quantitative measures are required to express these changes in terms of both costs and benefits so that net benefits can be derived. The above elements would be integrated into a policy analysis model. Such a model would aid in the examination of alternative policies, strategies, resource allocations, and projected program accomplishments expressed in more distal terms than the present proximal measures of decisions made." The same sort of mind-numbing language about "managing" might well have been used by the chemical industry to deflect public (and stockholder) concerns about the effects of its products on human life and our increasingly fragile environment.

While this performance was under way, Professor Pimentel's eyes would meet mine. He sat there smiling, wondering why he was wasting his time like this and thinking there was no way his research would have any impact on senior EPA people.

I finally got to ask Pimentel what he would have done in our shoes. He said two things could be done that would immediately reduce the threat of pesticides by at least 50 percent. First, pesticides ought to be given only to farmers who had a prescription from their county agent detailing precisely why those chemicals were necessary to treat the farmer's land. Second, the EPA should ban toxaphene, a DDT-like chemical that for several decades had left a heavy footprint of poisoning and death.

EPA had taken DDT off the market in 1972 and in one way or another had heavily restricted some twelve other major pesticides in the first ten years of the agency's existence. Now, Pimentel said, the time to ban toxaphene had come. In 1944, something like 250 million pounds of all farm chemicals were sprayed in the United States. Barely forty years later, in the early 1980s, 200 million pounds of toxaphene *alone* was being broadcast on our farms every year.

Like DDT, toxaphene accumulates at high levels in animals and moves readily by winds and rain around the globe. Toxaphene, which looks like amber, is not readily soluble in water, but it mixes nicely with other chemicals; indeed, it is made up of some 177 different chemicals, each of which has its own toxic history. Nearly 70 percent is chlorine, a deadly chemical in its own right. The impact this toxic bomb has on humans is dramatic: it causes leukemia and changes in the structure of human chromosomes, resulting in genetic disease. It damages the nerves and brain of all animals, sterilizes water animals, and has devastating effects on fish and wildlife.

"[T]here is clear and compelling evidence that toxaphene is acutely and chronically toxic to a wide variety of important fish and wildlife species at concentrations to which these species are likely to be exposed when the pesticide is used in several crops at historical or legally permitted levels," an EPA report said in 1980. "Continued toxaphene use fatally threatens members of endangered species."[7]

A great deal of toxaphene migrates to water on the back of soil erosion, polluting streams and rivers and lakes. However, a quarter of what gets into the ground is carried by prevailing winds to the four corners of the earth. For several decades, atmospheric transport moved toxaphene from the cotton fields of the American South to the water and fish of the Great Lakes. Scientists found toxaphene in the atmosphere above the western North Atlantic at a level ten times higher than any other pesticide.

In soil, toxaphene can linger for as long as ten years. In lakes, it has the potential to remain biologically active (that is, deadly) from two years to two centuries. Estimates are that toxaphene will radiate disease and death in Lake Michigan for 104 years and in Lake Superior for 185 years. This is particularly troubling given the web of life it contaminates: fish absorb toxaphene, bigger fish eat smaller fish, and humans and wild animals (such as eagles and bears) eat the bigger fish.[8]

Indeed, water animals are especially vulnerable to toxaphene poisoning because it bioaccumulates in their tissues at staggering rates. Yearling brook trout, for instance, absorb toxaphene at 4,000 to 16,000 times the water concentration, rainbow trout at 10,000 to 20,000 times, and brook trout fry at 15,000 to 20,000 times. In channel catfish, toxaphene biomagnifies at a factor of 2,000 to 50,000, and fathead minnows collect toxaphene at 3,700 to 69,000 times the water concentration. Oysters absorb into their flesh 146 parts per million of toxaphene from water with only 0.05 parts per million of toxaphene—in just ten days, which is to say, oysters collect toxaphene at nearly 3,000 times the amount of toxaphene found in the water.

Tragically, fish absorption seems to be the only way to "dispose" of toxaphene, which, obviously, is no way at all. In other words, once toxaphene gets into drinking water, there is practically no way to get it out.

Given the Reagan administration's utter disinterest in industrial regulation, David Pimentel knew he was talking to a blank wall when he told EPA they ought to ban toxaphene. The official said nothing, and our conversation with Pimentel came to an end.

And our toxaphene poisoning continued.

By 1982, close to 7 billion pounds of this poison had been used all over the United States. In 1974 and 1975 alone, more than 200 million pounds of toxaphene reached the land. In 1982, some two hundred merchants sold 200 million pounds of toxaphene through two hundred different products. About 80 percent went to the cotton farmers of the South; some of the remaining poison became a "dip" for millions of cattle. What was left became part of chemical arsenal used on about three hundred crops. This means that toxaphene was contaminating a lot of food, especially fish and meat.[9]

Because toxaphene produces thyroid cancer in rats, is widely distributed in the environment, bioaccumulates as it moves through the food chain, and has "specific adverse effects on fish," toxaphene should be restricted "more stringently" even than DDT, Endrin, Dieldrin, etc.," wrote John Doull, a professor of pharmacology and toxicology at the University of Kansas Medical School and a former member of the EPA's Science Advisory Panel.[10]

In other words, Doull said in early 1982, the EPA should ban toxaphene, and soon.

Even with Reagan in power, the slow and insidious toxaphene fallout was simply too much even for the timid scientists of the EPA, who in early 1982 decided to disclose what they knew about toxaphene: that the stuff was in the water, food, soil, and air of the entire country, and that the fresh fish and shellfish of entire regions were so contaminated they were unfit for people to eat.

EPA scientists were also sick of the word games being played by BFC Chemicals, the company in charge of persuading the EPA to adopt ludicrous "options" for regulating toxaphene (including canceling toxaphene use on rice and cranberries, two crops on which toxaphene was virtually never used). BFC's lawyers asked the EPA's top pesticides official, Edwin Johnson, to limit regulation to "monitoring" toxaphene. Translation: do nothing. Or, they said, the EPA could limit regulation to changing the label on the pesticide can. This was almost literally the least they could do.

These requests so infuriated David Severn and Joseph Reinert, two EPA scientists following toxaphene in the environment, that after talking to BFC, they sent a note to Johnson in which they put their cards on the table: BFC's proposals about toxaphene "would make no useful contribution to our state of knowledge," Severn wrote.

"Our concern about the environmental transport of toxaphene is dramatically illustrated by the recently recognized buildup of toxaphene residues in fish in the Great Lakes, even though little or no toxaphene is used in that region," Severn continued. "In fact, recent data from an isolated landlocked lake on Isle Royale, an island in Lake Superior near the Canadian border whose only known input of water is from the atmosphere, show 3.2 ppm [parts per million] toxaphene in adult lake trout. The toxaphene residues in the Great Lakes almost certainly result from atmospheric transport from the southern states. Toxaphene has been consistently found in rainwater collected along the eastern seaboard, and at levels 10–100 times greater than DDT or PCBs."

Severn warned Johnson that merely tinkering with toxaphene regulation—which BFC wanted—would do nothing to reduce the risk to people and nature. "Given the nature of our concern about its atmospheric dispersal throughout the environment, normal risk reduction methods would not be effective," Severn wrote. "Label restrictions such as requiring application lay-off distances or any type of limiting monitoring effort could not reduce the levels of environmental exposure for this pesticide. Environmental exposure can only be reduced effectively by reducing the amount of toxaphene used."[11]

Severn and Reinert were brave, and they were right. But they were also conventional scientists working within a dysfunctional system. They knew what the political fallout would be when that information became public. They knew that if their suggestions were taken seriously, BFC would lose money, and the implications of that loss would reverberate like a tsunami at the EPA. Congressmen and senators would demand their pound of flesh.

I talked about toxaphene with Stanley Weissman, the legal adviser to Edwin Johnson. He understood that toxaphene was an American tragedy. But we also saw clearly that Johnson would not dare initiate proceedings against toxaphene, and that it would be futile and dangerous for us to urge him to move in that direction. We knew toxaphene was a political problem that could probably be resolved only in a political context.

We passed the information about toxaphene to Illinois congressman Sid Yates, who to his credit acted quickly. Yates was the chairman of the appropriations subcommittee for the Department of the Interior and was well informed about environmental issues. As a congressman from Chicago, Yates was concerned about the shore of Lake Michigan, and once he learned about cancer-causing toxaphene and its contamination of the fish in Lake Michigan, he decided he would work to ban the chemical.

As so often happens in these cases, part of his interest was personal. Yates's wife had cancer, and in his mind, toxaphene was too close for comfort.

In August 1982, Sid Yates took his righteous anger with him to the floor of the House of Representatives, arguing for a ban on toxaphene.

"I am very emotional about this amendment," Yates said. "The reason I feel emotional is that I have just taken my wife home from the National Cancer Institute, where she has been found to have a malignancy. She and I played golf together up to about three weeks ago. We played on a Sunday afternoon, and the next day she did not feel well. We went into a doctor's office, and we found that she had this condition.

"How does this happen?" Yates asked his colleagues in Congress. "How can it happen? Where does cancer come from? It seems to come out of the blue—but we know better than that. We are being subjected to so many cancer-producing influences in our society today—like toxaphene."

Toxaphene is used widely in the South as insecticide sprayed on cotton crops, Yates said. "That in itself sounds entirely harmless, but it does not stay in place." Like DDT, toxaphene has "a very strong life," Yates said.

> The toxaphene that is sprayed on crops in the Southern States is lifted by the winds and carried for distances of over a thousand miles, to the city of Chicago. Then it is dropped by rainfall onto the city of Chicago, it is dropped on all the communities surrounding the Great Lakes, and it is dropped into the Great Lakes themselves.
>
> In Lake Michigan, in Lake Superior, whitefish and lake trout have been found to have toxaphene in quantities, according to the U.S. Fish and Wildlife Service under official surveys, of 10 parts per million. The accepted maximum level of FDA for this kind of a carcinogenic material is 5 parts per million. So that in the fish that swim in the Great Lakes, a thousand miles away from where this chemical is used, we find this cancer-producing material in the fish. It is in the food chain that is being used by people all over the country.
>
> This is the reason that I offer this amendment, to stop this chemical warfare. The House took a position against chemical warfare some time ago. This is a chemical that can harm men, women, and children.[12]

Yates's efforts resulted in a congressional action banning toxaphene, a rare moment of regulatory sanity. I never thanked Sid Yates for his courage, but I knew that what Yates did was one of those rare political events unlikely to happen again in my lifetime. He was right that cancer is not a curse of the gods, but a variety of different diseases that can be triggered by toxic substances in the environment, notably those employed in the chemical warfare of agribusiness. And he correctly characterized the sprays of the farmers as agents of chemical warfare.

It is not as if congressmen and senators do not have access to reliable information about pesticides. They, more than anyone else, have access to thousands of experts working for them in the Congressional Research Service and the Government Accountability Office. The National Academy of Sciences is also at their disposal. Moreover, members of Congress have command of appropriations and the agendas of committees with the power of investigation and oversight of every branch of activity inside and outside the government. Over the last forty years or so, after lengthy investigations, hearings, and research, the serious ecological risks and health hazards of farm sprays—including the deficient system of regulating these poisons—have caught the attention of elected officials including Senators Abraham Ribicoff, Walter Mondale, Philip Hart, Edward Kennedy, Paul Sarbanes, and Al Gore, and Representatives L. H. Fountain, John Moss, Bob Eckhardt, George E. Brown Jr., Sid Yates, Ted Weiss, Mike Synar, and Henry Waxman. Sadly, and repeatedly, their voices have been drowned out by those of politicians doing the work of corporate America.

Indeed, powerful politicians seldom challenge the chemical corporations that give birth to these toxic sprays. It is as if these companies have a license, granted by EPA, to decide what is going to live and what is going to die.

A case in point: On September 15, 1983, representatives of Ciba-Geigy, a Swiss corporation and one of the world's largest pharmaceutical and pesticide manufacturers, told EPA scientists they had a new cotton insecticide, dubbed CGA-112913, that was almost ready for registration. Like the ghastly pesticide Dimilin, this new concoction worked by preventing young insects from forming their lifesaving hard cover known as an exoskeleton. This insecticide, Ciba-Geigy figured, would have to be sprayed on cotton fields at least ten times per growing season.

According to Norman Cook, the same EPA ecologist who defended honeybees, the chemical was extremely toxic to aquatic invertebrates in amounts of less than 100 parts per *trillion*. Equally troubling, the toxin was also extremely persistent in the environment with a half-life of 6.2 years in pond sediments; bluegill sunfish absorb this poison at a rate of more than *100,000 times* its concentration in water.

Cook told Ciba-Geigy to "drop further development of this compound since the results to date show potentially devastating hazards to nontargets" such as beneficial insects and other animals. Cook also alerted other EPA scientists to keep their eyes open for CGA-112913 and similarly dangerous insecticides. "The Dimilin-like and DDT-like qualities of this [Ciba-Geigy] chemical cannot be over-emphasized," he wrote.[13]

Despite this history, the EPA approved and registered CGA under the name chlorfluazuron. To say I was astonished by this act would be an understatement. Despite what I had seen, I wanted to believe there was some wisdom left among decision makers in the EPA. I was wrong.

Make no mistake: the "nontarget" costs of spraying lethal poisons in the environment are often extraordinarily high. In a cotton field, everything but the bugs feeding on cotton is a "nontarget": that includes not only birds, beneficial insects, other crops, and wildlife but also farmers, farmworkers, and their children. In fact, poisoning of "nontargets" continues to take place in thousands of streams, rivers, forests, and farms when the annual ritual of billions of pounds of toxic sprays hit the shining surface of the water and the green carpet of the land.

Despite "alarming" evidence that farm poisons get into our soil and disrupt or kill the very microorganisms responsible for making the soil fertile, official agriculture remains silent on this tragedy.

"It is important to consider that in intensive agriculture such as the Midwestern corn/soybean production system, heavy applications of chemical pesticides and fertilizers are made to the same land year after year," Rosmarie von Rumker, an EPA consultant, has pointed out. "Most of the chemicals remain in the upper 1–3 inches of topsoil, and their routes and rates of degradation under field conditions are often not known. It is surprising and somewhat alarming how little information is available on the individual or collective effects of these chemicals on the soil microflora and -fauna [microplants and micro-animals in the soil] and on the long-term fertility of the topsoil, one of our most important resources."[14]

I remember an EPA colleague telling me that midwestern farmers had made their fertile land into a biological desert, the soil turned into nothing but a conduit to the corn and soybean seeds for synthetic fertilizers, insect sprays, and weed killers. Yet my colleague was no friend of organic farming; he mocked efforts to grow food without pesticides. He rose in the EPA ranks from the moment of its inception in December 1970 until his retirement more than thirty years later. His organization justified the use of pesticides in America, always siding with the manufacturers of pesticides, always concluding there was no way America could feed itself and the world without toxic sprays.

Although the EPA agreed to fund Rosmarie von Rumker and Sharon Hart and other university researchers who explored the issues of agricultural production and pesticides, the agency did little to publicize the data on the harmful effects of pesticides that were bulging from its files. In the end, senior EPA officials remained unwilling to help put an end to decades of covering up for agribusiness.

CHAPTER 11

The Hubris of the Reagan Administration

L ESS than twenty years after *Silent Spring* warned about the dangers of farm sprays, an EPA study revealed that more than 200 million Americans—at a minimum—were exposed to widely used poisons, including DDT-like chemicals and nerve toxins. Not just from farms, but from household bug sprays, greenhouses, and golf courses. Pesticides were no longer only saturating our food; they had soaked into every corner of our lives.[1]

"It is quite possible that household use of pesticides may have a more significant role in human exposure to pesticides than previously thought," the EPA study concluded. By this time the EPA already knew that in three large American cities, up to ten pounds of active pesticide ingredients get sprayed on every acre of the urban environment every year. EPA's urban soils monitoring program revealed excessive contamination of American cities with organophosphate (parathion-like) pesticides, DDT-like sprays, and PCBs.[2]

Nine of every ten households used pesticides, and more than three times as many Americans used pesticides inside their homes than in their gardens, one study showed. Other startling findings: Americans used more than five hundred different pesticide products. People living in the southeastern United States were exposed to more termite poisons and sprays of commercial insecticides than those living in other regions of the country. More than 35 percent of urban Americans used toxic mothballs; 90 percent sprayed disinfectants; 16.4 percent employed no-pest strips; and 28 percent used pet insecticide collars.

Throughout the 1970s, evidence had been mounting about the saturation of the soil with dangerous chemicals: 68 percent of soil specimens from Fitchburg, Massachusetts, contained detectable concentrations of nerve toxin (parathion-like) chemicals, DDT-like sprays, and PCBs. Some 98 percent of soil samples from Washington, D.C., had similar contamination. Samples from Springfield, Illinois; Camden, New Jersey; Richmond, Virginia; and Hartford, Connecticut, had similarly dangerous levels of parathion-like pesticides, DDT-like sprays, and PCBs.[3]

Hiding inside the country's seventeen thousand greenhouses—many of them managed by land grant universities—were large amounts of dangerous pesticides, including nerve toxins such as malathion, which is also a carcinogen.[4]

In other words, the time was overripe for a president to show leadership on industrial contaminants, to stand up for public health, to reinvigorate oversight of corporate malfeasance.

As the world quickly learned, Ronald Reagan was exactly the wrong man for this job. Rarely has our government allowed and encouraged the actions of the chemical industry so openly as it did during Reagan's tenure in office. He opened the door wide to corporate influence throughout the government, and especially at the EPA, which began a precipitous functional decline. Reagan gave corporations the reins of power at the agency, and they immediately began tearing the EPA apart. Outside the agency, the hired political guns in Reagan's Office of Management and Budget also set about demolishing environmental protection, justifying such vandalism by the self-serving mythology of the "cost/benefit analysis," which masked a naked ideological shift toward pesticide merchants and agribusiness.

Early in the Reagan administration, Vice President George H. W. Bush launched his task force on "regulatory relief," and the federal government was opened up for giveaways to corporate polluters. Reagan's political men and women were encouraged to run rough-shod over regulators they found in their way.

The EPA was an ideal target not because the agency was in the vanguard of environmental protection or industrial reform; it had hardly ever fulfilled its mission of making industry less toxic to human health or the natural world. The EPA was a target because its very mission, "environmental protection," was anathema to America's polluting industries.

"[T]here were plainly people in the administration, within EPA, who believed that the EPA itself should be dissolved, that the statutes that it implemented were senseless, and that the federal government had no business in environmental management," said Sheldon Novick, a top lawyer of the EPA from Region III. "Those people, who found enforcement of federal law particularly distasteful, expressed that the EPA should be dismantled, beginning with its enforcement functions."[5]

With this goal in mind, Reagan appointed a lawyer from Colorado, Anne M. Gorsuch (later Burford), to run his EPA; Reagan also appointed a lobbyist from California, Rita Lavelle, to run the EPA's toxic waste programs. Both understood that their mission was not to empower the EPA but to dismantle it. And they set about their work with zeal. Virtually all of Gorsuch's subordinates at the EPA came from the ranks of the industries they were charged with overseeing. My colleague William Sanjour said Reagan's EPA was being run by "hooligans."[6]

Gorsuch was tough: even as the country's leading environmental regulator, she wore fur coats, smoked two packs of Marlboros a day, and drove a government-issue car that got just fifteen miles to the gallon. Denver's *Rocky Mountain News* once said that Gorsuch "could kick a bear to death with her bare feet."

Gorsuch cut budgets for research and enforcement, slashed the number of cases filed against polluters, and sped up the pace of approvals for pesticides. She once boasted that she had reduced the thickness of the book of clean water regulations from six inches to a half inch. A colleague of mine, Richard Laska, once told me that Gorsuch "burned" a report he had prepared about acid rain. I can only assume he used the word "burned" metaphorically. Yet her agency once famously tried to set aside a 30-by-40-mile rectangle of ocean due east of the Delaware-Maryland coast where incinerator ships would torch toxic wastes, apparently out of view of nosy onlookers.[7]

Gorsuch drastically weakened the EPA's enforcement organization and did away with all employees working with the public. Meanwhile, in a series of sumptuous lunches and cocktail parties with the barons of America's hazardous waste kingdom, Rita Lavelle made deals that prevented the EPA from continuing its already inadequate efforts to ensure that effluent from millions of tons of toxic garbage did not go directly into the country's drinking water.[8]

Senior EPA officials had become "immoral," a senior EPA scientist, Lionel Richardson, a senior administrator and scientist who had been turned into a paper pusher, explained to me. Richardson had witnessed the arbitrary termination of a very useful though expensive project on alternatives to chemicals, and he was angry. "Nothing, or almost nothing, prevents them from getting in the end what they want from those working for them," he told me. "They promise their underlings favors and then slowly test them for loyalty. Would they lie, for instance? Or cover up? Or get rid of documents? You must understand this: We don't deal with very much science, and the little science we occasionally manufacture to support our decisions, we often screw up. The key to what's happening here is people, and how a couple of guys at the top have literally succeeded in destroying EPA's legal opportunity to regulate pesticides. I don't know what connections these people have with the chemical companies. But I do know they use scientists pretty quick."[9]

The Republican White House, however, ordered the EPA to cover up the mess by resorting to the imperial claim of "executive privilege." Reagan wanted to keep government documents out of the glare of congressional oversight. This meant that industry corporate lobbyists could see EPA documents, but Democratic congressional committee staff could not.[10]

This of course made House Democrats mad as hell. Since Democrats held the majority in the House of Representatives, a number of powerful subcommittee chairmen launched a series of investigations that revealed the gross negligence of Reagan's audacious men and women at the EPA.

John Dingell of Michigan was particularly effective. As chairman of the Subcommittee on Oversight and Investigations of the Committee on Energy and Commerce, he understood correctly that the White House's withholding of EPA documents from Congress was simply a way to cover up serious malfeasance. Dingell's subcommittee staff confirmed his suspicions. Top EPA officials "violated their public trust by disregarding health and the environment, manipulating the Superfund program [for the management of hazardous wastes] for political purposes, engaging in unethical conduct, and participating in other abuses."[11]

During the Reagan years, dangerous chemicals became so ubiquitous that they were even contaminating people inside buildings and during their leisure time. According to an EPA-funded study done at Colorado State University, female greenhouse workers in Colorado were giving birth to low-birth-weight babies at a significantly higher rate than average, the study concluded. They also had more than twice the average number of miscarriages or stillbirths.

What could have been causing this distress? Colorado and other western states use many of the most popular toxins in the farmers' arsenal. Of an estimated 104,000 pounds of active parathion ingredients distributed to American nurseries in 1982, some 102,000 pounds went to horticultural establishments in the West. These included benomyl, captan, carbaryl, chlordane, Cygon (dimethoate), DDVP (dichlorvos), diazinon, Dibrom (naled), Di-Syston, Dursban (chlorpyrifos), Kelthane, malathion, Metasystox, Morestan, nicotine, Orthene, Paraquat, parathion, Phosdrin, Pirimor, piperonyl butoxide, Princep, Roundup, sulfur, Temic (aldicarb), Thimet, thiram, Treflan, Vendex, warfarin, and zineb.[12]

Like the names of drugs, the names of pesticides are designed to seem technical and indecipherable, mere hints of the petrochemicals of which they are constituted. Many of the toxins used in the Colorado greenhouses are known to cause "unreasonable adverse effects on man and the environment," violating the EPA's core mission.[13]

During the Reagan years, we were not safe from pesticides even when at play. In 1984, an EPA-funded study revealed that golf courses are sprayed with some 126 different pesticides, at least nine of which (chlorothalonil, MSMA, thiram, benomyl, pentachlorophenol, ethylene dibromide, maneb, oftanol, and dithane M-45) have been known to cause "unreasonable adverse effects on man and the environment."

How many people played golf on the country's thirteen thousand courses? About 16 million.[14]

The problem with pesticides on the golf courses is not merely the incredible variety and toxicity of the poisons being sprayed; it's also that "large amounts of pesticide chemicals are used on the courses and that these chemicals are applied quite frequently throughout the year."[15]

By the mid-1980s, in other words, the bad news had become too widespread to ignore. Pesticides were among the greatest threats to the health of the American people and their environment, a danger that—despite the public outcry over Superfund sites—was more serious than that of hazardous waste. EPA's own "Operating Guidance" document for fiscal year 1987 listed pesticides as the number one priority for policies designed to reduce "risks from exposure to *existing pesticides and toxic chemicals*."

Disaster exploded in Arkansas in 1986, when FDA inspectors discovered shocking levels of heptachlor, an extremely toxic poison, in the milk fat of dairy cows fed a mash poisoned by the pesticide. How bad was the contamination? The mash contained heptachlor levels a thousand times greater than the permissible level. The milk itself had poison levels 75 times greater than legally acceptable.

The FDA ordered the seizure and destruction of the heptachlor-laced milk and cream in Arkansas. This travesty, which cost dairy farmers and cattle raisers of Arkansas about $16 million, forced another agricultural crisis to the surface. If American agribusiness were actually interested in producing healthy food, EPA would not be running a poison empire. Instead, we have a brutal business composed of mechanized factories that are, in effect, mining the land.

Owners of factory farms think nothing of "dressing" seed, that primordial molecule of life, with all sorts of toxins, especially fungicides. In the United States in the 1980s, no less than 8.2 billion pounds of seed were treated with fungicides and insecticides. This includes virtually all seed for corn, cotton, sorghum, vegetables, and peanuts. Also, more than 80 percent of potato and rice seed and approximately 30 to 35 percent of all wheat, rye, oats, barley, and soybean seed are treated with pesticides. Considering that a bushel of treated seed sells for $70, and that quite a bit of that seed is genetically designed to be useless for germination at the end of each planting season, the temptation to feed cattle with all that poisonous waste seed is powerful indeed. The FDA has been catching farmers giving cows seed loaded with poisons for years.

Today, of course, the chemical treatment of seeds remains the same, though more sophisticated and far wider. In 2004, for example, 1.3 billion pounds of seed a year were treated with 631,000 pounds of a single chemical, thiram.[16]

Of all the seeds "dressed" with poisons against disease and insects, seed corn is king. In 2012, the United States used 25 million bushels of corn seed for planting. This translates to 1.4 billion pounds of corn. About 90 percent of all seed, including corn seed, is "dressed." Thus, altogether, in the second decade of the twenty-first century, several billion pounds of seed are annually treated with pesticides.[17]

Every year farmers and seed companies ended up with something like 2 million bushels of "obsolete" chemically treated corn
seed. What to do with so much valuable but dangerous seed? Farmers
didn't intend to plant it but, at least before 1981, neither could they
legally give it to cows; the seed was coated and pumped with several
fungicides and insecticides in amounts that would make the cows'
milk, cream, and meat toxic to people. So corn farmers and seed
companies resolved the dilemma with a straightforward political solution: they buttonholed the Reagan administration through the
American Seed Trade Association—and the rest was easy. Companies
claimed that they had effective "detreating" methods that neutralized
the toxicity of poisoned seeds, and so these companies were allowed
to feed the toxic stuff to cows. On November 6, 1981, the EPA once
again gave in to the administration's "regulatory relief" agenda and
allowed corn farmers to feed their livestock the corn seed treated
with the fungicide captan, a carcinogen that is far more powerful
than thalidomide in causing fetal deformities. About five years later,
in 1986—at a time when desperate Arkansas officials and FDA
bureaucrats were contemplating dumping millions of gallons of
heptachlor-laced milk—EPA managers realized they simply could not
trust industry habits of "washing" or "roasting" the captan-soaked
corn seeds.

The danger, of course, was not merely related to high quantities
of captan. Like magic beans, corn seed is "dressed" with several coats
of deleterious protection. Captan and other pesticides are joined by
powerfully toxic "inerts" and "dyes." Ironically, even more poisons are
created during the ludicrous and ineffective "detreating" process.
The "magic beans" are then fed to livestock.

The problem of poison-soaked corn seeds became so appalling
that even timid EPA bureaucrats began thinking in early 1987 how to
undo the harm they had legalized six years before. Could they revoke
the "captan tolerance" for corn seed and thus once again make it illegal to feed livestock poisonous corn seeds?

As the EPA debated this, about half the obsolete captan-treated corn seed in the United States (close to a million bushels) was exported to Holland to feed Dutch animals. Here's how it worked: companies would buy the million bushels of captan-treated seed corn, "detreat" the seed, mix this seed with other feeds, then package the final product and sell the mixture to Holland.

This is important not just because another country showed gross negligence by purchasing poisoned seed. It also illustrates the global trade in poisons—many of which end up not just in our food, but in the food of the world.[18]

EPA managers knew that this poisoned milk disaster was slowly unfolding and that Americans were paying the price. Even by the mid-1970s, a study showed that DDT-like chemicals (dieldrin, heptachlor, heptachlor epoxide, oxychlordane, lindane, BHC, PCBs, HCB, trans-nonachlor) were showing up in the milk of a majority of fourteen hundred nursing women in a hundred fifty American hospitals. The numbers were shocking: 80 percent of the mothers had, on average, 164 parts per billion of dieldrin in their milk. The mean level for BHC, lindane, HCB, and trans-nonachlor varied from 56 to 193 parts per billion. But the most startling (and frightening) discovery was the presence of DDE, the carcinogenic form of DDT, in the milk of 99 percent of the mothers. The average amount of DDE in the mothers' milk was 3,521 parts per billion. (There were no legal limits to pesticides in mothers' milk. DDT and other organochlorines were allowed at about 7 parts per million limits in crops.)[19]

A couple of years later, the EPA found pentachlorophenol, an acutely toxic insecticide, fungicide, and wood preservative, in the urine of about 120 million Americans.[20]

Another study painted a grim picture of the health of the country's Hispanic population. The Reagan administration had funded the study in order to feign loyalty to the Hispanic community, though Reagan's environmental agenda had little to do with either public health or the environment. The administration assigned the task to John Todhunter, the EPA's assistant administrator from 1981 to 1983.

Todhunter had arrived at EPA after serving as an assistant professor of biology at Catholic University. He also served on the board of scientific advisers of the American Council on Science and Health, a front organization for the agrochemical industry. His work at EPA continued his life's work, which was to fight for the interests of the industry.[21]

On January 19, 1983, Todhunter signed a memorandum and agreement with the National Center for Health Statistics for a study of the toxic contamination of the country's Hispanic population. The study cost EPA more than $6 million, seven years of lab work, and fifty person-years of labor. The scientific results were predictable, and deeply troubling: more than 90 percent of the Latinos in the sampling areas had pentachlorophenol in their urine, and nearly all those living in some areas of Texas, New Mexico, Colorado, and Los Angeles had DDE, the cancer-causing form of DDT, in their blood. (Two Hispanics from Los Angeles also had 18 and 33 parts per billion of PCBs in their blood.)[22]

Up to 80 percent of Hispanics living in San Antonio and Houston, Texas, were poisoned by the nerve toxin dursban (also known as chlorpyrifos), a Dow Chemical product used for termite and corn insect control, and much more. Some 27 percent of the rest of the Hispanic population of the country had dursban in their urine. This compound, known to be "acutely toxic to fish at extremely low levels," has also been linked to brain abnormalities in the children of exposed mothers. Virginia Rauh, a professor of medicine at Columbia University and head researcher of the 2012 study of chlorpyrifos, reported that mothers who breathe or eat chlorpyrifos can deliver the poison through their blood and across the placenta to their infant's bloodstream. Five or ten years after chlorpyrifos poisons the infant, "structural changes" take place in the brain, affecting those areas responsible for "attention, language, reward systems, emotions and control." Nearly twenty years later, the EPA banned chlorpyrifos for residential use. Farmers, however, keep chlorpyrifos in their armory.[23]

The study of Hispanics only confirmed evidence that minorities and poor people were—and are—exposed to more poisons than affluent whites. "So striking is the association of the pesticide residues with social class that one might predict the occurrence of greater residues of DDT and its metabolites in those diseases which are associated with poverty," John E. Davies, a physician funded by the EPA, had concluded in a earlier report.[24]

So, did all this evidence cause major regulatory action at the EPA? Of course not. Once the study's findings began to sink in, when Reagan's people could see that the results were bad, they contemplated terminating or abandoning it. Although they "restricted" the use of pentachlorophenol in 1984, they said—and did—nothing about the contamination of so many millions of people with that acutely toxic poison.[25]

Donald Marlow, an EPA laboratory manager, told me in July 1984 just how upset he was that senior EPA managers did not, in his opinion, have the brains—or the courage—to act on evidence that pentachlorophenol was in the bodies of a large segment of the country's Hispanic population. He was right: the EPA had enough evidence against pentachlorophenol to ban it. But the "dummies," he said, "did nothing."

The Reagan EPA did nothing because that's what the Reagan EPA always did: nothing. Not long after this, John Todhunter, who had overseen the study, was brought before a congressional panel over his decision to delay—for three years—restrictions on the cancer-causing pesticide ethylene dibromide. This pesticide, which was injected into the ground in citrus groves to kill worms (and used as a fumigant on grain milling equipment), was known to have caused cancer, birth defects, and other disorders in animal studies. It had not only been found in Florida water supplies; EPA scientists had discovered it in bread given to children as part of school lunch programs.

One congressman accused Todhunter of buckling to the demands of industry and the Reagan White House; another accused him of destroying his calendar, a practice that may have violated federal law. "What you had was a series of secret meetings which resulted in the reversal of a decision reached on the record," Jonathan Lash, an attorney with the Natural Resources Defense Council, told *The New York Times*. "That is not the way the government is supposed to work."[26]

Then Todhunter was accused of ordering EPA studies altered to downplay the dangers of formaldehyde. Todhunter was said to have held a private meeting with representatives of the formaldehyde industry (which, not coincidentally, had contributed to the American Council on Science and Health, on whose board Todhunter had once served). After the meetings, Todhunter decided to take no regulatory action on formaldehyde, which has been used for decades to make plywood and particleboard, among many other products.

Once this news broke, Todhunter—like so many other Reagan appointees at EPA—abruptly resigned. Newspapers noted that Todhunter had been accused of "holding private meetings with industry groups before deciding not to regulate formaldehyde as a suspected cancer-causing agent. Also being investigated was his receipt of a $1,664 payment from a former employer after starting work at the EPA. The firm subsequently received a $40,000 no-bid contract from Todhunter's office." Todhunter "denied any involvement," newspaper reports noted.

Five years later, the EPA finally decided to call formaldehyde what it is: a "probable human carcinogen."[27]

"To see what has gone wrong inside the Environmental Protection Agency, there is no need to peer through the acrid vapors that stream from its every window," *The New York Times* opined during the tenure of Todhunter and Reagan's other EPA appointees. "Seldom since the Emperor Caligula appointed his horse a consul has there been so wide a gulf between authority and competence."[28]

CHAPTER 12

From Reagan to Bush

F ARMERS have always sought any advantage they can find to help them grow more food. Sadly, given the regime of intensified agricultural chemicals, this has meant a relentless tide of hazards for both nature and society. In the late 1930s, for example, there were no more than three thousand to four thousand acres of land devoted to rice production in the Missouri Bootheel, which is 4,125 square miles in size. Not much changed in rice growing in Missouri until the early 1970s.

Suddenly, in a single decade, farmers in the Bootheel increased the acreage given to rice production from 5,000 acres to 75,300 acres, a growth of 1,500 percent. Very little idle land survived. By 2005, Missouri rice farmers—and their corporate overseers—ranked sixth in earnings in the country, taking in about $100 million per year. These farmlands are blessed with plenty of water, and the farmers get plenty of government subsidies. But they have also been using massive amounts of weed killer, much of it applied by aerial spraying in the month of June.[1]

Just to the north of Missouri, Iowa is also almost entirely under cultivation: of its 36 million acres, nearly 34 million are farmed. In 1978, 13.5 million acres of this land was devoted to corn alone. That year, Iowa farmers treated 96 percent of their corn with weed killers, spraying the weed killer 2,4-D on 1.3 million acres of emerging corn. (Recall that 2,4-D made up half of Agent Orange, the weed killer weapon the United States used to burn out the jungles of Vietnam.)

Since 1978, farmers in Iowa (and elsewhere) essentially abandoned traditional mechanical weed removal, going all in for the "no-till" method of intensive spraying of weed killers like 2,4-D before sowing their seed corn. Despite evidence that these poisons end up in our drinking water, chemical companies in the early 1980s taught farmers to spray weed killers and other chemicals through center-pivot irrigation sprinkler systems, thus worsening an already bad situation.

It wasn't just the Midwest that was choking on industrial chemicals. In 1983, during the Reagan administration, a long-term EPA study called the Regional Environmental Management Reports documented America's environmental disaster in frightening detail. Some 65 percent of nearly six hundred industries in Florida, Georgia, South Carolina, North Carolina, Alabama, Mississippi, Tennessee, and Kentucky "were discharging wastes containing substances lethal to aquatic life."

Wastes, both solid and liquid, were also overwhelming New Jersey, which was running out of clean drinking water; the state had been forced to close 74 public water supply wells since 1971, 90 percent because of contamination by organic and industrial chemicals. Of New Jersey's 391 legal and illegal landfills, fully 75 were suspected of contaminating groundwater—every year—with seven billion gallons of contaminated "leachate." On top of this, 356 dumps were annually leaking another 6 billion gallons of contaminants into groundwater supplies. New Jersey's other problems? More than twenty-five hundred accidental petroleum and chemical spills in 1981 alone; leaking underground storage tanks and pipelines; and decrepit wastewater disposal systems.

Over the next several decades, the EPA reported, of the 750 million gallons a day of groundwater used for drinking water, fully 40 to 50 million gallons a day "will be lost because of pollution."

New York fared little better in the report. It was hard to find a fish in the state that was not already toxic: fish in Adirondack lakes were contamination with cadmium, lead, and mercury; shad in the Delaware River had elevated arsenic levels; trout in the Finger Lakes were poisoned with DDT and chlordane; fish in Lake Champlain and the Hudson River were blighted with PCBs; blue crabs had high levels of cadmium.[2]

And on and on it went. The rivers and lakes of the entire country had become a mirror clouded and dark from chemical pollution. Researchers found PCBs and DDT-like chemicals in the Pacific Northwest's Columbia River sturgeon; the PCBs killed the eggs of the fish and also decimated mink and otter. In all, there were more than fifteen thousand sites in the United States where PCBs were buried or dumped, ceaselessly releasing their poisons into the environment. EPA inspectors may need several hundred years to clean up PCBs from the environment of the Pacific Northwest alone.

Evidence of the country's widespread contamination by farmers' chemicals was sobering, but at least the Regional Environmental Management Reports correctly identified a root problem: the nation's pesticides law was little more than an avenue for legal pollution.

Under the law's Section 18 "emergency" or "crisis" exemptions, federal agencies and states allow the spraying of untested chemicals. But as I described in chapter 2 with regard to asana, the lethal pyrethroid spray, a great volume of untested poisons (and a great deal of money) can come down to what industry and regulars decide constitutes an "emergency."[3]

All too often, what "emergency" means to a company is "whenever we want to test a chemical so we can recover the money we spent on research and development."

The pitch goes like this. Companies (and their lackeys in state government) come to the EPA with a simple request: "Since existing pesticides seem to be ineffective, this new chemical is the only one left to save the farmers from disaster." Individual states then ask EPA for a

Section 18 exemption, and regulators bow down and do the state's (and thus the companies') bidding. The demand for the use of untested poisons typically came primarily from Kentucky, Tennessee, Mississippi, Alabama, Georgia, Florida, South Carolina, and North Carolina. The states of Washington, Oregon, Alaska, and Idaho were also exploiting Section 18 "emergency" exemptions with a vengeance.[4]

Predictably, the definition of an "emergency" or a "crisis" is left to the industrial farmers and chemical companies themselves. This policy is merely another way the agricultural and chemical industries have found to line their own pockets without interference from the government agencies supposedly overseeing them. Among the biggest beneficiaries of this dangerous practice are domestic and foreign companies such as Shell Chemical Company, Ciba-Geigy, DuPont, Mobay, and Chevron.

With so much money at stake, these companies can be relentless in their lobbying. During the Reagan administration, emergency exemption requests went through the roof, increasing 376 percent from 1978 to 1983. In 1984 alone, EPA approved 770 such requests.[5]

ICI Americas and FMC Corporation, for example, successfully persuaded farmers and governors of different states to secure EPA's "emergency" permission for the introduction of their deadly product Ambush (permethrin) 259 times between 1978 and 1982.[6]

In 1981, my esteemed colleague Adrian Gross urged his EPA bosses to ban permethrin because it caused cancer in experimental animals. Gross showed that a child weighing about 40 pounds who ate a California orange contaminated with a tiny amount of ethylene dibromide (used to fumigate the Mediterranean fruit fly in the summer of 1981) would receive a dosage 50 to 70 times the legal limit.

Gross distributed his findings to several congressional subcommittees on Capitol Hill, and of course he got what was coming to him. Usually reporters showed up after the release of his lengthy memoranda, but nothing more; this time, Gross was stripped of his position as chief of the EPA's toxicology branch. Since it would have been politically embarrassing for the EPA to fire him, he was simply given an empty room and an empty job, left to rot in comfortable silence.

No doubt companies like ICI Americas and FMC Corporation made a bundle of money when they persuaded EPA to "register" permethrin. Beyond the "registered" sprays, the tons of "emergency" pesticides that rain down on American food constitute a grand experiment on the nature and the people of the United States. At least registered pesticides have come through some kind of scientific scrutiny, however flawed. But when the chemicals are unregistered, we know nothing at all about them.

Given all the evidence against it—including EPA's own legal team vigorously opposing the emergency ruling—the permethrin debacle became a public scandal. Calling permethrin safe seemed to "fly in the face of the most elementary principles of [the] scientific method," an infuriated Connecticut Senator Christopher J. Dodd wrote to an EPA administrator. Dodd found the EPA's decision "alarming." How was the public supposed to trust its own government "when the very data this conclusion was drawn from appears to have been patched together at best?"[7]

Dodd's question goes to the EPA's core failure: using bad science to mask pro-industry policies. Sadly, Dodd did not follow up, and Congress never seriously contemplated challenging corporate influence over America's environmental policies. EPA researchers who wrote reports (in 1983 and 1987) on popular, untested pesticides said the agency simply did not have the ability to monitor the use of those chemicals.

The result of all this has been the ever-broadening and intensifying spraying of powerful weed killers, with the usual toxic side effects: chemical runoff into streams, rivers, and groundwater; spray drift hurting humans living near the farms; contaminated gardens, organic farms, and animals; and the crippling and killing of wildlife.

In Montana, North Dakota, Wyoming, Utah, and Colorado, major bird kills were still being caused by DDT and DDT-like chemicals in the 1980s—a decade after DDT had been banned. DDT poisoning of insect-eating birds and waterfowl covered the entire West Coast. Researchers found extremely high levels of DDT in the brain (up to 230 parts per million) as well as in the tissues and eggs of the heron, the whitefaced ibis, and numerous other birds.

In California, the drinking water wells of the San Gabriel Valley were laced with industrial chemicals, trichloroethylene and tetrachloroethylene and carbon tetrachloride, a fumigant used in treating seeds. Nearly a third of the 349 wells bringing drinking water to two dozen community water systems—which served 4.5 million people—had one or more of these potent poisons in them. Also in California, a worm killer called dibromochloropropane (DBCP) was found in more than 750 drinking water wells in the San Joaquin Valley. DBCP made news because it sterilized workers who made it in a factory in Lathrop, California. When I taught for a time at Humboldt State University, one of my students told the class about having to drink DBCP-contaminated water because his family had no other option.[8]

The U.S. Fish and Wildlife Service documented numerous episodes of acute poisoning of birds by farm sprays. In the summer of 1982, hundreds of rare sage grouse died in south central Idaho; so did Canada geese, songbirds, and fish in Yakima, Washington, and geese in Ontario, Oregon. Since the introduction of a nerve poison for the killing of cattle grubs, the population of American magpies declined by about 50 percent.

By 2000, the Fish and Wildlife Service estimated that every year, roughly one in ten birds that come into contact with farm sprays are killed. That's about 67 million birds.[9]

The aerial application of mosquito-killing sprays was also sending toxins drifting into lakes and estuaries, especially those of central and southeast Florida and other southern states. Many of the mosquito killers are nerve poisons, toxic to crustaceans, fish, and birds, and DDT-like compounds, crippling or lethal to nearly all wildlife. In addition, both neurotoxic and DDT-like chemicals poison drinking water. Similarly, private and commercial aerial application of pesticides on crops caused "environmental incidents" throughout the country, especially in EPA's Region V, which includes Illinois, Indiana, Ohio, Wisconsin, Michigan, and Minnesota.

Farmers of these states also "incorporate" granular pesticides into the soil, which means that after rains, huge amounts of poisons end up in streams, rivers, and lakes, contaminating and killing fish and wildlife.

The residents of Scottsdale, Arizona, learned this the hard way. People exposed to drifting pesticides suffer effects that are "diverse, intense, disabling, and distressing," wrote Stanley H. Schuman, a professor of epidemiology at the Medical University of South Carolina, who studied this dilemma on behalf of the EPA in 1979.

"There is considerable *mental stress and distress* associated with belonging to some as yet undefined percentage of the population in a neighborhood or a community [hit by chemical drift]," Schumann wrote. "In addition to experiencing bouts of illness associated with repeated pesticide exposure, [the people of that neighborhood] suffer various forms of antipathy and intolerance. Whereas others may be annoyed or irritated by odors, eye irritation, and respiratory discomfort, these people are functionally disabled. Such a person finds one's self placed on the defensive with little medical or social support."

Very little has changed with pesticide drift in the last thirty-five years; if anything, the situation has gotten worse. In the Central Valley of California, a woman named Teresa Avina complained in 2008 that she got sick from the drifting pesticides every day and that drifting pesticides were responsible for the miscarriages and cancer afflicting her neighbors in the town of Huron, located at the center of San Joaquin Valley.[10]

In 2012, in rural Minnesota, spray poisons put people at risk throughout the growing season. Pesticides drift invisibly from the agricultural fields to residential areas, contaminating their air, water, and food. Rural Minnesotans say they endure "heavy dousings of agricultural pesticides."[11]

Drifting pesticides also damage wildlife. Pesticides from California's Central Valley, for instance, travel fifty to a hundred miles to the Sierra Nevada mountains, where they poison frogs, threatening these sensitive animals with extinction.[12]

If anything, the pesticide industry had simply—once again—rebranded itself, appropriating the vocabulary of ecology but remaining as ruthless as ever in its defense of toxins. Pesticide companies formed a group with the Orwellian name CropLife America, but the group continues to insist that endangered species are not endangered, that spray drift is not a problem, and that EPA is nothing but a hindrance to business.[13]

All of this jibed perfectly with the philosophy of the administration of President George W. Bush, which came to power in 2001. President Bush made it clear early on that federal regulators would continue to turn a blind eye to industrial pollution. It could not have been otherwise. In the grand tradition of Washington politics, many in Bush administration "regulatory" agencies had made a great deal of their money in the very polluting industries they were now charged with overseeing.

Bush's opening gambit was handing the EPA to Christine Todd Whitman, the personable former governor of New Jersey. Whitman was a reliable Republican; while in New Jersey (one of the most polluted states in the country), she had cut the staff and budget of the state's Department of Environmental Protection (DEP). Evaluating her environmental stewardship, a coalition of environmental groups gave her a C minus.

PEER, the Washington-based Professional Employees for Environmental Responsibility, judged Whitman just as harshly. In a 1997 survey of the employees of New Jersey's DEP, the group's director said that Whitman fully supported "corporate violators" of the law and applied "pressure to block enforcement of anti-pollution laws, [and] back-door efforts to gut regulations."[14]

With Whitman at the head of the EPA, pro-industry Republicans in charge of Congress through 2006, and the courts packed with environmental regulation skeptics, the state of American environmental protection under Bush fell to levels I had not seen since the days of Reagan. The Bush administration gave away millions of acres of public lands to oil and timber industries for drilling and logging; the Endangered Species Act almost became extinct; Yellowstone and Grand Teton National Parks were opened to sixty thousand snowmobiles; and some two thousand miles of streams in the Appalachian mountains became choked with mining waste.

The Bush administration also stopped enforcing environmental laws, and Republicans—and not a few Democrats—shamelessly defended those breaking these laws. In early 2002, after twelve years of service, Eric Schaeffer resigned as director of the EPA's Office of Regulatory Enforcement because of the dirty politics being played between the White House, the Energy Department, and energy companies. "Congressmen have become de facto lobbyists for home state polluters," Schaeffer said.

The White House had paralyzed the EPA and worked hard to weaken the federal Clean Air Act, Schaeffer told Whitman in his resignation letter. Nine power companies, for example, had expanded their plants without upgrading their pollution controls, which clean air laws required. When the EPA filed suit against these companies, the White House undermined EPA's determination to bring those corporate criminals to justice. In addition to emitting 2 million tons of the powerfully damaging greenhouse gas nitrogen oxide, the companies "emitted an incredible 5 million tons of sulfur dioxide every year (a quarter of the emissions in the entire country)," Schaeffer wrote.

These coal plants' 7 million tons of sulfur dioxide and nitrogen oxide caused more than 10,800 premature deaths, at least 5,400 incidents of chronic bronchitis, more than 5,100 hospital emergency visits, and over 1.5 million lost workdays, Schaeffer wrote. To this toll could be added "severe damage to our natural resources, as acid rain attacks soils and plants and deposits nitrogen in the Chesapeake Bay and other critical bodies of water."[15]

Needless to say, the energy barons running the Bush administration—especially Vice President Dick Cheney, the former head of energy services giant Halliburton—were undeterred. Their tactics, borrowed from the Reagan playbook, involved public deception, intimidating the EPA staff, and weakening or scrapping the law for the benefit of their friends in industry. The EPA could hardly be said to be "working in the public interest," Schaeffer wrote in *The Washington Monthly* soon after leaving the agency.[16]

In the spring of 2006, the presidents of unions representing about nine thousand EPA scientists and other professionals appealed to the EPA administrator to curtail the immense volume of organophosphate pesticides getting into the nation's food supply—especially since infants and children are so vulnerable to those poisons. The union presidents did not demand that the nerve toxins be banned entirely; they merely appealed for stricter regulation. Industrial muscle, they said, had blinded the EPA to its moral responsibility to protect the public's health.

In early August, the Bush administration rejected this argument and extended the government's approval for most of those chemicals, choosing once again to side with industry over the country's health.

As it had under Reagan, the EPA started to crumble. A new "disinvestment" mandate required that EPA reduce or eliminate its own research libraries and laboratories and shrink the number of scientists serving the agency. That way corporations would be even freer to pollute. Without research libraries, EPA would be blind, incapable of knowing who did what when. These libraries were stocked with tens of thousands of scientific studies and government documents—all relating to issues of public health and environmental protection. The EPA ordered the contractors running its libraries to trash entire document collections, delink documents from websites, and auction off library furniture and bookcases. In short, the Bush managers of EPA pillaged the nation's information resources on public health and the environment.

The Bush administration also targeted EPA's laboratories, knowing full well that without its labs, the EPA would become impotent.[17]

The long-term consequences of this sort of environmental "management" were predictable, and dire.

In 2004, the Center for Biological Diversity, a nonprofit scientific organization based in San Francisco, concluded that the Bush EPA's ties to the agrochemical industry had led to the widespread pesticide contamination of the country's waterways.

"Pesticides are contaminating our air and water while the EPA fails to adequately regulate their use to protect our environment," the Center reported. "Amphibians are a barometer of environmental health—adverse impacts to amphibians are a sign that our ecosystems are under stress. The EPA's attempt to ignore the documented and disturbing impacts of pesticides to amphibians by dismissing the science will not alleviate this systemic problem."

These problems were not limited to wildlife, the report confirmed. Neurological and sexual developmental dysfunction also affected humans, especially children. Infertile women were "27 times more likely to have mixed or applied herbicides in the two years prior to attempting conception than women who were fertile. Farmers, manufacturers and applicators of pesticides have an increased risk of certain types of malignancies, especially lip, prostate, or testicular cancer, lymphoma, leukemia, brain tumors, pancreatic cancer, sarcoma and multiple myeloma."

Bush's EPA consistently appeared to work more vigorously for agrochemical industries than for human or environmental health, the report concluded; indeed, much of the data supporting pesticide permits was "compiled by the registrants themselves. The EPA often dismisses environmental concerns in the face of hard science, and steadfastly refuses to adopt any mandatory measures to limit pesticide use."[18]

For example, rodenticides, used by farmers and nonfarmers alike to poison mice and rats, were decimating California's raptors. Predatory birds including eagles, hawks, falcons, owls, and vultures were eating many of these poisoned mice and rats, causing a "secondary poisoning."

Beginning in 2003, public reaction to the death of predatory birds finally forced Bush's EPA to begin restricting these poisons, a policy that formally took effect in 2011. Yet despite eight years of public outrage and (reluctant) federal restrictions, three chemical companies, Reckitt Benckiser, Spectrum, and Liphatech, simply refused to comply. EPA regulators claimed to be "shocked" that the companies were "thumbing their noses at them."[19]

CHAPTER 13

The Obama Administration: Yes, We Can?

O N the eve of the 2012 elections, the EPA administrator, Lisa Jackson, started an offensive to try to prove that her boss, Barack Obama, cared about public health. On October 21, 2011, she denounced Republicans for delaying the implementation of smog rules. She also said it was necessary to clean up pollution from power plants.

Two months later, I received an email bulletin from Stephanie Cutter, a former EPA employee who in 2011–2012 served as a deputy campaign manager for President Obama's reelection campaign. "Today, President Obama announced a once-in-a-generation step forward for the environment and public health—the first-ever national standards for mercury, arsenic, and other toxic air pollution from power plants," Cutter wrote. "This new rule has been 20 years in the making, but couldn't have come a moment sooner."

For far too long, Cutter wrote, out-of-date power plants "have polluted our air with toxins like mercury and arsenic: nasty stuff that causes everything from cancer, heart attacks, and neurological damage." She placed the blame for this squarely on the shoulders of Republicans, who, she said, have been "fighting us tooth and nail to block new environmental protections like this one, while their industry allies have poured millions into rolling back time-tested safeguards already in place."

Cutter was right: the time had come to do something about the "nasty stuff" of mercury and arsenic poisoning millions of Americans, giving them cancer and neurological diseases. But when it comes to environmental protection, Obama was still asleep at the wheel. Why did his administration wait three years to point out the clear and documented dangers of unregulated power plants?

It was true that Republicans in Congress and the Republican candidates for president (and eventually their nominee, Mitt Romney) were unified against regulating industrial pollution. But from the vantage point of my twenty-five years of experience within the EPA, I can state unequivocally that both Democrats *and* Republicans fight tooth and nail to block anything like real environmental protection. That is the reason it has taken twenty years to broadcast the word that arsenic, mercury, chromium, nickel, and acid gases are bad for our children. In fact, the EPA had known for more than twenty years that half the country's twelve hundred coal- and oil-fired electricity plants did not use modern pollution controls. EPA had also known that breathing the air the factories emit causes cancer and other deadly diseases.[1]

After the doom and gloom accumulated over eight years of the George W. Bush administration, things appeared to change with Obama's election in November 2008. Obama pledged to discard Bush's environmental policies, and environmentalists breathed a sigh of relief.

"Because of the widespread and unnecessary use of over 5 billion total pounds of pesticides a year, hazardous chemicals invade our lives through the contamination and poisoning of our bodies, air, land, water, food and the built environment," read a letter to Obama signed by 102 environmental organizations early in the new president's tenure. "We humans share with other inhabitants of this ecosystem immensely elevated toxic body burdens, and excessive rates of environmentally-induced illnesses, such as cancer, infertility and reproductive problems; immune, hormonal and nervous system disease; respiratory illness and asthma; and learning disabilities and autism."

Administrative practices and leadership are urgently needed, the letter continued, to reverse decisions that have compromised America's public health and environment and to "change a regulatory culture that accepts unnecessary harm [and] the politicization of science, all of which have resulted in wholly inadequate protection of public health and the environment. Priority must be given to reversing and correcting the blatant disregard for law that has been incorporated into regulatory decisions. And most importantly, leadership is needed to direct federal agencies to prioritize the development of safer, clean, healthy and viable systems that sustain our health, air, land, water, food and the built environment."[2]

Unfortunately, President Obama had other priorities that did not include environmental integrity or the protection of public health. Bush had caused so much economic damage that the country teetered on the verge of economic collapse; when Obama stepped into the breach, he rushed for advice to Wall Street. His first chief of staff, Rahm Emanuel, had made $18.5 million in less than three years at a Wall Street bank. Emanuel's successor, William M. Daley, was the son and brother of powerful Chicago mayors and had worked for JPMorgan Chase. Daley was succeeded in early 2012 by Jack Lew, the former director of the Office of Management and Budget; Lew once worked for Citigroup. With such powerful Wall Street voices whispering in his ear day after day, it's no surprise that Obama left environmental protection and public health entirely out in the cold.[3]

At least as influential as the bankers were the voices from industrial agriculture. Among the people Obama appointed to important regulatory positions were Carol Browner, Bill Clinton's EPA administrator and now Obama's senior adviser on energy and the environment; Tom Vilsack, agriculture secretary; Roger Beachy, director of the National Institute of Food and Agriculture; Michael Taylor, the FDA's senior adviser on food safety; and Islam Siddiqui, the agricultural negotiator in the office of the U.S. Trade Representative.[4]

What bound these officials together was their bias toward agribusiness and their commitment to the genetic engineering of food—in other words, they shared Monsanto's view of the world. Sure enough, in the spring of 2013, Obama signed what critics called the Monsanto Protection Act, which protects companies from being sued if their genetically modified seeds lead to health problems. Food safety groups like Food Democracy Now collected more than a quarter million signatures on a petition calling for the president to veto the bill; they argued that not enough is known about the possible health risks of genetically modified seeds. Eliminating the public's ability to halt the selling or planting of these seeds, the groups said, was removing the one sure way of checking this hugely profitable but potentially dangerous forced march toward the genetic engineering of our food.[5]

We knew this was Bush's view, of course: State Department cables reveal that the Bush administration threatened the European Union with sanctions unless EU governments allowed the planting of Monsanto's genetically modified seeds in Europe.[6] But the phalanx of Monsanto men and women working for Obama simply confirms that it does not really matter who presides over the White House or Congress. Corporations rule the kingdom. While still serving as Obama's solicitor general, Elena Kagan wrote a brief requesting the Supreme Court to lift a ruling by an appeals court forbidding the planting in California of Monsanto's genetically engineered Roundup Ready alfalfa. In August 2010, Kagan was confirmed as a Supreme Court justice. She sits beside Justice Clarence Thomas, who once worked as a lawyer for Monsanto.[7]

Indeed, when it comes to genetic engineering, "the Obama administration has not been better than the Bush administration, possibly worse," wrote Jeffrey Smith, an expert on the health effects of bioengineered food. The triumph of Monsanto within the government is bad for our health and bad for the environment. Let me explain further by introducing Don Huber.

※

Don Huber knows a lot about biological weapons, and he knows a lot about plants. A retired colonel from the Army's biological warfare corps, Huber taught plant diseases and soil microbiology at Purdue University for thirty-five years. He has also been the coordinator of the U.S. Agricultural Research Service National Plant Disease Recovery System, a program of the USDA. Of all the things he knows about biological weapons and crops, he is most concerned about the destructive effects of pesticides on the biological systems of plants.

Huber worries, for example, about the effects of glyphosate—popularly known as Roundup, one of the country's most popular weed killers for both farmers and home gardeners. Glyphosate is also a powerful driver of genetic engineering; its creator, the global conglomerate Monsanto, has bioengineered "Roundup Ready" soybeans, corn, and other crops to resist Roundup's killing power. For years, farmers have cleared their fields of weeds by spraying them with glyphosate and then planting Monsanto brand crop seeds that are resistant to the poison.

Monsanto has been using seeds, crops, pesticides, and genetic engineering to spread its web over the entire planet, promising more food to those who buy its modified seeds and chemicals. But like other agribusiness giants, Monsanto seems blind to the harm its products cause to humans and the natural world. For example, Monsanto has convinced millions of farmers, the American government, and the European Commission that glyphosate is safe. Yet the picture is not so clear.

Studies published in 2010 show glyphosate causes birth defects in frogs and chicken embryos at amounts smaller than farmers and gardeners leave in food. Older studies document other dreadful effects of glyphosate, including cancer, endocrine disruption, damage to DNA, and deleterious malformations of the reproductive, neurological, and developmental systems of animals and humans. Researchers also link glyphosate to miscarriages in humans and livestock. Monsanto and government authorities have known about the toxic effects of glyphosate since the 1980s. And both the industry and regulators have kept the public in the dark.[8]

Genetic engineering, in other words, represents imperial politics of the worst kind, aiming at no less than the control of the world's food by agribusiness. In early January 2012, Catholic cardinal Peter Turkson accused the merchants of the genetic engineering of crops of breeding economic dependence and a new form of slavery. However, Monsanto remains implacable.[9]

With decades of experience in biological warfare and crop diseases, Don Huber was convinced in 2011 that glyphosate had probably brought to life a potent pathogen threatening the health of American agriculture. This pathogen is new to science, he said. Its most insidious effect is prompting devastating diseases in genetically engineered crops including soybeans and corn. Huber also linked this pathogen to diseases striking farm animals and, possibly, human beings.

On January 17, 2011, Huber wrote a letter to Secretary of Agriculture Thomas Vilsack. "For the past 40 years, I have been a scientist in the professional and military agencies that evaluate and prepare for natural and manmade biological threats, including germ warfare and disease outbreaks," Huber wrote. "Based on this experience, I believe the threat we are facing from this pathogen is unique and of high risk status. In layman's terms, it should be treated as an emergency."

Huber explained that the pathogen is "a medium size virus" and "a micro-fungal-like organism" that can reproduce itself. It has been found in livestock feed made by soybeans and corn genetically engineered to withstand glyphosate ("Roundup soybean meal and corn"). In addition, the pathogen has been found in pigs, cattle, and other animals that have been struck by spontaneous abortions and infertility. The pathogen "may explain the escalating frequency of infertility and spontaneous abortions over the past few years in US cattle, dairy, swine, and horse operations," Huber added. "These include recent reports of infertility rates in dairy heifers of over 20%, and spontaneous abortions in cattle as high as 45%."

"It is well documented that glyphosate promotes soil pathogens and is already implicated with the increase of more than 40 plant diseases," Huber continued. Furthermore, glyphosate "dismantles plant defenses" against disease by immobilizing vital nutrients, which means the growing crop is starved of the nutrients it must have to defend itself against disease and to be nutritious. Such impoverished crops, says Huber, are causing "animal disorders."

Someone leaked the letter Huber sent to Secretary Vilsack. Huber then sent his original letter to the European Union and the European Commission with a cover letter, dated April 20, 2011, explaining why he had felt compelled to write so urgently to the U.S. Secretary of Agriculture.

"I feel I would be totally irresponsible to ignore my own research and the vast amount of published research now available that support the concerns we are seeing in production agriculture," Huber wrote. He cited evidence showing this new pathogen kills chicken embryos in 24 to 72 hours. The pathogen also intensifies many of the diseases afflicting crops, including an affliction known as Goss's wilt that in 2010 caused American farmers to lose fully a billion bushels of corn.

Huber pleaded for help investigating the risks of the pathogen, and for a moratorium on genetically engineered crops, especially alfalfa, which Huber considered America's most valuable forage crop. Allowing the use of Roundup Ready alfalfa "could strike a mortal blow to struggling dairy and beef operations."

Huber's hopes were quickly dashed. Two weeks after he sent his letter to Vilsack, he received a letter back from the USDA: the government was determined to side with Monsanto on alfalfa. The letter assured Huber that the decision was based "on sound science informed by peer-reviewed research."[10]

I don't know Huber personally, but in early December 2011, I watched him being interviewed by Dr. Joseph Mercola; the clip can be viewed on YouTube. Huber is a cautious, comprehensive master of detail. As an accomplished scientist, he uses peer-reviewed research for drawing conclusions. But he is angry that farmers skeptical of using modified seeds, and scientists who study genetic engineering, are effectively being muzzled.

"It's almost as though you have to belong to that religion [of genetically engineered crops] if you're going to do any research or publish your research," Huber said.[11]

Given his background, Huber can't help but see parallels between biological warfare and crop diseases; glyphosate is doing to crops in America what only an enemy would have liked to do to undermine our agriculture and food security. Huber later emailed me to say that ten days after he received the USDA's letter, the agency deregulated alfalfa and other crops. The spread of Roundup Ready seeds would promptly explode.[12]

Huber responded to the USDA with a long and impassioned letter citing 135 scientific studies supporting his position. He was furious at the intimidation of scientists working on the risks of bioengineered crops, especially on the links between glyphosate and the now-unregulated alfalfa.

"The current crop and animal production environment is NOT normal and NOT sustainable!" Huber wrote. "We are experiencing an escalating incidence of crop, animal, and human diseases, the emergence and reemergence of diseases once rare or under practical control, and new diseases previously unknown to science."

Increasing incidences of disease in animal production programs, especially cattle, dairy, and swine, had become associated with low manganese or other micronutrients, Huber wrote. Manganese deficiencies are associated with infectious diseases, bone and tissue deformities, reproductive failure, and death. Discovered just a decade previously, this new "electron-microscopic-sized 'organism'" was causing infertility and miscarriage in animals. "The excessive use of glyphosate is a major contributor to the increased severity and epidemics of plant and animal diseases, reduced nutrient quality, high mycotoxin levels, and toxic chemical residues we are experiencing in production agriculture," Huber wrote. "I urge your reconsideration of the decision to deregulate Roundup Ready alfalfa based on the principle of 'Scientific Precaution' until essential research can be completed relative to its safety, equivalency, and sustainability."[13]

Huber must have known that asking the USDA to undo the deregulation of alfalfa was hopeless. The Monsanto-controlled agency would not tolerate scientific resistance. So, on November 1, 2011, Huber left for England, where he made a presentation to the All-Party Parliamentary Group on Agroecology of the British House of Commons, in which he repeated the conclusions he had reported to the USDA, the European Union, and the European Commission.

Now outside the suffocating atmosphere of USDA, Huber expressed himself in less diplomatic language. Glyphosate "predisposes plants to disease" and "stimulates pathogens" in the soil, he said. Glyphosate compromises the defense of crops against disease and kills the targeted plants by acting as a biological war agent—in a sense, by boosting disease organisms in the soil while killing disease resistance organisms.

For the last thirty years, glyphosate has been sterilizing the land of beneficial organisms essential for the health of crops. These microorganisms are the pathways through which plants absorb essential micronutrients and are responsible for fixing up to 75 percent of the nitrogen that legumes such as soybeans, alfalfa, and peas need for protein. By killing microorganisms, glyphosate reduces the ability of crops to absorb essential micronutrients such as calcium, nickel, copper, iron, manganese, and zinc from the soil. These micronutrients are absolutely essential not only for the health and nutritious quality of crops, but for the health of animals and people eating these crops. Huber also connected the micronutrient deficiencies in crops to the birth of stillborn calves and animal disease.

Like Morton Biskind sixty years earlier, Don Huber spoke of "a new factor" in our civilization causing havoc in nature, human health, and global food security. The new factor for Biskind in 1953 was the "miracle" of DDT; for Huber in 2011, the danger was posed by a pathogen associated with another "miracle" chemical named glyphosate. In both cases, we have the sick feeling that little, if anything, has changed. The same irresponsible agribusiness policies reign, threatening the very integrity of our food and our health.

Like all good scientists, Huber sees agriculture and the human body as systems. "It's how that ecological system is modified and changed that brings us a new level of diseases and problems with sustainability of our agriculture, our own health, and well-being," he writes.

Huber denounces the betrayal of public trust by government and industry and academia. He cites a letter composed by more than two dozen entomologists complaining that the money their universities receive from genetic engineering companies effectively prohibits them from doing research that might question the safety of the companies' products.

"Technology/stewardship agreements required for the purchase of genetically modified seed explicitly prohibit research," the letter said. "These agreements inhibit public scientists from pursuing their mandated role on behalf of the public good unless the research is approved by industry. As a result of restricted access, no truly independent research can be legally conducted on many critical questions regarding the technology, its performance, its management implications, and its interactions with insect biology. Consequently, data flowing to an EPA Scientific Advisory Panel from the public sector is unduly limited."

A telling comment was attached to this letter: "The names of the scientists have been withheld from the public docket because virtually all of us require cooperation from industry at some level to conduct our research. How willing we've been to sacrifice our children and future generations, and to jeopardize the sustain ability of our entire agricultural infrastructure that is the very basis of our existence as a society."[14]

Huber, now an emeritus professor at Purdue, wrote to me in August 2012 to say that all his efforts with the USDA had "fallen on deaf ears." The USDA was busy deregulating genetically modified crops, and scientists working at universities with industry contracts were in hot water: "Several scientists have been limited in what they can say or share, while others have been denied promotion or tenure," Huber wrote. Thankfully, he said, his own research was still privately funded, "since we couldn't take a chance on it being shut down earlier."[15]

Huber's dire warning is like a sword hanging by a thread. The USDA "regulators" of genetically engineered crops continue with business as usual. In early 2012, they were ready to approve the dangerous herbicide 2,4-D (which, you will remember, was half of Agent Orange) for a new genetically modified corn. This action is certain to double the adverse effects of genetically modified crops. 2,4-D may even trump glyphosate as the greatest chemical threat to American agriculture. Its history of more than seventy years as a chemical weapon, and as a weed killer contaminated by the lethal 2378-dioxin, doesn't bode well for America.

The effects of genetically engineered crops on American agriculture have already acted like an earthquake. The huge increase of herbicides has introduced "super weeds" that are very difficult to kill and that are now spreading across 13 million acres of land in 26 states. In 1996, the year genetically engineered crops took off, there was one super weed. In 2012, there were twenty-six.

Another major ecological effect of dumping countless millions of pounds of powerful weed killers in rural America—especially in a Midwest and South blanketed by more than 170 million acres of genetically modified crops—is the near destruction of the monarch butterfly. Herbicides kill milkweeds, where monarch butterflies both feed and lay their eggs. No milkweed, no monarchs. It's as simple as that. It's as hard to imagine living in a world without monarchs as it is to imagine living in a world without bees. The future of both depends absolutely on what we decide to do about these obnoxious poisons.

In 2011, USDA approved a genetically modified corn for ethanol production that speeds up the process of turning starch to sugar. However, contamination of food corn by the ethanol corn can dissolve starches and "ruin food for starch uses," according to Lynn Clarkson, president of Clarkson Grains of Gerro Gordo, Illinois. "If you were the Japanese [who buy a lot of American corn], would you want to be buying from an area that grew this corn, that approved this corn?"[16]

These are good questions, and they are not being asked by Dow Chemical, maker of both 2,4-D and 2,4-D-resistant corn and soybeans. Nor are they asked by Monsanto, the maker of Roundup and Roundup Ready soybeans. Dow has convinced the "regulators" of America, Canada, and the European Union that 2,4-D is safe. And now that the overuse of glyphosate has been triggering an "invasion" of glyphosate-resistant farm weeds, Dow is pushing Canada to approve its "Enlist" field corn, which is genetically engineered for both 2,4-D and glyphosate; the company claims this new concoction will kill the unwanted super weeds. The strategy is "to target weeds that have not yet developed immunity." The Save Our Crops Coalition opposes Enlist because it fears 2,4-D will poison fruit and vegetable farmers and will add to the already heavy toxic burden on honeybees.[17]

Indeed, all genetically modified crops harm the natural world and human health, in large part because they (by definition) invite and encourage the spraying of toxic pesticides. But their supporters also mislead regulators and society with claims about the seeds themselves that fail to stand up to scientific scrutiny. Industry says that GMO crops are no different from crops developed by natural breeding. They are safe to eat, they say; they need fewer pesticides than conventional crops and make a positive contribution to reducing global warming and world hunger.

The truth, however, is different. Three British scientists reviewing the scientific evidence about genetically modified crops have concluded that the far-reaching claims of safety and efficacy and usefulness of the genetically modified crops are not true. Genetically modified crops are "laboratory-made, using technology that is totally different from natural breeding methods," they wrote.

Genetically modified crops can also be toxic. Charles Benbrook, a former Capitol Hill staff scientist, has shown that, in the period between 1996 and 2011, the GM crops in the United States increased the use of pesticides by about 7 percent, or 404 million pounds a year. When it comes to nutrition and productivity, genetically modified crops are also no better than conventional crops. They create herbicide-tolerant super weeds. They increase the disease suscepti-bility of crops, harm soils and ecosystems, and reduce biodiversity. They have not been shown to have a positive impact on hunger or global warming. And—in the end, and as always—genetically modi-fied crops "are not adequately regulated to ensure safety."[18]

If the arrival of GMOs is the most insidious development we've seen in recent years, it is hardly the only area in which the Obama admin-istration has lost its way. In January 2010, the Center for Biological Diversity complained that Obama's pesticide policy violated the Endangered Species Act.

"Many endangered species most affected by toxic pesticides are already struggling to cope with habitat loss and rapid climate changes," one of the scientists at the Center, Jeff Miller, pointed out. For too long, EPA oversight "has been abysmal, allowing the pesti-cide industry to unleash a virtual plague of toxic chemicals into our environment."[19] In 2011, seventy environmental groups sent a letter to the EPA administrator, Lisa Jackson, in which they pointed out that emerging science tells us that pesticides "have transgenerational effects, so low level exposures today may be transmitted via epige-netic modifications that harm subsequent generations."[20]

When little changed, the Center for Biological Diversity sued the EPA, charging failure to safeguard species all over the country. The suit was joined by the Pesticide Action Network, another nonprofit conservation organization.

"Endangered species and biological diversity are strong indica-tors for the health of the natural-resource base on which we all

depend," Heather Pilatic of the pesticide group wrote. "To the extent
that we fail to protect that base we erode the possibility of prosperity
for future generations. This suit thus presents a real opportunity for
American agriculture: By enforcing the law and counting the real
costs of pesticide use, we strengthen the case for supporting a transition towards more sustainable pest-control practices like crop
rotations and beneficial insect release."[21]

The heart of the matter with endangered species is that there is
a law, the Endangered Species Act, that forbids activities harming
species already considered threatened and endangered. Pesticides,
designed to kill all life, are a great threat and danger to the vulnerable
birds and wildlife protected by the Endangered Species Act. So the
January 2011 lawsuit against the EPA and administrator Lisa Jackson
tried to get the EPA to follow the law and thus slow down the ceaseless poisoning of endangered species by pesticides.

The plaintiffs, the Center for Biological Diversity and the
Pesticide Action Network North America, urged the court to order
the EPA to reestablish its "consultation" with the U.S. Fish and
Wildlife Service and the National Marine Fisheries Service. This
cooperation is required by law, and for good reason: after all, EPA
reports the effects of the pesticides it has registered on endangered
and threatened species. This exchange of information, done correctly
and honestly, would ensure that "EPA's oversight of pesticides does
not jeopardize the continued existence of any endangered or threatened species or result in the destruction or adverse modification of
designated critical habitat of these species."[22]

Predictably, the pesticide lobby went on the offensive to interfere in the lawsuit, Jeff Miller said. Miller launched a campaign to
persuade leaders of environmental groups to cosign a letter to EPA in
order to show a "united front against the pesticide lobby." In the letter
to Lisa Jackson, the EPA administrator, Miller repeated his complaint
that EPA-approved pesticides threaten both the natural world and the
American people.[23]

EPA-approved pesticides are linked to cancer, endocrine disruption, and other serious health effects in humans, particularly children, the elderly, farm families, and farmworkers, Miller said. Emerging science further indicates that low-level exposures may be transmitted via epigenetic modifications that harm subsequent generations.

"Species are dying off at over 1,000 times the normal background rate; pollinators and other indicator species such as frogs are suffering dramatic declines. Not since the dinosaurs disappeared has our planet seen this kind of species collapse," Miller wrote. "This historic loss of biodiversity and degradation of human health must be viewed as intimately intertwined: species and biodiversity loss undermine the productivity and resilience of the natural resource base on which we all rely."[24]

This is not a light charge; indeed, it cuts to the core of the EPA's mission. Environmental organizations representing millions of Americans have been telling the EPA that Americans care about the natural world. They don't want the EPA approving pesticides harming more than two hundred "imperiled species." In addition, the environmentalists say, the EPA also knows that pesticides are threatening hundreds of endangered species, some of which are facing extinction. Pesticides also endanger some of America's treasured animals such as the Florida panther, killer whale, California condor, gray wolf, red-cockaded woodpecker, bull trout, and Atlantic salmon.[25]

Yet once again the EPA—perpetually under pressure from pro-industry members of Congress—chose not to act. And still the chorus of anger rose. "Two billion pounds of pesticides are sold in the United States every year, killing millions of animals and driving hundreds of endangered species closer to extinction," Kieran Suckling, director of the Center for Biological Diversity, wrote in a September 2011 letter to other environmental groups. "The government is doing nothing to stop it. Paralyzed by political pressure from chemical giants Monsanto, Syngenta and a host of lobbying firms, the EPA and the U.S. Fish and Wildlife Service are pointing fingers at each other instead of taking action. Pesticides kill 72 million birds each year, but are especially dangerous to endangered species that have already been reduced to small, struggling populations. In response to our lawsuit, the agency [EPA] began reviewing impacts on endangered species, and even initiated steps towards banning atrazine. Then the massive chemical lobby stepped in. Republicans in Congress threatened both the EPA and the Fish and Wildlife Service. Now both agencies have stopped doing anything at all for fear of angering the chemical industry."[26]

Of course, congressional Republicans continued the GOP's long-standing effort to neuter the EPA or get rid of it altogether. What better way to serve their corporate masters? Former Speaker Newt Gingrich called for "completely abolishing the Environmental Protection Agency," the League of Conservation Voters complained in March 2011. "Republican leaders in the House took a big step toward making Gingrich's plan to eliminate the EPA a reality by slashing funding for environmental and public health safeguards. Their call for a 30 percent cut to the EPA budget—the largest cut in 30 years—would jeopardize the water we drink and air we breathe, endangering the health and well-being of all Americans."

Indeed, in order to meet the legal requirements of the Clean Air Act—and thus prevent the 7,200 annual deaths, 11,000 emergency room visits, and 38,000 acute instances of asthma—EPA sought a new standard for ozone pollution of 65 parts per billion. This was one of Obama's EPA's rare high points. New smog rules would mean "the difference between sickness and health—in some cases, life and death—for hundreds of thousands of citizens," Lisa Jackson, the EPA's director, wrote in the *Los Angeles Times*. The link between health and air pollutants—especially neurotoxins like mercury and lead and the danger of soot, nitrogen oxides, and volatile organic poisons—is "irrefutable," Jackson wrote. She urged Americans to stop Republicans from undermining the EPA and denounced the owners of nearly half of America's power plants that are still operating without pollution controls such as scrubbers.[27]

This strategy was nothing new. Electric power companies have been lobbying for decades against public health rules designed to reduce pollution, said Ilan Levin, associate director of the Environmental Integrity Project, a nonprofit organization founded in 2002 by former EPA enforcement lawyers in Washington, D.C.[28]

As the flap over smog reached a climax, Republicans in the House passed a bill to "scrap" EPA rules. The Republican bill was "a blatant giveaway to polluters that will cost thousands of American lives and hundreds of billions of dollars in preventable health care needs," Congressman Earl Blumenauer (D-Oregon) responded.[29]

Despite the urging of advocates inside his own political constituency, Obama buckled. William Daley, Obama's chief of staff, and Cass Sunstein, his regulatory czar, sided with the polluters. They feared that the economic power of the regulators—and even worse, the backlash from industry and wealthy donors—would harm Obama's reelection campaign. With this misplaced calculation—indeed, with this betrayal of public trust—Obama's promise of new smog standards all but disappeared from view.[30]

The New York Times opined that the capitulation on smog was evidence of both Obama's "mediocre" record on environmental enforcement and its all-too-frequent capitulation to the demands of industry. (Two years earlier, the Obama administration—citing worries about terrorism—refused even to reveal the locations of forty-four coal ash dumps containing billions of gallons of toxic sludge. In the same year, Obama torpedoed real progress at the Copenhagen climate conference.)[31]

There is good reason for industry to fear public scrutiny of power plants, which are responsible for 50 percent of mercury air pollution and 77 percent of acid gas emissions. The EPA claims there are more than sixteen hundred facilities that are "high priority violators" of the Clean Air Act. Some three hundred of these facilities have been violating the law for a decade or more. In 2009, factories reported to EPA that they released into the atmosphere about

600 million pounds of poisons including arsenic, benzene, formaldehyde, and lead.[32]

In 2011, seeking to lower the amount of carcinogens including
mercury, arsenic, chromium, and nickel that power plants dump into
the air, the EPA issued the Mercury and Air Toxics Standards (MATS
or MACT).

The proposal infuriated Oklahoma Republican senator James
Inhofe, a prominent climate change denier and major supporter of
the coal, oil, and gas industries. Repeating the usual script, Inhofe
claimed the effort to clean up power plants was "specifically designed
to kill coal as well as all the good paying jobs that come with it." Inhofe
formed a group of twenty-nine senators—whose names remain
secret—determined to repeal the EPA rule and to forbid EPA from
issuing additional rules to protect air quality. Senator Inhofe also
resisted new rules to regulate soot, the invisible killer particles of
smoke, chemicals, and metals coming primarily out of the stacks of
factories and diesel trucks. The American Coalition for Clean Coal
Electricity, a Washington, D.C., lobbying organization for the coal
industry, joined Inhofe in describing the EPA standards as part of an
"aggressive regulatory agenda" harming the economy.[33]

The environmental community saw Inhofe's proposal as potentially disastrous. The EPA standards would save "tens of thousands of
lives and avoid hundreds of thousands of asthma attacks," said John
Walke of the Natural Resources Defense Council. The American
Lung Association described Inhofe's strategy as "extreme," reporting
that the EPA standards protect millions of lives from toxic air poisons
such as mercury, which "damages children's neurological development and intelligence." The ALA also affirmed that soot levels
currently considered "safe" still cause heart attacks, strokes, and
asthma and that new soot standards would "prevent more than 35,000
premature deaths and save $280 billion in health-care costs."[34]

Unimpressed with the benefits of cleaner air, Senator Inhofe
accused Obama's EPA of "persistently going to the extreme." His

sentiments were echoed by the coal industry, which described the EPA standards as part of an "aggressive regulatory agenda" harming the economy. Once again, as it has for forty years, the EPA was held up as nothing more than an impediment to industrial growth. And once again, it will be our health, and our environmental integrity, that will suffer. Once again, industry and the political establishment they command have played their most reliable hand: if you can intimidate an administration—even one that has promised change—change will never come.[35]

Better Living and a Healthier Natural World Through Small Family Farms

I N a major report on childhood exposure to toxic chemicals that was released in April 2011, the American Academy of Pediatrics lambasted the country's "non-evidence-based system for chemical management." The academy was especially critical of the pathetic Toxic Substances Control Act (TSCA), a pro-industry law that hasn't been updated since 1976. Using the chemical industry's own estimate of the massive amounts of chemicals used every year in the United States, the academy raised a red flag over the implications of spreading 27 trillion pounds of petrochemicals on the United States every year. This ocean of synthetics does not even include pesticides, pharmaceuticals, fuels, or chemicals used in food production.

"As children grow and mature, their bodies may be especially vulnerable to certain chemical exposures during critical windows of development," the academy wrote. "Neurologic and endocrine systems have demonstrated particular sensitivity to environmental toxicants at certain stages of growth. These differences in biological susceptibility and exposures in children versus adults support the need for strong consideration of children in chemicals policies. This principle must underpin all chemical-management legislation and regulation."[1]

It's not just the young who are most vulnerable to our toxic legacy. Minorities and the poor have more poisons in their bodies not merely because of the food they eat, but also because of where they live. Their communities have long been the dumping grounds for America's industrial pollution. For example, West Anniston, Alabama, had the misfortune of being a center for the manufacture of PCBs. West Anniston was also an Army depot for chemical weapons. In 2003, the military began burning its chemical weapons. The people of West Anniston, who are mostly black, pay the price for being surrounded by pollution, many of them dying young from cancer and other diseases.

Bob Herbert, an African American columnist for *The New York Times*, visited West Anniston and other black communities burdened by dumping. He rightly concluded that placing garbage dumps, oil refineries, and other hazardous manufacturing operations in the midst of black communities was a continuation of the Jim Crow policies that "have existed in one form or another, legally or illegally, since slavery.

"The evidence has been before us for decades that black people, other minorities and some poor whites have been getting sick and enduring horrible deaths from the filth that they breathe, eat, drink and otherwise ingest from the garbage dumps, landfills, incinerators, toxic waste sites, oil refineries, petrochemical plants and other world-class generators of pollution that have been deliberately and relentlessly installed in the neighborhoods where they live, work, worship and go to school," Herbert wrote. "Government and industry alike have used black and poor neighborhoods as dumping grounds for the vilest and most dangerous of pollutants."[2]

The latest crisis at the EPA—and one with disproportionate impact on the country's young, its poor, and its minorities—concerns the current fever over a procedure for gas drilling known as hydraulic fracturing, or "fracking." Once again, giant industries are disregarding or sneaking around the law and ignoring science and the public health. Once again, government regulators are looking the other way. And once again, the public health—and particularly its drinking water— hang in the balance.

As hot as this issue is today, the struggle over fracking goes back decades. And one of its sorriest chapters began at the EPA, with a morally compromised study of drinking water contamination.

The EPA has known since the 1980s that wastes created by drilling for oil and gas are toxic and should not be allowed to flow into rivers or groundwater. Yet to this day, the oil and gas industries have pressured their puppets in Congress to exempt drilling from most environmental laws.

In 1994, the Legal Environmental Assistance Foundation sued the EPA for its refusal to regulate the gas drilling industry. Several years later, the Eleventh Circuit Court of Appeals recommended that EPA bring the gas drillers under its control. EPA ignored the court but agreed to look into the potential effects of drilling chemicals on drinking water.[3]

"Fracking a well" means pointing a cannon at the source of the suspected gas, usually found in stone formations thousands of feet under the ground, often in or near aquifers of drinking water. Huge amounts of water mixed with tons of chemicals and sand blast their way through a downward shaft under tremendous pressure and demolish the stone that encloses the gas. Some of the three hundred compounds used in hydraulic fracturing include diesel fuel, a dangerous mixture of benzene, toluene, ethyl benzene, and xylene. Other materials in fracking fluids include acids, formaldehyde, polyacrylamides, chromates, and other potentially toxic or carcinogenic substances.

Rather than reveal these chemical cocktails to a public that will inevitably see the stuff in their rivers (and in their tap water), companies routinely put their fracking chemicals on a list of "trade secrets" and refuse to divulge their names or compositions. And while the EPA's Toxic Release Inventory used to inform us about what chemicals companies release in our environment, even that basic source of information is dead: the oil and gas industries long ago maneuvered their way out of being subject to this fundamental environmental law.[4]

Here's how that travesty came about. The EPA started a fracking study in 2001 and completed it in 2004, during the administration of George W. Bush, a former oilman, and Dick Cheney, whose former company, Halliburton, had pioneered the fracking process. Predictably, the administration's 2004 study found that injecting toxic fluids into gas wells "poses little or no threat" to drinking water and "does not justify additional study at this time."[5]

This finding dismayed Weston Wilson, a scientist who had been with the EPA for thirty years. Wilson, an environmental engineer in the Denver office with long experience with oil and gas drilling, had observed carefully how EPA did its study. He knew the politics of the gas drilling industry, and how tightly those politics were linked to the execution of the EPA study.

Since Wilson's home state of Colorado had grand fracking ambitions—and since the state's coal beds producing natural gas are located within drinking water aquifers—Wilson had good reason to worry. He wrote to three Colorado politicians, Senator Wayne Allard, Senator Ben Nighthorse Campbell, and Representative Diana DeGette, and attached a report entitled "EPA Allows Hazardous Fluids to be Injected into Ground Water."[6]

The Bush administration's EPA report, Wilson wrote, was "scientifically unsound" and ran afoul of the Safe Water Drinking Act that prohibits the contamination or poisoning of our drinking water. The EPA had not only failed to adequately assess the risks of the toxic fracking fluids, it had used a panel of outside experts who openly favored the drilling industry. Five of the seven members of the study panel "appear to have conflicts of interest and may benefit from EPA's decision not to conduct further investigation or impose regulatory conditions," he wrote.

EPA's failure to regulate the injection of fluids into gas wells "may result in danger to public health and safety," Wilson continued, noting that fracking "can also create new pathways for methane migration into aquifers containing good quality ground water."

Beyond the dangers to Colorado residents, Wilson predicted that EPA's "flawed analysis" would open the floodgates for the gas drilling industry, who no longer had to concern themselves with drinking water contamination. Sure enough, Congress (and Dick Cheney) used the EPA's 2004 report to shape the Energy Policy Act, which exempted gas drillers from regulation under the Safe Drinking Water Act. This public health abomination became known as the Halliburton loophole.[7]

It didn't take long for the scientific community to raise the alarm about the dangers of all these chemicals in drinking water supplies. Theo Colborn, a Colorado resident and a nationally recognized expert on the effects of poisons on the human endocrine system, has identified 171 products composed of 245 chemicals used in fracking fluids. Close to 90 percent of the volatile chemicals cause irritation to the skin, eye, sinuses, nose, throat, lungs, and stomach and cause effects on the brain and nervous system ranging from headaches, blackouts, memory loss, confusion, fatigue or exhaustion, and permanent neuropathies, she told a congressional panel in 2007. More than half can cause disorders to the cardiovascular, kidney, reproductive and immune systems.[8]

Do we really want this toxic cocktail pouring into our drinking water? Congress doesn't seem to mind; it ignored Colborn's warnings. And in the years since, politicians from both parties have pushed the gas companies' fracking mission with an evangelical fervor, using their full voice to convince the world that America is the Saudi Arabia of natural gas. Most congressional members of panels reviewing studies are associated with the industry. Oklahoma, a major gas drilling state, illustrates this sordid policy. The state's Republican senators, James Inhofe and Tom Coburn, have spent their political careers defending gas drilling, always pressuring EPA to stay clear of their pet industries. In return, the drilling industries have rewarded them handsomely. As a result, in Oklahoma and other states, the "mystery liquids" of toxic gas and oil drilling wastes continue to contaminate the nation's waters.[9]

Nationwide, the mania for gas well drilling has simply over-whelmed state officials. New Mexico, for instance, has 99,000 gas wells but only eighteen inspectors. How can they possibly safeguard the state's drinking water?[10]

While some elected officials pay lip service to protecting the public health, it's hard to be convinced by such expressions of good faith. "We have a supply of gas that can last America one hundred years, and my administration will take every possible action to safely develop this energy," President Obama said in his 2012 State of the Union speech. "I'm requiring all companies that drill for gas on public lands to disclose the chemicals they use. America will develop this resource without putting the health and safety of our citizens at risk. We don't have to choose between our environment and our economy."

Given the Washington establishment's history—and his own—Obama's promises for health and safety did not sound sincere. He made no effort to get rid of the Halliburton loophole, so fracking fluids are *still* (unbelievably) exempt from the Safe Drinking Water Act. And as his EPA prepares another study of fracking and drinking water, gas industry lobbyists and their congressional clients are adding more pres-sure to simply confirm the results of the morally bankrupt 2004 study.

In this gold-rush climate, it's hard to imagine drinking water advocates getting anything like a fair hearing. Senator Inhofe, long a fiery booster of the petrochemical industry, has cautioned the EPA not to use outside experts "who have been longtime critics of hydrau-lic fracturing." When the EPA announced in December 2011 that they had linked fracking to water contamination near Pavilion, Wyoming, Inhofe described the findings as "offensive."[11]

So here we are: once again giant corporations are acting with impunity, muscling local officials and members of Congress to nullify environmental regulations. Just as banks considered "too big to fail" wrecked the lives of millions of Americans, the hucksters in the gas industry are moving fast into the country's farm fields. They dig for gas and petroleum and poison the drinking water and air. People living near gas wells—many of them poor, many of them bought off by companies waving fistfuls of cash for drilling rights—now find themselves living in sacrifice zones. They are the first victims of gas drilling: if they detect bad smells or their drinking water catches fire, they complain to state and EPA officials, but these officials have already made their allegiance clear, and their allegiance is not to the victims of poisoned water wells.

The upshot of all this is that today there are more than a thousand cases of fracking-related water contamination in thirty-four states, and documented cases of both human harm and severe health effects on wildlife and farm animals. In Colorado alone, where drilling increased by 50 percent between 2003 and 2008, there were more than fifteen hundred fracking spills.[12]

In Pennsylvania, as elsewhere, fracking wastes contain dozens of compounds of unknown toxicity, including arsenic, barium, and strontium. Yet gas drillers in Pennsylvania still dump these radioactive wastes into rivers that provide drinking water for more than 16 million people.[13]

These crimes take place in part because gas drillers are literally beyond the reach of both state and federal governments.

In Wyoming, a small farmer named John Fenton has twenty-four gas wells on his farm, and his drinking water is full of poisons, including drilling fluids, drilling muds, and high levels of the cancer-causing benzene. Since the contamination, Fenton's property has lost half of its value; he has to buy drinking water, though he still bathes in the contaminated water. Around his community, he has seen people with "a lot of neurological problems, neuropathy, seizures, people losing their sense of smell, sense of taste. People with their arms and legs going numb."

Local officials, meanwhile, continue to tell Fenton his water is potable. When Fenton persuaded the EPA to test his water and investigate the fracking of gas wells under his land, the agency agreed with him: fracking had poisoned his water.

The political response to this evidence was predictable. House Republicans held a public meeting on the Fenton water testing case, but when the "public" actually showed up—in the form of Josh Fox, the producer of *Gasland*, a documentary on the devastation caused by natural gas drilling—the elected officials had Fox arrested.[14]

In May 2012, the Obama administration proposed regulations requiring drillers to reveal the composition of their fracking chemicals thirty days before they blasted the underground deposits of oil and gas with those chemicals. Once again, industry pressure diluted the effort, and lobbyists for ExxonMobil and other drillers convinced the White House to reverse the regulation. The drillers would name their fracking chemicals only *after* they completed their work.[15]

Once again, we find ourselves asking fundamental questions: What does such a policy say about our country's priorities? Who are such laws meant to protect? As with pesticides, so with fracking: America needs to reinvent itself, to reverse the pervasive and insidious influence of the petrochemical-agribusiness complex.

So here, in the end, is a central question: How can we make the EPA a truly independent, Federal Reserve–like organization, charged with (and actually capable of) defending nature and public health? How can we create a health and safety mechanism that neither the president nor members of Congress nor—critically—industry lobbyists would be able to compromise?

Here are a couple of suggestions that have emerged from my long career spent watching the current system fail:

A great scientist or a distinguished citizen with a long record of defending public health and the environment ought to be selected for a ten-year post administering a politically neutral EPA. A vigorous and sustaining EPA would be a measure of a vigorous and sustaining democracy. Like the Fed chairman, this person—not the president— ought to appoint agency deputies and ought to appropriate enough money to allow our scientists to rebuild the EPA's laboratories, research capabilities, and libraries. Contact between EPA and industry lobbyists should be off-limits, as should the influence of the White House. And senior EPA officials should not be allowed to work for the industry for five years after their government work has been concluded.

If these ideas seem utopian, it can only be because we have become so numbed (or defeated) by the stranglehold that industry has had on our economic, agricultural, and energy systems. Yet if we simply consider industry's legacy—its deceit, its political manipulation, its contribution to broad and long-lasting harm to our health and the environment—it is imperative that we have this conversation. The American public simply cannot afford to serve any longer as the subject of unbridled chemical and technological experimentation.

We've long known that radiation from the testing of nuclear weapons created genetic defects that are passed down through the generations, creating debilitating diseases, physical anomalies, intellectual retardation and other medical genetic problems.

But with the testing of the various toxic compounds released into the human economy and environment, we now also know that pesticides "injure man's genetic material in precisely the same way that radiation does," my EPA colleague John Hou-Shi Chen, a distinguished geneticist, told me more than thirty years ago. "And what is so awful about such a genetic injury is that it is permanent—it can't be recalled, corrected or somehow restricted to the victim, unless you also castrate that individual. So now with a greater number of pesticide poisons loose in the environment, we as a society are creating a generation of people who will be weak in facing the future. We are then changing, irreversibly, the future itself. The price for that change is—or should be—unacceptable to any people with dignity and respect for themselves and love for their children."

I agree with this wisdom wholeheartedly. For decades, the EPA was my personal university, where I learned the hard way why America and the rest of the industrialized world have become hooked on dangerous farm sprays. No science or policy has been allowed to interrupt this corruption. In fact, science and policy themselves have been made a prop to the pesticides industry and agribusiness.

This is a tragic turn of events, especially given the evidence. Tomes of scientific studies have shown farm sprays for what they really are: biocides, which cause and promote insect infestations of crops; give cancer to animals and humans; and leave a trail of death among fish and wildlife.

Just as petroleum companies pay for fake "science" that muddies the debate about climate change, most studies funded by the chemical industry muddy the debate about pesticides. Meanwhile, the U.S. Department of Agriculture and the EPA continue to take up the cause of agribusiness, with catastrophic consequences for family farmers, who have been almost completely swallowed up (or driven into bankruptcy) by industrial-scale farms. In the twentieth century, 98 percent of black farmers and more than 60 percent of white family farmers were forced off the land. The few large farmers and agribusinesses left in charge of rural America are hooked on pesticides precisely because these enable them to control their vast estates.

A widely held myth in industrial agriculture holds that the larger the farm, the better for agriculture and society. In the late 1970s, Arnold Aspelin, the EPA's chief economist, wanted to know if the size of a farm had anything to do with the amount of pesticide that could be found in its onions. He asked Sharon Hart of Michigan State University to look into it.

Hart interviewed growers and observed what they did to produce onions. Her analysis challenged two premises that have long been central to American agriculture: that chemicals provide the only science-based road to food production, and that America's food is the safest in the world.

In her February 1980 report "An Approach to Solving Onion Production Problems in an Energy and Chemical Limited Future," Hart painted a very unsettling picture of American agriculture.

Farmers had become so addicted to chemicals that they rarely asked what their consequences might be. If one chemical didn't work, farmers would simply try another. "Everyone assumes another chemical will prevent the onion industry from disaster," she wrote.[16]

In the end, farmers know that chemicals lose their effectiveness, since insects build up resistance to them, and some farmers worried about using too much. Farmers could not believe "the public wants to eat those onions with all that spray on it," Hart wrote. "'With all the chemicals we use, people eat it anyway,' one farmer said. 'Working with poisons seems so hopeless,' said another. 'Who knows the outcome of working with chemicals?'"

Food is usually the main route pesticides find to poison people. Such poisoning often has no immediate or obvious effects; tiny amounts of pesticides can be neutralized by the liver, stored in the body's fatty tissues, or excreted in urine. What's less clear is how the body handles these toxic residues as they accumulate over time. But the long-term effects, including cancer and other illnesses, are unmistakable.

EPA has long known about the poisoning of our food, but it has done far too little to prevent it. Both EPA and the agribusinesses it regulates deny that the pesticides in food are harmful, but this stance is based on faulty and even prejudicial science designed mainly to protect the pesticide makers from lawsuits.

Indeed, the tide of farm chemicals kept flowing. "We keep adding pesticides till costs exceed return—same as we did with fertilizers," one farmer told Hart. "We just spray for insurance," another said. "It would be better if we knew when to spray." An oft-repeated refrain: "We don't want to use sprays, but we can't afford not to."

Purely in terms of economics, what Hart found was startling: the larger the farm, the more sprays per acre, and the heavier the costs; the smaller the farm, the less pesticide sprayed per acre, and the less cost to the farmer. Farms under 24 acres paid about a third (per acre) of what farms over 50 acres paid for pesticides, yet the

largest farms sprayed nearly five times as much as the smallest grower
and nearly twice as much as a medium-size grower.

Large and medium-size growers used twice as much fungicide as
the small farmer. Hart stressed that the "intensity and level" of sprays
of the "large capital-intensive grower" was "significant." In the end, if
an informed consumer had a choice between eating onions from a
large farm (sprayed with 52 different chemicals) and onions from a
small farm (sprayed with 11 different chemicals), the owner of the
larger farm "would probably not be able to sell his onions."

Time was, farmers knew enough to graze cows next to onion
fields. They knew that cow dung provided food parasites that controlled the onion maggot. Once industrial farms insisted on devoting all
their fields to a single crop (such as onions), the onion maggot flourished and created an ideal market for toxic sprays.

Given these results, Hart wondered why her academic colleagues
seemed so enthralled by chemical companies rather than working to
help make farming less hazardous. University researchers, she
concluded, were hooked on "agri-chemical research" and spent more
energy protecting the profitability of the chemical companies than the
needs of farmers.

These are excellent insights. Universities regard large companies as cash cows that fund their research and pay their salaries. As far
back as 1980, Don Paarlberg, a senior official of the U.S. Department
of Agriculture, admitted that the land grant universities failed their
mission, boosting the industrialization of agriculture instead of serving family farmers. "The [Department of Agriculture's] Extension
Service," he said, "with its advice that a farmer should have a business
'big enough to be efficient,' undoubtedly speeded up the process of
farm consolidation and reduced the number of farms. In the class-
room, emphasis on modern management helped put the traditional
family farm into a state of total eclipse."[17]

Conventional American farmers have become mindlessly
attached to a certain view of nature and the world: they have

essentially become an extension of the chemical and agribusiness industries. The Department of Agriculture Extension Service has county agents in every significant farming community who are "very effective communicators of the USDA line," wrote David Menotti, the second most senior lawyer at EPA dealing with pesticide issues. "That line has always been the familiar DuPont slogan 'Better things for better living through chemistry.'"

Many agricultural pesticides have been used for years, Menotti wrote, and farmers have, in essence, become addicted to them.

"We are understandably watched anxiously by farmers, much in the same manner that mechanics would feel threatened by the OSHA [Occupational Safety and Health Administration of the Department of Labor] initiative to take away their socket wrenches."[18]

From July 2003 until December 2004, the EPA sent me to the University of Maryland to teach a graduate seminar on global environmental issues, most of them related to food and agriculture.

At Maryland, which in theory is a land grant school, most of my forty former colleagues in the Department of Natural Resource Sciences had nothing to do with family farming. Only two tenured professors offered courses from time to time that were relevant to organic farming; the rest refused to use the words "sustainable farming," "organic agriculture," or "family farming" in describing what they do.

These agricultural professors keep teaching and researching "nutrient" management as if they are trying to hide the ceaseless suffocation of the Chesapeake Bay, Maryland's water treasure and one of the country's ecological, fishing, and recreational jewels, by the wastes of the chicken factory farms in Delaware, Maryland, and Virginia. Poisons come to Chesapeake Bay from as far away as New York and Pennsylvania, but the real danger lurks next door in the animal farms, which are all but invisible to academics at the University of Maryland.

In 2005, Maryland had 5.5 million people and about 12,000 growers. How many were organic farmers? Eighty-nine. More than 35 percent of farm receipts in Maryland come from industrial chicken farms, which produced 292.9 million "broilers" in 2002. Yet Maryland's industrial chicken factories left a vast footprint of ecological devastation in the Chesapeake Bay watershed and social upheaval in what used to be rural Maryland. And any consumer given the opportunity to visit a "chicken factory" would be sufficiently appalled to swear off eating the chicken "products" extruded from its machinery.

It's as if the beauty, history, and extraordinary value of family farming and unimpaired nature as sources of life, democracy, and culture—what the Greeks would call Mother Earth—ceased to matter whenever someone threw money or power at scientists. The same thing happens when the state adopts nature-killing policies such as subsidizing and enabling corporations and industrial-scale farmers to take over rural America. Nearly all debate becomes muted.

When universities put most of their research money into studying "no-till" farming (which Sharon Hart correctly called "a chemical-intensive system"), farmers are convinced to prepare their fields with a flood of weed killers rather than with traditional cultivation. "The no-till system relies totally on chemicals," Hart wrote. "The EPA has demanded research on the chemical effects of no-till on soil micro-organisms on corn, which, according to the researcher involved, 'is a bunch of nonsense, anyway. We'll show them that these chemicals don't affect nothing!' Researchers generally evaluate options in terms of private (as opposed to social) economic return only."

Hart ended her report on a melancholy note. Farmers can only mirror a "mismanaged society." They need guidance and direction and appropriate research from the land grant universities, which, sadly, take their cues from pesticide companies and the rest of the agroindustrial complex. Ideally, the EPA, the USDA, and the state governments ought to intervene by teaching farmers how to practice safe agriculture. In reality, the academic-agribusiness complex is rife with "cultural arrogance," failing to see that its system "cannot continue in a future energy and chemical limited environment—if we are to maintain a viable culture for future generations."

Hart's report was not what EPA wanted to hear. The American farmer has been the economic and cultural paradigm for most of the world, they reasoned. Why change anything?

Yet Hart's modest but original study leaves little doubt that the hegemony of the industrial-scale farmer—with his demands for petroleum-based pesticides and fertilizers, his machines, and his huge chunks of land—is becoming toxic to the survival of farming in America. In fact, she found the myth had it backward: the larger the farmer, the more pesticides sprayed on the crops—and therefore the more poisons in our food and drinking water.

Pesticide sprays' effects against insects and weeds, as I have shown, do little to improve the nation's agricultural productivity; their effects on the natural world and human health, however, are deadly serious. The chief role of chemicals has to do with politics and money. Chemicals lubricate the relentless production of vast amounts of processed food (and dollars) from very few species of crops and very few species of animals on large factory farms.

Occasionally, this unethical and dangerous system is revealed for what it is, as when industry corruption burst its seams in the 1970s, or when the Reagan administration did everything it could to abolish the EPA in the 1980s. Since those demoralizing moments, the agency has become a toothless tiger, only pretending to fight on behalf of the environment and public health. EPA officials know global chemical and agribusiness industries are manufacturing science. They know their products are dangerous. Yet industry power either corrupts or silences EPA scientists, who are forced then to bury or ignore the truth. Scientists find themselves working in a roomful of funhouse mirrors, plagiarizing industry studies and cutting and pasting the findings of industry studies as their own.

These are the behaviors of a traumatized organization. And these are the reasons why, fifty-two years after *Silent Spring*, farm sprays remain ubiquitous, their makers remain more powerful than ever, and we remain overwhelmed with diseases in humans and imbalances in nature.

President Barack Obama—indeed, any president—needs to take human health and family farming much more seriously. He needs to discard the toxic policies of agribusiness in favor of small-scale agriculture that raises healthful food without injuring humans and wildlife or contributing to climate change. Traditional (and often organic) farmers—until seventy-five years ago, the only farmers there were—are slowly beginning to make a comeback. They have always known how to raise crops and livestock without industrial poisons. They are the seed for a future harvest of good food, a healthy natural world, and democracy in rural America—and the world.

Acknowledgements

The story of the U.S. Environmental Protection Agency is not very complicated or very long. The difficulty has been in decoding and documenting the corruption behind the scientific facade of the EPA.

I am grateful to my EPA colleagues who passed their stories on to me. Many thanks also to others outside the walls of the EPA for their ideas, encouragement, and friendship: Brent Blackwelder, Jay Feldman, Jefferson Boyer, the late Nikolaos A. Stavrou and the late Congressman George E. Brown, Jr., Dee Lusby, Michael Fox, Nick Maravell, the late Bill Devall, Theo Solomos, the late Rudolph Becking, Barbara Childers, Carol Van Strum, Paul Merrell, the late Al Krebs, the late Michael Warren, the late Robert Metcalf, Mohamed Abou-Donia, Michael Hansen, Timothy Weiskel, Cecilia Gregorio, Jeff Gritzner, David Pimentel, Miguel Altieri, Gary Grant, Fred Wilcox, Nicolaos G. Alexopoulos, Daniel F. Yuhasz, Tony Perreira, John Cobb, Harriett Crosby, Raisa Scriabine, Richard Olson, Richard Hazlett, Don Huber, Ian Panton, and Rosemary Mason.

Gloria Fulton typed the first draft of this book. I thank her for that act of generosity and kindness. Janette Sherman—a physician and research scientist documenting the carcinogenic effects of the nuclear and chemical industry—read part of this book and gave me useful comments. I thank her for her friendship and wisdom. James Wade also read the book and made it better.

I am grateful to my literary agent Jonah Straus, who brought the book to the attention of Peter Ginna, editorial director and publisher of Bloomsbury Press. Ginna asked probing questions that helped me improve the book. He also brought me in touch with McKay Jenkins, who employed his superb writing talent in editing and polishing the text. I also thank Nikki Baldauf, Emily DeHuff, and Rob Galloway of Bloomsbury Press for their meticulous work.

I am very grateful to my wife, Crista. My tenure at the EPA was extremely trying, and the unexpected fallout engulfed her as well. She put up with my anger and anguish. She kept the family together and helped me in the enjoyment of life.

Finally, I thank my children, Mark Andreas and Corinna Lia, as well as the students I taught at Humboldt State University, the American University, George Washington University, the University of New Orleans, Bard College, the University of Maryland and Pitzer College. It is to them—children and students—that I dedicate this book. In addition, I wrote this book in grateful memory of two men, both government bureaucrats, who made a difference: Adrian Gross, my EPA colleague who revealed the systemic corruption of the chemical industry, and William Carl Heinrich Hueper, who fought the good fight at the Department of Health and Human Services in defense of our health.

Young people have to replace the culture of pollution and undemocratic politics of their parents and create a new EPA as part of an Earth-venerating civilization; otherwise the world, and the United States in particular, will have a bleak future—or no future at all

Notes

PREFACE: A COUNTRY BATHED IN MAN-MADE CHEMICALS

1   Alexander Hamilton, James Madison, and John Jay, *The Federalist*, edited by
    Benjamin Fletcher Wright (Cambridge, MA: Harvard University Press, 1961),
    451. Paul C. Light, professor of public service at New York University, took
    Hamilton's warning (of a government ill executed being a bad government) seri-
    ously and wrote a timely and important book about the decline of government in
    the United States: *A Government Ill Executed: The Decline of the Federal Service
    and How to Reverse It* (Cambridge, MA: Harvard University Press, 2008).

2   *Annual Review of Medicine* 21 (1970): 409–32.

3   Eula Bingham, Marvin S. Legator, and Stephen J. Rinkus, "Women and the
    Workplace" (Occupational Safety and Health Administration, Department of
    Health, Education and Welfare, Washington, D.C., June 17–18, 1976).

4   Robert U. Ayres and Udo E. Simonis, eds., *Industrial Metabolism: Restructuring
    for Sustainable Development* (Tokyo: UN University Press, 1994), p. xii.

5   U.S. Department of Agriculture, *Concentration in Agriculture: A Report of the
    USDA Advisory Committee on Agricultural Concentration* (Washington, DC,
    June 1996); William Heffernan, "Consolidation in the Food and Agriculture
    System" (Report to the National Farmers Union, February 5, 1999).

6   In 1988, some 14,000 people worked for EPA's technical staff. This was an
    impressive team of physicians, toxicologists, and economists. There were also
    ecologists, chemists, biologists, and plant pathologists, lawyers, engineers, statis-
    ticians, and hydrologists. The team in 1988 had a $2.7 billion budget for programs
    dealing with hazardous waste, water, and air, radiation, pesticides, and other
    toxic substances. From 2006 to 2010, EPA had around 18,000 employees and a
    budget of $7.7 billion (in 2006) and $10.3 billion (in 2010). The overwhelming
    majority of these technical people were stationed in Washington, D.C.

7   In 1982, there were thirty companies in charge of the production and sale of

pesticides in the United States. These major producers supplied 3,300 formulators who distributed their products to some two million farmers. There were also 100 other producers connected to 29,000 distributors who sold their pesticides to 75 million households and 40,000 pest control companies. All this production and trade relied on the EPA approval of 1,400 chemicals made into some 35,000 products. The production of 1.5 billion pounds of pesticide "active ingredients" in 1982 employed 15,000 people, earning $5.8 billion for the 30 major pesticide corporations. Agriculture used 62 percent of all pesticides; industry and government 24 percent; and 14 percent went to supply homes and gardens. EPA, Office of Pesticide Programs, "Regulatory Impact Evaluation," September 17, 1982, Figure 1.

8   EPA, "EPA's Toxics Programs: An Unparalleled Task" (Office of Pesticides and Toxic Substances, December 17, 1979).

9   William Hueper, "Adventures of a Physician in Occupational Cancer: A Medical Cassandra's Tale" (unpublished autobiography, 1976, Hueper Papers, National Library of Medicine), pp. 290–91, 300.

10   EPA, Office of Pesticide Programs, "Point Source Pesticide Use Sites," October 28, 1987.

11   EPA, Office of Pesticide Programs, "Estimated Usage of Pesticides in Homes," February 7, 1984.

12   Other key elements in America's toxic universe:

Pesticides: About 1,850 toxic chemicals; 400 manufacturers; and 4,200 formulators devising more than 34,000 products.

Air pollutants: 10,000 to 15,000 man-made chemicals in the air, hundreds of which are toxic to life and 50 to 100 of which are carcinogens. Air pollutants come from millions of mobile and tens of thousands of stationary sources.

Hazardous waste: About 57 million tons every year. There are 353,000 large generators of hazardous waste and 10,000 companies transporting hazardous waste. In 1979, the country also had about 50,000 landfills.

Water pollutants: About 336,000 industrial plants emitting toxic water pollutants, 129 of which were of "particular concern."

Drinking water: There are some 200,000 "non-community" water systems and 60,000 community water systems in America. The potential for the contamination of drinking water is theoretically "as great as [the] number of chemicals in commerce." Government agencies have detected 700 organic chemicals in drinking water.

Ocean dumping: Every year about 8 million tons of sewage sludge (in which there are high residual concentrations of toxic chemicals) and industrial waste end up in the 5 ocean sites of this country.

13   Nena Baker, *The Body Toxic: How the Hazardous Chemistry of Everyday Things Threatens Our Health and Well-Being* (New York: North Point Press, 2008), pp. 39–40. See also Katharine Mieszkowski, "Plastic Bags are Killing Us," *Salon*, August 10, 2007; Elizabeth Royte, "A Fountain on Every Corner," *New York Times*, May 23, 2008; Athanasios Valavanidis et al., "Persistent Free

Radicals, Heavy Metals and PAHs Generated in Particulate Soot Emissions and Residue Ash from Controlled Combustion of Common Types of Plastic." *Journal of Hazardous Materials* 156 (1–3): 277–84 (August 15, 2008).

14 William Lijinsky, "Environmental Cancer Risks—Real and Unreal," *Environmental Research* 50, 207–9 (1989).

15 Samuel S. Epstein, "Losing the War Against Cancer: Who's to Blame and What to Do About It" (Chevy Chase, MD: Rachel Carson Council, 1987), p. 1.

16 I joined EPA in May 1979. The reasons I initially applied to the EPA were mostly practical. I had worked on Capitol Hill, but the job left me unfulfilled. An EPA employee living in my neighborhood in Alexandria, VA, put me in touch with an EPA office, which hired me immediately. My first assignment was working with a team of scientists seeking information from the owners of pesticides. From that very moment I began to understand how science—and the government—are used mostly to benefit a few giant companies running the chemical industry.

17 I temporarily sought asylum in the academic community. I took up an offer from Allen Jennings, the director of the EPA's Biological and Economic Analysis Division, to take a year's leave of absence. Humboldt State University in Northern California became my home for 1988–89. Neither Jennings nor I expected I would come back to the EPA. I went off to California by myself, leaving behind my wife and my two teenage children. Teaching gave me rare moments of happiness that overshadowed all my unhappy experiences at the EPA. I told myself I had to stay on teaching. Finally I had found my calling. I made good friends at the university but soon discovered that my department, which emphasized the teaching of sociology and social work, did not really want a historian on the roster. And my knowledge of environmental policy and its impact on both public health and society seemed of little interest to my colleagues. At the end of the year I returned to the EPA.

18 Citing every document I have seen would be impossible, of course, since citing the entire database of documents would take up an entire archive. I donated most of my papers (about 20 boxes) to the Friends of the Earth in Washington, D.C. FOE has now given the documents to the American Heritage Center of the University of Wyoming. I also donated a few documents to the University of Maryland.

19 "Make no mistake about it—actions to protect consumers of food products by canceling the registrations of pesticides shown to be carcinogens will not be universally applauded," Menotti wrote. "On the contrary, interest groups in the agricultural sector—egged on by the USDA—will raise a great fuss, and attempt to persuade the world that our actions are technically unsound and motivated by a passionate desire to eliminate pesticides as tools of agricultural production." See memo from David Menotti to Jodie Bernstein, September 23, 1977.

20 Aldo Leopold, "The Conservation Ethic," *Journal of Forestry* 31 (1933): 635–37.

21 Aldo Leopold, *A Sand County Almanac* (New York: Oxford University Press, 1966), p. 185.

22   David L. Coppage and Clayton Bushong, "On the Value of Wild Biotic Resources of the United States Affected by Pesticides" (EPA, Office of Pesticide Programs [early 1980s]).

23   Ibid.

CHAPTER 1: THE EPA NOBODY KNOWS

1   Federal pesticides law (the Federal Insecticide, Fungicide, and Rodenticide Act, for example) forbids the use of "ineffective" pesticides. But 30 years ago, the EPA—bowing to pressure from the Reagan administration—ended its review of data on whether pesticides were effective. So a central rule of the pesticide law has effectively been rendered meaningless.

2   The 1947 FIFRA introduced the registration and labeling of sprays. After Rachel Carson broke the news in 1962 that pesticides were damaging the natural world, Congress amended FIFRA four times between 1964 and 1996. (The changes in 1996 had to do with the amounts of pesticides entering and staying in food.) FIFRA became the Food Quality Protection Act, which legalized carcinogens in processed food.

3   Other statutes fundamental to environmental protection include the Resources Conservation and Recovery Act of 1976, which enabled the EPA to regulate the treatment, storage, transportation and disposal of hazardous waste; the Comprehensive Environmental Response, Compensation, and Liability (Superfund) Act of 1980, which allows the EPA to respond promptly to hazardous waste emergencies and clean up the dangerous waste; the Wilderness Act of 1964; the Wild and Scenic Rivers Act of 1968; the National Environmental Policy Act of 1969; the Safe Water Drinking Act of 1986; the Marine Protection, Research, and Sanctuaries Act or the Ocean Dumping Act of 1972; the Endangered Species Act of 1973; the Federal Food, Drug, and Cosmetic Act (section 408 of this act authorizes the EPA to set "tolerances" or "legal" amounts of pesticides in the food we eat); the Noise Control Act of 1972; the Nuclear Waste Policy Act of 1982; and the Pollution Prevention Act of 1990.

4   Assistant EPA administrators oversee International and Tribal Affairs; Administration and Resources Management; Enforcement and Compliance Assurance; Environmental Information; Air and Radiation; Water; Chemical Safety and Pollution Prevention; Research and Development; and Solid Waste and Emergency Response. During my time at EPA there was no Office for Environmental Information, and the Office of Chemical Safety and Pollution Prevention was known as Prevention, Pesticides and Toxic Substances.

5   In contrast to the mission of the EPA of "protecting man and nature" from the ills of industrial civilization, the USDA does not bother with ideals. At least since World War II, it has been a defender of industrial-scale farmers, agribusiness, and corporate America, the very agents that have been subverting the

EPA. During the presidency of Richard Nixon in the late 1960s and early 1970s, the Secretary of Agriculture, Earl Butz, told the farmers to "get big or get out." That very unwise advice remains the guiding principle of American farmers.

6   The EPA gives its civil service employees tenure and some protection from arbitrary and capricious managers and rules. This certainly helped me survive the ceaseless attacks on and reorganizations of the agency. During the 19 years I served at the EPA headquarters, I lived through the minor and major upheavals that hammered the agency into a more industry-friendly, industry-obedient organization.

7   Natasha Singer, "Medical Papers by Ghostwriters Pushed Therapy," *New York Times*, August 4, 2009; David Gutierrez, "Busted: Wyeth Used Ghostwriters to Place Over 40 'Scientific' Articles in Medical Journals," *Natural News*, July 8, 2010.

8   Exponent has also been paid $1.5 million by the British government to look into the link between maneb-paraquat mixtures and Parkinson's disease.

9   Sheila Kaplan, "Company Pays Government to Challenge Pesticide Research Link to Parkinson's," *Investigative Reporting Workshop* (American University School of Communication), February 11, 2011.

10 See http://www2.hn.psu.edu/faculty/jmanis/poldocs/uspressu/SUaddressRNixon.pdf.

11 Editorial, "Ignoring Science on Clean Air," *New York Times*, January 17, 2006.

12 Fred A. Wilcox, *Waiting for an Army to Die: The Tragedy of Agent Orange* (New York: Vintage Books, 1983), xiv.

13 "New DDT Report Confirms Data Supporting 1972 Ban, Finds Situation Improving," EPA press release, August 11, 1975.

14 Jim Sibbison, "Revolving Door at the EPA," *The Nation*, November 6, 1989.

15 In the case of waste management alone, the revolving door between waste management businesses and the EPA hurts "millions of people who live near the toxic waste dumps." See Sibbison, "Revolving Door at the EPA," *The Nation*, November 6, 1989. More on Thomas's conflict of interest can be found at the Center for Responsive Politics website: www.opensecrets.org/news/2013/02/monsanto.html.

16 John Quarles, *Cleaning Up America: An Insider's View of the Environmental Protection Agency* (Boston: Houghton Mifflin, 1976), xi.

17 Douglas Campt, director, Registration Division, OPP, "Final Review of the April 1981 Florida Statewide Pesticide Use Report," memorandum to Edwin Johnson, director, OPP, EPA, August 14, 1981.

18 See the April 26, 2007, report of the Center for Public Integrity: http://www.publicintegrity.org/2007/04/26/5622/methodology.

19 The ecological idea at the heart of integrated pest management has been so strong that IPM is still studied in government, industry, and land grant universities. Like its sister, organic farming, IPM tried to wake up people to the ecological predicament of our earth. Its career at the EPA was limited but important in setting a few people on the right course. Now organic farming leads the way.

20 See http://www.epa.gov/pesticides/factsheets/ipm.htm.

21   U.S. House of Representatives, Committee on Interstate and Foreign
      Commerce, Subcommittee on Oversight and Investigations, *Federal Regulation
      and Regulatory Reform*, House Document No. 95–134 (Washington, DC: U.S.
      Government Printing Office, 1976), 145.

22   See http://www.epa.gov/pesticides/factsheets/ipm.htm.

23   Congressman John Moss to Congressman Hartley O. Staggers, Subcommittee
      on Oversight and Investigations, Committee on Interstate and Foreign
      Commerce, House of Representatives (Washington, DC, December 1978).

24   The term "use" was all about counting the amounts of pesticides sprayed by
      farmers and lawn owners. In time, understandably, even this name became a
      target for criticism from the environmental community, so the EPA changed
      the name to something that sounded more scientific: "Economic and Biological
      Analysis Division."

25   See http://www.epa.gov/opp00001/regulating/laws/fqpa/backgrnd.htm.

26   One of the most pernicious strategies industry has devised to delay regulation is
      simply to bury the EPA in paperwork. The scheme leads industries to dump "so
      much irrelevant data to EPA, and with such frequency, that new assessments
      become mired in never-ending controversy," Rena Steinzor, a law professor at
      the University of Maryland and president of the Center for Progressive Reform,
      testified before the House Subcommittee on Investigations and Oversight. This
      practice makes chemical assessments endless and incomplete and, in time,
      obsolete for regulatory purposes. "The more important a public health program,
      the more likely it is to be the subject of relentless, intemperate, and unjustified
      attacks [by the industry and its congressional and White House allies]," Steinzor
      said. See Rena Steinzor, Testimony before the U.S. House of Representatives,
      Committee on Science, Space, and Technology, Subcommittee on Investigations
      and Oversight, "EPA's IRIS Program: Evaluating the Science and Process
      Behind Chemical and Risk Assessment," Washington, DC, July 14, 2011.

27   These compounds led to a bizarre and nearly tragic example of skewed thinking
      at the agency. In 1974–75, Leonard R. Axelrod, a senior EPA official, working
      closely with Wayland Hayes, a biochemistry professor at Vanderbilt University,
      almost managed to have ETU and the EBDC fungicides tested on patients in a
      gynecological-obstetrics hospital in Mexico City. Axelrod was ready to fund
      such testing with $100,000 of EPA money. In a July 1, 1977, letter to Senator
      Warren G. Magnuson, Barbara Blum, deputy administrator of EPA, blamed
      Axelrod, who died in 1975, for "lack of good judgment."

28   Given this level of disconnect, even the EPA's Christmas party that year was
      fraught. At the party, I bumped into a chemist who had become distraught over
      threats he had received from his section head: write approvingly of a set of stud-
      ies done by a private industry contractor, he was warned, or be fired. The
      chemist told me the work done by the contractor was "garbage." The company
      had so badly messed up the data that he had had to overhaul the reviews
      himself. Yet when he saw the final report, his own work had been typed right in
      as if it were the company's own work. The chemist was well aware, just as I was,

that he could not change the corrupt practices he had witnessed. It wasn't just the company that was doing bad work, after all, it was our colleagues as well. When he complained to his supervisors about this utterly unacceptable practice—and about the systematic covering up of the company's shoddy work—his supervisors did nothing. Instead, from 1998 to 2005, they actually gave the same company contracts totaling tens of millions of dollars.

CHAPTER 2: PEST CONTROL: A MATTER OF MERCHANDISING

1   Letter from Jarzabek to the EPA, July 2, 1980.

2   Letter that Attorney Catherine Alexander, the victim's lawyer, wrote to EPA, April 6, 1983.

3   William Roessler, "Pesticides Strategy" memorandum to Director, Program Development, U.S. EPA, Office of Pesticide Programs, December 20, 1974. See also Adrian Gross, Chief, Toxicology Branch, Hazard Evaluation Division, Office of Pesticides and Toxic Substances, "Intentionally Added Ingredients *re* Registration Standards" (memorandum to Edwin L. Johnson, Deputy Assistant Administrator for Pesticide Programs, March 27, 1980); John McCann, Acting Chief, Chemical and Biological Investigations Branch, "Comments on Handling Mixture in Registration Standards Documents" (memorandum to James G. Touhey, Director, Benefits and Field Studies Division, OPP, August 25, 1980); Kenneth Bailey [pharmacologist, OPP], "Inerts" (undated draft note to Janet [Auerbach]); Kenneth Bailey, "Proposed Plan to Regulate Intentionally Added Inert Ingredients" (Drafts: April 1981 and March 1982); Jeff [Kempter, OPP, handwritten note to] Janet [Auerbach], Ann [Lindsey], "Inerts Policy Paper" (July 7, 1981); Ann Dizard, [Special Pesticides and Review Division, OPP], "Inert Ingredients" (March 10, 1982); Amy Rispin, [OPP], "Inerts" (October 16, 1984). All these notes, memoranda, and papers are similar, indeed repeating the same issues and concerns, all hoping for a regulatory review, which is yet to come.

4   Elizabeth May from Baddeck, Nova Scotia, Canada, sent a letter to Congressman Toby Moffett in early 1977 in which she described the work of John Crocker. See also an article by John Crocker: John F. S. Crocker et al., "Reye's syndrome: A clinical review," *Canadian Medical Association Journal* (February 15, 1981) 124 (4): 375–82, 425.

5   I have seen no evidence that Crocker's studies were flawed. Crocker is a member of the National Reye's Syndrome Foundation Scientific Advisory Board.

6   In theory, registered pesticides are not intended to foul enzymes of the liver. Synergists are. But a synergist like piperonyl butoxide is an inert. And we know what they (pesticides and synergists) do from their studied effects on insects. In the case I cite, it's the combination of pyrethrins and piperonil butoxide.

7   David Pimentel, "Environmental and Economic Costs of the Application of Pesticides Primarily in the United States," *Environment, Development and Sustainability* (2005) 7: 229–52.

8   A. D. Pickett, "A Critique on Insect Chemical Control Methods," *Canadian Entomologist* 81 (March 1949): 67–76.

9   The story of Mexican cotton can be found in a 1971 report by University of California scientist P. L. Adkisson, "Agricultural Chemicals—Harmony or Discord," published by the University of California, Berkeley, 1971.

10   Maurie Semel, "History of the Colorado Potato Beetle in New York: Control and Development of Resistance to Insecticides on Long Island," Long Island Horticultural Research Laboratory, Riverhead, New York, February 4, 1980.

11   R. L. Doutt and Ray F. Smith, "The Pesticide Syndrome—Diagnosis and Suggested Prophylaxis," in *Biological Control*, edited by C. B. Huffaker (New York: Plenum, 1974), 3–5.

12   Ibid.

13   Christopher J. Bosso, *Pesticides and Politics* (Pittsburgh, PA: University of Pittsburgh Press, 1987), 63–64, 70, 106.

14   Van den Bosch's academic credentials were solid. His University of California, Berkeley and Riverside, colleagues—all distinguished scientists in using biology for the control of pests—praised him as "one of the foremost experts in the field of biological control." They also agreed that in agriculture and development, "making a fast buck still overrides all other considerations." Robert van den Bosch, *The Pesticide Conspiracy* (first published in 1978; Berkeley: University of California Press, 1989), 27, 59. See also Rosmarie von Rumker, "Farmer's Pesticide Use Decisions and Attitudes on Alternative Crop Protection Methods" (Environmental Protection Agency, Office of Pesticide Programs, 1974).

15   Quoted in Van den Bosch, *Pesticide Conspiracy*, vii–xvi.

16   McGregor's "Insect Pollination of Cultivated Plants" is a masterpiece of science and practical farming that will never become obsolete. His knowledge of bees, farmers, and pesticide drug pushers was impeccable and intimate. Yet he spoke to the wind. S. E. McGregor, "The Bee Poisoning Problem in Arizona and Its National Significance," *American Bee Journal*, April 1978, pp. 235–36.

17   Rosmarie von Rumker, *Farmer's Pesticide Use Decisions and Attitudes on Alternative Crop Production Methods* (Report to EPA, July 1974), 137–38. See also Abt Associates study on the dependence of farmers on chemical companies for advice, EPA: Office of Pesticide Programs, 1981.

18   Metcalf died in 1998. His colleagues at the University of Illinois, where he ended his career, said he was "renowned for alerting the scientific community to the environmental consequences of pesticide abuse" (*Entomology Newsletter*, 1999; University of Illinois at Urbana-Champaign).

19   Emil M. Mrak, ed., *Report of the Secretary's Commission on Pesticides and Their Relationship to Environmental Health*, Parts I and II, U.S. Department of Health, Education and Welfare (Washington, DC: U.S. Government Printing Office, December 1969), 245.

20   U.S. Senate, Committee on Labor and Public Welfare, *Migrant and Seasonal Farmworker Powerlessness* (Hearings Before the Subcommittee on Migratory Labor, 91st Congress, First and Second Sessions on Pesticides and the

Farmworker, August 1, 1969, Part 6-A, Washington, DC, U.S. Government Printing Office, 1970), 3024.

21   See the summer 1987 issue of the Newsletter of the College of Arts and Sciences of the University of Illinois.

22   *Apicultural Abstracts* 805 (1971).

23   *Journal of Economic Entomology* 64 (1971).

24   H. B. Petty, "Soil-insecticide use in Illinois corn fields, 1966–72," University of Illinois, College of Agriculture, Extension Service, 1974.

25   Cassandra Stuart, "Development of Resistance in Pest Populations," http://www.nd.edu/~chem191/e2.html (January 2003).

26   David Pimentel, "Environmental and Economic Costs of the Application of Pesticides Primarily in the United States," *Environment, Development and Sustainability* (2005) 7: 229–52.

27   George P. Georghiou, "Insecticide resistance and Prospects for Its Management," *Residue Reviews* 76 (1980): 131–45.

28   Nuzrat Yar Khan, "An Assessment of the Hazard of Synthetic Pyrethroid Insecticides to Fish and Fish Habitat," in *IUPAC Pesticide Chemistry: Human Welfare and the Environment*, edited by J. Miyamoto et al. (New York: Pergamon Press, 1983), 437–50.

29   Keith R. Solomon, *Canadian Journal of Fisheries and Aquatic Sciences* 42 (1985): 77–85.

30   "Incremental Risk Assessment for Asana Use on Grasshoppers," memo from James Ackerman to Rebecca Cool, Pesticides Registration Division of EPA.

31   Despite a uniform policy of risk assessment and cost-benefit analysis, there remained internal doubt about the scientific process within the agency. In the late 1980s, for example, an analyst at the OPP wrote a document in which he questioned everything about decisions at EPA. "What data were used (field trial, FDA monitoring, market basket)? Were data corrected for processing (washing, cooking)? Were actual data or estimates used to make the corrections? How large were the sample sizes used to estimate residues? Are crops large enough that consumption estimates are reliable? If field trial data were used did we factor in storage stability or field recovery and what data did we use to do so? If FDA monitoring data were used do we know that samples are representative of national average residues? What was the basis for the meat/milk exposure estimates and how representative are they? Is the meat/milk exposure confined to a small population? Do infants and children receive a significantly higher proportional exposure and what is it? If processing data are old are the data still representative of current processing procedures? If effect or concern is acute is the sample size large enough to identify likely maximum exposures? Do monitoring data include all metabolites/breakdown products of concern? Do we understand the metabolism adequately?" The writer of these questions—which also included questions about toxic effects, exposure, human and ecological risk, risk assessment, and use and economic impacts of pesticides—might have been teasing his colleagues, never hoping for answers. On the other hand, the questions show the extraordinary difficulty of

trying to establish safety in eating food sprayed by toxins, which, in the case of pesticides, nullifies the very effort considering these toxins are created to be biocides. So no matter the questions and the data one collects and analyzes, the result will be toxic. "Looking into the Black Box: Factors Considered in Risk/Benefit Decision-Making," OPP, late 1980s.

32   Possible Use of Risk/Benefit Analysis for the Issuing of Tolerances and Food Additives Under Sections 408 and 409 of the Food, Drug, and Cosmetic Act; Memorandum from John W. Lyon to Edwin L. Johnson, September 13, 1977; Methodology and Data Sources for Benefit Analyses of Pesticides; Memorandum from Arnold L. Aspelin to Philip Ross, September 29, 1986; "Looking into the Black Box: Factors Considered in Risk/Benefit Decision-Making," briefing paper [late 1980s]; Sal Biscardi, "On Risk," *Inside the Fishbowl*, April 1990 [National Federation of Federal Employees, Local 2050]: Biscardi was a toxicologist with the OPP, EPA.

33   Remember that "active ingredients" are a very small amount of the toxic materials going into the making of what we call pesticides. So we can safely assume that consumers of pesticides in California in 1983 used several billion pounds of toxic substances. See California Department of Food and Agriculture, Division of Pest Management, "Report of Pesticides Sold in California for 1983."

34   Organic farming, which rejects toxic sprays, is the road back to democratic family farming and good food. But organic farming has a long way to go in becoming more than an agricultural sector that produces a limited amount of food at a price that makes it affordable only for affluent consumers. Overcoming this limitation requires an exponential increase in independent organic farming and a distribution infrastructure to support it. Given the financial and political clout of the industrial food and chemical industries, the organic movement faces colossal odds. See "Region 6 Comparative Risk Project: Overview Report," November 1990.

35   Rosmarie von Rumker, *Farmer's Pesticide Use Decisions and Attitudes on Alternate Crop Protection Methods* (EPA report, July 1974), 139.

CHAPTER 3: THE DIOXIN MOLECULE OF DEATH

1   Jim Weaver letter to William Ruckelshaus (August 11, 1983). EPA, Office of Pesticide Programs, Benefits and Field Studies Division, "Report of Assessment of a Field Investigation of Six-Year Spontaneous Abortion Rates in Three Oregon Areas in Relation to Forest 2,4,5-T Spray Practices" (February 28, 1979).

2   This dioxin contamination was hardly a mystery. The EPA had known since 1969 that 2,4,5-T was contaminated by TCDD; the agency finally began regulating 2,4,5-T in 1971, but then fiddled around for 22 years before finally banning the compound in 1993. Dow Chemical challenged the early EPA suspension of 2,4,5-T. The argument focused on the EPA's inability to reliably measure the amounts of dioxin in the environment. From 1975 to 1977 the EPA did manage to measure dioxin in the environment at levels in the parts per trillion.

3   Janet Gardner, "Answers at Last?" *The Nation*, April 11, 1987, pp. 460–62. See also Geoffrey York and Hayley Mick, "Last Ghost of the Vietnam War," *Globe and Mail*, July 12, 2008.

4   "Agent Orange and the Vets," *Washington Post*, July 21, 1979, A14.

5   "Coalition to Study Effect of Agent Orange on G.I.'s," *New York Times*, July 17, 1979, A10.

6   In 1981, Dow Chemical and the EPA asked the presiding administrative law judge for a recess in the cancellation hearings so the company's lawyers could negotiate a settlement. I suspect that during the secret negotiations between the EPA and Dow Chemical, the chemical giant got the agency to sign on the dotted line. The EPA and Dow Chemical must have agreed that the agency would not regulate 2,4-D, far less ban it as it had 2,4,5-T. (Had researchers found TCDD residue traces at Five Rivers, of course, banning the compound would have been unavoidable.) But the EPA had made up its mind not to regulate 2,4-D even before the conclusion of a study of the disaster at Five Rivers. The cozy arrangement between Dow and the EPA, you might say, had made the Five Rivers "failure" inevitable.

7   The EPA "forced our branch chief, Jack Griffith, to go to the University of Miami, supposedly to head the EPA's 'farmworker epidemiological research,'" Vandermer said. "The reason why I escaped that early purge was simple. They thought I was a chemist rather than a biologist. So a clerical error saved my life for two years. But they did not leave me alone."

8   June 2, 1980, memorandum from Frank L. Davido, pesticide incident response officer.

9   John C. Martin, the EPA's inspector general, investigated the agency's efforts to deal with the 2,4,5-T problems of the Oregon women in 1978–79. He reported to the EPA deputy administrator, Alvin Alm, that "EPA's regulatory actions involving cancellation and reregistration of 2,4,5-T and Silvex began in 1979. Extensive delays have resulted from litigation and the administrative hearing process. Over this period of some four years [1979–83], EPA has not completed this [2,4,5-T] regulatory action." (John C. Martin to Alvin L. Alm, memorandum, "Office of Inspector General's Review and Inquiry into EPA's Handling of the Five Rivers Incident," U.S. EPA, November 22, 1983.)

10 July 17, 1979, letter of the Five Rivers women quoted in "Analysis of EPA's Handling of the Five Rivers Investigation" (EPA, Office of Pesticide Programs, November 22, 1983), 3.

11 Letter of Congressman Jim Weaver to EPA administrator William Ruckelshaus, August 11, 1983.

12 In addition to naming the animals, the EPA table summarizing the results of the sample analysis cites "sediment," "sludge," and "products of conception." See Table VII. Analysis of TCDD in Biological and Environmental Samples (Alsea, Oregon Phase II Project, in letter of Congressman Jim Weaver of Oregon to EPA administrator William Ruckelshaus, August 11, 1983). See also Carol Van Strum and Paul Merrell, "No Margin of Safety" (Toronto, Canada: Greenpeace, 1987), IV, 20.

13   Strum and Merrell, "No Margin of Safety," IV, 19. See also Exposure Assessment Branch, "Analysis of EPA's Handling of the Five Rivers Investigation," Hazard Evaluation Division, OPP, November 22, 1983, 18.

14   "Bay St. Louis would occasionally extract some of these samples but this was not the case with this group," Hall wrote. "Dr. Gross extracted and analyzed the samples and sent the results to EPA. Dr. Gross was subsequently called by an attorney representing a plaintiff in one of the dioxin suites going on in the Northwest. As a result, Dr. Gross released the data [generated in his laboratory,] apparently thinking all the samples were from Oregon." Homer Hall, "Note to Mike Conlon [deputy director, OPP] Regarding the ABC News Release and EPA Press Release on Dioxin Samples from Oregon—5 Rivers," August 19, 1983.

15   For several years I collected data on biological alternatives to pesticides. Not once did the biologists and economists doing the cost-benefit analysis take me seriously. They had already decided, before the evidence, that one chemical would be simply replaced by another chemical. I had the same feeling in countless meetings when the toxic evidence of chemicals would be cited, but no corresponding action would follow. Staff scientists would say, "Let's wait to hear from the upper management," and leave it at that.

16   EPA, Office of Pesticide Programs, "Analysis of EPA's Handling of the Five Rivers Investigation" (November 22, 1983).

17   EPA, Inspector General, "Report on OIG [Office of the Inspector General] Review and Inquiry into the Five Rivers Incident" (November 22, 1983). See also "Analysis of EPA's Handling of the Five Rivers Investigation" (Exposure Assessment Branch, Hazard Evaluation Division, Office of Pesticide Programs, November 22, 1983).

18   I spoke to Hale Vandermer several times in late 1980 and after. I also spoke to other scientists involved with the Oregon study. They confirmed what I heard from Hale. Their branch was dismantled. The scientists were made paper pushers.

19   EPA, Office of Research and Development, "The Carcinogen Assessment Group's Risk Assessment on 2,4,5-Trichlorophenoxy Acetic Acid (2,4,5-T) and 2,3,7,8-Tetrachloro-Dibenzo-P-Dioxin (TCDD)" (February 23, 1979). See also letter from S. M. Jalal to Edwin Johnson, September 26, 1983.

20   "Straight Talk About 2,4-D," 2012 Industry Task Force II on 2,4-D Research Data.

21   To the astonishment of knowledgeable scientists and environmental activists, EPA "reregistered" 2,4-D in 2005. And on August 8, 2007, EPA announced that the "weight of the evidence" did not support that 2,4-D was a human carcinogen. *Federal Register*, August 8, 2007, vol. 72, no. 152, pp. 44510–11.

22   By June 1983, the EPA had a report that included the finding of the studies at both Alsea and Five Rivers. The report only increased the friction between the EPA and the women at Five Rivers. Sure, some of the samples had come from Michigan. But there was also dioxin in the sludge samples from Oregon. During 1984–85, Donald A. Marlow, chief, Chemical Operations Branch, Office of Pesticide Programs, reanalyzed those sediment samples from Five Rivers, Oregon, and found 1.6 and 1.1 parts per trillion of TCDD. EPA,

Office of Pesticide Programs, Environmental Chemistry Laboratory, "Analytical Results for 2,3,7,8-TCDD in Reanalyzed Sediment Samples from Five Rivers / Alsea, Oregon" (Samples Received 8/30/84 from Region X, February 14, 1985).

23 EPA, Office of Public Awareness, "Environmental News," February 15, 1979.

24 J. Milton Clark, "A Report on Polychlorinated Dibenzo-P-Dioxins (PCDDs) and Polychlorinated Dibenzofurans (PCDFs) as They Relate to the Great Lakes Area" (USEPA Region V, Office of Toxic Substances, June 18, 1981). The evidence for Hernandez's passing the report to Dow comes from Clark's handwritten note "Conference Call with Dow" dated August 10, 1981. See also "Hernandez may be forced out of EPA," United Press International, March 20, 1983. See also "Scheuer Says EPA Aide Let Dow Delete Dioxin Tie in Draft Report," *New York Times,* March 16, 1983, http://www.nytimes.com/1983/03/16/us/scheuer-says-epa-aide-let-dow-delete-dioxin-tie-in-draft-report.html; http://news.google.com/newspapers?nid=1842&dat=19830320&id=JGIeAAA AIBAJ&sjid=ocgEAAAAIBAJ&pg=3095,3885510.

25 David Kee to Valdas V. Adamkus, "Briefing on Region V Dioxin Problem, Report, and Recommendations" (June 10, 1981).

26 Valdas V. Adamkus to David Kee, Regional Administrator, EPA, Region V, "Statement Before the Subcommittee on Oversight and Investigations, Committee on Energy and Commerce, US House of Representatives" (March 18, 1983). See also "EPA Aides Charge Superiors Forced Shift in Dow Study," *New York Times,* March 19, 1983, http://www.nytimes.com/1983/03/19/us/epa-aides-charge-superiors-forced-shift-in-dow-study.html.

27 News of Hernandez's resignation can be found here: Martin Crutsinger, "Three More EPA Officials Asked to Resign." Associated Press, March 25, 1983. http://news.google.com/newspapers?nid=1665&dat=19830325&id=5HEjAAAAIBAJ &sjid=NiQEAAAAIBAJ&pg=6636,3685204. See also http://www.nytimes.com/1983/03/25/us/acting-epa-chief-is-said-to-be-ready-to-quit-post-today.html.

28 *New York Times,* January 10, 1984. After three years of public debacles at EPA, Reagan brought back its first administrator, William Ruckelshaus, expecting that shrewd move would divert attention from his administration's wrecking of environmental protection in the United States.

29 Janet Gardner, "New Agent Orange Research: Answers at Last?" *The Nation,* April 11, 1987, 460.

30 In 1979, as noted earlier, EPA had suspended the use of 2,4,5-T and another similar weed killer, Silvex, in forests, rights-of-way, pastures, home gardens, turf, and aquatic vegetation. Dow Chemical tried to get this decision overturned in court but lost.

31 EPA, Office of Water Regulations and Standards and the Office of Solid Waste and Emergency Response, in conjunction with the Dioxin Strategy Task Force, "Dioxin Strategy" (August 15, 1983), iv, 4.

32 See Cate Jenkins, "Consultant Abuses at EPA and Cover-Up," letter to Congressman John D. Dingell et al., October 7, 1988.

33 "Carcinogen Assessment Group's Risk Assessment on 2,4,5-Trichlorophenoxy Acetic Acid (2,4,5-T), and 2,3,7,8-Tetrachloro-dibenzo-p-dioxin (TCDD)" (memorandum from Elizabeth L. Anderson, Executive Director, Carcinogen Assessment Group, to Harvey L. Warnik, Special Pesticide Review Division, EPA, February 23, 1979).

34 Cate Jenkins, "Newly Revealed Fraud by Monsanto in an Epidemiological Study Used by EPA to Assess Human Health Effects from Dioxins" (memorandum to Raymond Loehr, Chairman, Executive Committee, EPA Science Advisory Board, February 23, 1990).

35 Cate Jenkins, "Criminal Investigation of Monsanto Corporation—Cover-up of Dioxin Contamination in Products—Falsification of Dioxin Health Studies" (memorandum to John West and Kevin Guarino, EPA Office of Criminal Investigations, November 15, 1990).

36 Cate Jenkins, "Impact of Falsified Monsanto Human Studies on Dioxin Regulations by EPA and Other Agencies—January 24, 1991, NIOSH Study Reverses Monsanto Study Findings and Exposes Certain Fraudulent Methods" (memorandum to John West and Kevin Guarino, EPA Office of Criminal Investigations, January 24, 1991).

37 Memo from William Sanjour, "The Monsanto Investigation," July 20, 1994.

38 Jenkins had become so concerned about this treatment, she told me, that she began secretly taping conversations she had with her EPA colleagues. I sympathized with Jenkins as I, too, had suffered similar humiliations: supervisors ordering you to do clerical jobs, checking up on the use of the EPA computer, telephone, the time of arrival and departure, etc. One of those supervisors would stop in the middle of the street and check his watch the moment he saw me. Another supervisor in the early 1980s even checked if I had done postdoctoral studies at Harvard. An official from Harvard called me and asked me why the EPA was anxiously asking about my Harvard studies. Did I really study at Harvard, the EPA official wanted to know.

39 See http://www.combatmonsanto.org/docs/doc%20scan/Dioxine/Jenkins%20 v.%20EPA/Jenkins%20vs%20EPA%20case.pdf.

40 Sanjour, "The Monsanto Investigation," 21, 24. See also http://www.greens.org/ s-r/078/07-49.html.

41 See http://www.nytimes.com/1988/08/14/obituaries/elmo-r-zumwalt-3d-42-is-dead-father-ordered-agent-orange-use.html; http://articles.latimes.com/ 1988-08-14/news/mn-793_1_agent-orange.

42 "Affidavit of Admiral Elmo R. Zumwalt, Jr.," August 28, 1991 (in the U.S. District Court for the Eastern District of New York, *Shirley Ivy et al., Plaintiffs, v. Diamond Shamrock Chemicals Company et al., Defendants*. CV-89-03361 (E.D.N.Y.) (JBW) [B-89-00559-CA (E.D. TEX)].

43 Kate White, "Monsanto Vows 93 Million Dollars to Nitro Residents," *Charleston Gazette-Mail*, February 24, 2012.

44 EPA, "EPA, Dow reach agreement for dioxin cleanup" (Region 5, Chicago, July 13, 2007). Barrie Barber, "EPA Quits Dioxin Talks," *Saginaw News*, January 5,

2008. "Dioxin Cleanup Near Dow Chemical Plant remains on Slow Track," *Saginaw News*, March 17, 2008.

45   Eartha Jane Melzer, "EPA Misses Dioxin Deadlines," *Michigan Messenger*, January 11, 2011.

46   *Michigan Messenger*, January 7, 2011.

47   "E.P.A. Chemist Who Warned of Ground Zero Dust Is Reinstated," *New York Times*, May 8, 2012.

CHAPTER 4: DDT: A NEW PRINCIPLE OF TOXICOLOGY

1   The letter was sent to the EPA administrator in Dallas by Jenny L. Stegman, acting regional director of the Department of the Interior's Fish and Wildlife Service in Albuquerque, New Mexico, July 7, 1980.

2   Morton S. Biskind, "Public Health Aspects of the New Insecticides," *American Journal of Digestive Diseases* 20 (November 1953): 331–41, 332.

3   Rachel Carson, *Silent Spring* (first published 1962, Boston: Houghton Mifflin, 1987), 5–13.

4   Ibid., 7–8.

5   Ibid., 10, 297.

6   *Time* magazine, June 30, 1947. The ad was taken out by the Pennsylvania Salt Manufacturing Company.

7   *Agricultural Chemicals*, December 1951, in *The War on Bugs* by Will Allen (White River Junction, VT: Chelsea Green Publishing, 2008), 170. See also "The Editor Comments," *Agricultural Chemicals*, December 1951, in Allen, *War on Bugs*, 170.

8   EPA, *DDT: A Review of Scientific and Economic Aspects of the Decision to Ban Its Use as a Pesticide* (EPA-540/1-75-022, July 1975).

9   Ibid., p. 11.

10   *United States v. Goodman*, 486 F. 2d at 855 (7th Cir. 1973).

11   Steven G. Herman and John B. Bulger, "Effects of a Forest Application of DDT on Nontarget Organisms," *Wildlife Monographs* 69, October 1979, p. 49.

12   Richard Balcomb, "Dicofol: A review of the biological effects associated with the contaminants DDT and DDE" (EPA, Office of Pesticide Programs [1985]), p. 1.

13   See Dick Beeler, "DDT Post Mortem," *Agricultural Age*, July 1972, in Allen, *War on Bugs*, 174. See also Frank Graham, Jr., "The Witch-hunt of Rachel Carson," *The Ecologist*, March 3, 1980.

14   Paul Shepard and Daniel McKinley, eds., *The Subversive Science: Essays Towards an Ecology of Man* (Boston: Houghton Mifflin, 1969), 230.

15   Jantzen letter to Clayton Bushong on May 18, 1983.

16   Eventually, Kelthane disappeared. I don't know if it was officially banned, as it was an inert.

17   Donald Roberts, "A New Home for DDT," *New York Times*, August 20, 2007.

CHAPTER 5: WHY ARE THE HONEYBEES DISAPPEARING?

1   Private communication, January 19, 2011, and January 14, 2013.

2   In 2000, a study by Cornell University estimated that every year bees pollinate crops—especially fruits, nuts, and vegetables—worth about $14 billion. See S. E. McGregor, *Insect Pollination of Cultivated Crop Plants*, Agriculture Handbook No. 496, Agricultural Research Service (Washington, DC: U.S. Department of Agriculture, July 1976), 1–2. See also Robert Dismukes et al., "Crop Insurance for Hay and Forage," Economic Research Service, U.S. Department of Agriculture, October 25, 1995. See also David Pimentel, "Environmental and Economic Costs of the Application of Pesticides Primarily in the United States," *Environment, Development and Sustainability* 7 (2005): 229–52.

3   The vulnerability of honeybees to deleterious changes in their environment makes them like alarm bells of harm to other insects, and, indirectly, to birds, plants, and other species. See Laura Maxim and Jeroen van der Sluijs, "Seed-dressing systemic insecticides and honeybees," in European Environment Agency, "Late lessons from early warnings: Science, precaution, innovation," Denmark, 2013, 401–38. In 2006, the Honeybee Genome Sequencing Consortium reported that honeybees are more sensitive to environmental pollution than other animals. Honeybees are of paramount importance because they pollinate crops and wild plants, and pollination is essential to both human nutrition and global ecology. George M. Weinstock et al., "Insights into Social Insects from the Genome of the Honeybee *Apis mellifera*," *Nature* 443 (October 26, 2006): 931–49. See also U.S. Department of Agriculture, "California Almond Forecast," May 8, 2009.

4   Hesiod, *Works and Days*, 230–35, translated by Apostolos N. Athanassakis (Baltimore, MD: Johns Hopkins University Press, 1983).

5   Aristotle, *Historia Animalium* 9.623b5–27b22; 631a9–b3, edited by D. M. Balme (Cambridge: Cambridge University Press, 2002).

6   Pappos, "On the Sagacity of Bees in Building Their Cells," in *Mathematical Collection*, translated by Thomas Little Heath, *A History of Greek Mathematics*, vol. II, *From Aristarchus to Diophantus* (Oxford: Clarendon Press, 1921), 389–90.

7   "Transactions of the Massachusetts Horticultural Society," 1917. This quote is also cited in *Insect Pollination of Cultivated Crop Plants* by S. E. McGregor (USDA, 1976), 1.

8   S. E. McGregor and C. T. Vorhies, Arizona Agricultural Experiment Station Bulletin 207, 1947.

9   S. E. McGregor, *Insect Pollination of Cultivated Plants*, Agriculture Handbook No. 496, Agricultural Research Service, U.S. Department of Agriculture (Washington, DC: U.S. Government Printing Office, July 1976), pp. 1, 4.

10 Gerhard Schrader, the chemist who invented these poisons, worked for the German chemical giant IG Farben.

11 Eldon P. Savage et al., "Chronic Neurological Sequelae of Acute Organophosphate Pesticide Poisoning: A Case-Control Study" (EPA, May 1980). Steven D. Jellinek,

assistant administrator, Office of Pesticides and Toxic Substances, wrote to the EPA administrator, Douglas M. Costle, September 8, 1980, that compared to a control group of people, the "100 previously poisoned persons" selected for the study "demonstrated significantly greater impairment of the higher integrative or neuropsychological functions, i.e., average impairment, verbal IQ, full scale IQ . . . reading recognition, etc."

12   One study demonstrating the toxic effects of pesticides on farmworkers was done by Clarence B. Owens, "The Extent of Exposure of Migrant Workers to Pesticide Residues" (EPA, January 1981). Finally, two memos by the EPA scientist Barbara Britton (August 15, 1985, and October 30, 1985) summarize the science of the deadly ecological and human health effects of parathion.

13   In a June 2, 1986, memorandum about the "Statistical Evaluation of Parathion," EPA scientists cited research data of the 1960s confirming that parathion in crops transforms itself into two very toxic compounds.

14   August 15, 1985, letter from Barbara Britton, a scientist at EPA's Office of Policy, Planning and Evaluation, to Jay Ellenberger, Office of Pesticide Programs; January 16, 1986, letter from Britton to Bruce Kapner, EPA Office of Pesticide Programs.

15   Encapsulated methyl parathion, an extremely toxic homologue of parathion, remains toxic in stored pollen for close to two years. As early as 1978, 41 parts per million of methyl parathion was discovered in pollen, 1 part per million in honey, and 1 part per million or less in wax from honeycombs. Honeybee research experts have implied that residues of pesticides (whether encapsulated or nonencapsulated) "are a relatively common occurrence in honey." See Clayton Bushong, "Penncap-M and Other Encapsulated Pesticides: Issues and Recommendations," memorandum to Peter E. McGrath, Director, Hazard Evaluation Division, OPP, EPA, July 27, 1979. Norman Cook of the Ecological Effects Branch drafted this memorandum. His two memos, September 20, 1978, and October 11, 1978, were critical.

16   The EPA has generated a great deal of paperwork about the agency's approval of neurotoxins deleterious to bees. See "Penncap-M: Hazards to Humans and Bees," memorandum from Norman Cook to Acting Director, Hazard Evaluation Division, September 20, 1978; "Honey Bees and Penncap-M," memorandum from Norman Cook to Acting Director, Hazard Evaluation Division, October 11, 1978; "Modifications of Penncap-M Regulations to Protect Bees," letter from C. A. Johansen, professor of entomology, Washington State University, Pullman, Washington, to Arthur Losey, assistant director, grain and chemical division, Department of Agriculture, Olympia, Washington, February 8, 1979; "Meeting on March 2, 1979, Between Representatives of Pennwalt Corporation and the Agency Concerning the Classification of Microencapsulated Formulations of Methyl Parathion," memorandum from Mitchell B. Bernstein, Office of General Counsel, to the File, April 5, 1979; "Penncap-M: Status as of June 29, 1979," memorandum from Norman Cook to P. E. McGrath, June 29, 1979; "Preliminary Report for Penncap-M-Honey Bee Project," memorandum from Richard M. Lee to J. G. Cummings, July 20, 1979; "Penncap-M and Other Encapsulated Pesticides: Issues

and Recommendations," memorandum from Clayton Bushong to Peter E. McGrath, July 27, 1979; "Ecological Effects Branch Response to Pennwalt's 9/26/80 Response to May 9, 1980 Incremental Risk Assessment," memorandum from Norman Cook, John Leitzke, and Allen Vaughan to Jay S. Ellenberger, December 10, 1980; "Brief History of Penncap-M and Penncap-E," memorandum from Norman Cook to Ecological Effects Branch Files, February 13, 1981.

17 Johansen letter of February 8, 1979, to Arthur Losey, an agricultural official of the State of Washington.

18 March 12, 1978, letter from Elwood Sires, president, Washington State Beekeepers Association, to Bob Mickelson, director, Washington State Department of Agriculture.

19 Memo from Norman Cook to the director of the Hazard Evaluation Division, October 11, 1978.

20 Letter from Frank Robinson, January 6, 1981, to the EPA. Vernon W. Miller, "Deadly Penncap-M Poisons Illinois Bees," *American Bee Journal*, July 1983, p. 535.

21 Letter from Hardie to Dale Parrish, a senior EPA official, March 14, 1980.

22 "Botulism in Infants: A Case of Sudden Death?" *Science*, September 1, 1978, 799–801.

23 Norman Cook, "Penncamp-M: Status as of June 29, 1979," memorandum to Peter McGrath, Hazard Evaluation Division, Office of Pesticide Programs, EPA, June 29, 1979.

24 Norman Cook, John Leitzke, and Allen Vaughan, Ecological Effects Branch, "Ecological Effects Branch Response to Pennwalt's 9/26/80 Response to May 9, 1980, Incremental Risk Assessment," memorandum to Jay Ellenberger, Insecticides-Rodenticides Branch, Hazard Evaluation Division, OPP, EPA, December 10, 1980.

25 Bushong memo of July 27, 1979.

26 Richard Lee memo of July 20, 1979, to his lab chief, J. G. Cummings.

27 Robert L. Metcalf, "EPN Insecticide RPAR [Rebuttable Presumption Against Registration]" (consultant's report to Edwin Johnson, August 24, 1982).

28 Pierre Mineau and Cynthia Palmer, "The Impact of the Nation's Most Widely Used Insecticides on Birds," American Bird Conservancy, March 2013.

29 Henk Tennekes, *The Systemic Insecticides: A Disaster in the Making* (Zutphen, The Netherlands: Weevers Walburg Communicatie, September 2010), 70–71.

30 Damian Carrington, "Insecticide Regulators Ignoring Risk to Bees," *The Guardian*, December 12, 2012.

31 For the leaked EPA memo, see Pesticide Action Network, www.panna.org.

32 I spoke to Gutierrez by phone on December 27, 1984.

33 June 30, 1989, letter from Dee A. Lusby.

34 Lusby letter, August 31, 1990.

35 The organizations suing the EPA included the National Pollinator Defense Fund, American Honey Producers Association, National Honey Bee Advisory Board, and American Beekeeping Federation.

36   Earthjustice, "Beekeeping Industry Sues EPA for Approval of Bee-Killing Pesticide" (press release, San Francisco, July 8, 2013).

37   George Monbiot, "Neonicotinoids Are the New DDT Killing the Natural World," *The Guardian*, August 5, 2013.

CHAPTER 6: AGRICULTURAL WARFARE

1   See "Pesticide Induced Delayed Neurotoxicity" (EPA, Office of Research and Development, Health Effects Research Laboratory, 1976). The site for this study: http://books.google.com/books/about/Pesticide_Induced_Delayed_Neuro toxicity.html?id=ECIoGwAACAAJ.

2   See "The Report of the Leptophos Advisory Committee to the Administrator" (U.S. EPA, October 1976), which discusses the leptophos poisoning of workers. Page 28: "Humans exposed to leptophos exhibited typical signs of OP [organophosphate] poisoning." The report admits that two workers were paralyzed. One worker suffered "total paralysis in the lower extremities" and the other "partial paralysis of the lower extremities" (p. 52).

3   The members of the committee were Julius Coon of Thomas Jefferson University, Seymour Friess of the Naval Medical Research Institute, Tetsuo Fukuto of the University of California, Bernard McNamara of the U.S. Army Material Command, and Gerald Rosen of Duke University. Their report was dated October 1976.

4   A year with the migrants was enough to convince Owens that these terribly poor people had something going for them. "To travel over the country, to endure the hardships of the labor, the loneliness of the camps, the scorn and abuses from all quarters of our society just for the privilege of working takes an especially determined person," he wrote. "He takes pride in his work and he is proud, for how else could he endure?" Clarence B. Owens, "The Extent of Exposure of Migrant Workers to Pesticides and Pesticide Residues" (submitted to the National Science Foundation and Environmental Protection Agency, Washington, DC: May 1982), pp. 345–50.

5   Owens, "Extent of Exposure," p. 316.

6   The dysfunctional relationship between the Owens brothers and the two government agencies was surely compromised by race as well as chemical politics. A senior EPA scientist who reviewed the Owenses' proposal wrote on November 19, 1974, that the Owens brothers "are not now and may never be in a position to implement a study of sound scientific merit."

7   EPA report, September 21, 1977.

8   Eldon P. Savage et al., "Chronic Neurological Sequelae of Acute Organophosphate Pesticide Poisoning: A Case-Control Study" (Final Report, Epidemiologic Pesticide Studies Center, Colorado State University, Fort Collins, Colorado, May 1980).

9   See Hale Vandermer's memo, "Persons Acutely Poisoned by Organophosphate Pesticides Have an Apparent Delayed Impairment of Neuropsychological Function," August 8, 1980.

10   "Chronic Neurological Sequelae of Acute Organophosphate Pesticide
      Poisoning: A Case Control Study" (U.S. EPA, OPP, Final Report, May 1980).

11   Harvey L. Bank and Diane Melendez, "An Enzyme Immunoassay for the
      Detection of Malathion Specific Immunoglobulin" (January 1981).

12   U.S. Army, Environmental Hygiene Agency, "Behavioral and Biochemical Effects
      of Malathion" (Study No. 51-051-73/76, October 1975–April 1976), p. 11.

13   Satoshi Ishikawa et al., "Eye Disease Induced by Organic Phosphorous
      Insecticides," *Acta of the Ophthalmological Society of Japan* 75 (1971): 841–55.

14   We know this from James Boland, who was in the midst of the scientific and
      political bureaucracy of the EPA. In a memo of November 5, 1980, Boland, a
      scientist dealing with the management of the Colorado study, reported that
      "when the OP [organophosphate] preliminary study results were suspected last
      December, Ed Johnson used the OP study as one of the pillars upon which to
      build his farm worker program."

15   The problems for the EPA created by Dr. Cranmer's findings paralleled those the
      EPA faced as a result of the use of malathion in South Carolina. Malathion in the
      environment changes to malaoxon, a compound more toxic than malathion itself.
      Adrian Gross, who reviewed five malathion/malaoxon animal studies done by the
      National Cancer Institute, concluded in 1984 that both malathion and malaoxon
      cause cancer of the adrenal and thyroid glands in rats, and malathion alone
      causes liver cancer in mice. Not only is it extremely difficult to detect malaoxon
      in nature, but the compound also continues to kill or cripple biological organisms
      long after the disappearance of malathion. See Adrian Gross, "Carcinogenicity of
      Malathion" (memorandum to Kevin Keaney, OPP, EPA, April 24, 1984).

16   "The Environmental Protection Agency and the Regulation of Pesticides"
      (Washington, DC: U.S. Government Printing Office, December 1976).

17   Theo Colborn et al., "Developmental Effects of Endocrine-Disrupting
      Chemicals in Wildlife and Humans," *Environmental Health Perspectives*, 101,
      no. 5, October 1993, 378–84. See also "The Estrogen Complex," *Newsweek*,
      March 21, 1994, 76–77.

18   Laura Vandenberg, "There are no safe doses for endocrine disruptors,"
      Environmental Health News, March 15, 2012.

19   Theo Colborn, "Endocrine Disruption Fact Sheet," www.endocrinedisruption
      .com. Colborn is also the coauthor (with Dianne Dumanoski and John Peter
      Meyers) of the study of endocrine-disrupting chemicals titled *Our Stolen
      Future: Are We Threatening Our Fertility, Intelligence, and Survival? A
      Scientific Detective Story* (New York: Plume, 1997). See also Laura N.
      Vandenberg et al., "Hormones and Endocrine-Disrupting Chemicals,"
      Endocrine Reviews, 33 (3) (June 2012), edrv.endojournals.org.

20   Warren P. Porter, James W. Jaeger and Ian H. Carlson, "Endocrine, Immune,
      and Behavioral Effects of Aldicarb (Carbamate), Atrazine (Triazine) and Nitrate
      (Fertilizer) Mixtures at Groundwater Concentrations," *Toxicology and
      Industrial Health*, 15 (1–2) (1999): 133–150.

21   Joan M. Spyker Cranmer, "Integrated Study of Subtle and Delayed Effects

from Low-Level Exposure to Pesticides" (Final Report, EPA Contract # 68-01-1925 [1979]), p. 140.

CHAPTER 7: THE SWAMP: THE BIG BUSINESS
OF FRAUDULENT SCIENCE

1   From the April 1983 "Opening Statement" of the IBT court transcripts. The "Opening Statement" was several hundred pages long. The other major source for the IBT story was my extensive discussions with Adrian Gross. In addition, my IBT narrative is based on evidence in these documents: (1) Memorandum of Concern Regarding the Regulatory Follow-Up of the IBT Audit at Decatur [Illinois]; From: Edwin L. Johnson, Deputy Assistant Administrator, Office of Pesticide programs, EPA, March 1, 1978; (2) Status of International Biotest Investigation—Information Memorandum; From: Steven D. Jellinek, Assistant Administrator for Toxic Substances; To: The [EPA] Administrator, March 8, 1978; (3) Letter to Senator Edward M. Kennedy, Chairman, Subcommittee on Health and Scientific Research, Committee on Human Resources; From: Steven D. Jellinek, Assistant Administrator for Toxic Substances, EPA, October 23, 1978; (4) Quality Assurance Paper: Decision Memorandum; From: Marcia Williams, Director, Special Pesticide Review Division; To: Edwin L. Johnson, Deputy Assistant Administrator for Pesticide Programs, January 12, 1981; (5) Fact Sheet—IBT Program, OPP [December 1981]. I also read with interest these secondary sources: Sharon Begley, "Scandal in the Testing Lab," *Newsweek*, May 30, 1983; Eliot Marshall, "The Murky World of Toxicity Testing," *Science*, June 10, 1983, 1130–32; Eliot Marshall, "EPA Ends Cut-and-Paste Toxicology," *Science*, January 27, 1984; Keith Schneider, "Faking It," *Amicus Journal*, Spring 1983, 14–26; Schneider, "The Data Gap," *Amicus Journal*, Winter 1985, 15–25.

2   Gross discovered the IBT fraud in 1976. By the time he was talking to Manny Reyna, Gross was the most knowledgeable government expert about the magnitude and significance of the IBT crimes. A. E. Conroy, director of pesticides enforcement at the EPA, sent EPA's IBT files to the Justice Department on May 2, 1978. So the FBI was assisting in the investigation probably from 1978.

3   The story of Gordon came from Adrian Gross, who was present during the FBI's investigation of Gordon.

4   October 31, 1977, letter from Wilson to Edwin Johnson.

5   See memo on Status of the EPA Toxicology Data Auditing Program Enforcement Cases, April 2, 1979. See also "Grand Jury Indicts Velsicol, Six Persons," UPI, December 13, 1977, http://news.google.com/newspapers?nid=2209&dat=1977 1213&id=XnljAAAAIBAJ&sjid=53kNAAAAIBAJ&pg=5157,2629988.

6   Senior EPA officials went out of their way to diminish the gravity of the cut-and-paste malpractice. See: Letter to Congressman George E. Brown, Jr., Chairman, Subcommittee on Department Operations, Research, and Foreign Agriculture, Committee on Agriculture; From: Edwin L. Johnson, Director, Office of Pesticide Programs, February 24, 1983; and Letter to Congressman George E.

Brown, Jr., Chairman, Subcommittee on Department Operations, Research, and Foreign Agriculture, Committee on Agriculture; From: John A. Moore, Assistant Administrator for Pesticides and Toxic Substances, January 5, 1984.

7   Gross discovered the science scam in the huge corporate laboratory in Chicago while working for the FDA. Senator Edward Kennedy thanked Adrian Gross for his "professional competence, integrity and unyielding dedication." Exposing the EPA's dirty secret of licensing dangerous toxins brought Adrian Gross so much trouble for so long that it ultimately destroyed his career in the federal government. On September 6, 1985, Gross wrote a letter to the EPA administrator, Lee M. Thomas, in which he begged Thomas for some sort of "garden-variety, elementary justice." He never heard back. But Gross never gave up. He kept exposing the deficiencies of his colleagues, their sloppy science serving the poison merchants. His lengthy memos became his weapons. They circulated widely, always adding light to obscurity and replacing jargon with logical narrative. They were models of good science and clarity, explaining difficult technical issues in terms even a nonexpert could understand. See Opening Statement by Senator Edward Kennedy at Joint Hearings Before the Senate Subcommittees on Health and Administrative Practice and Procedure, January 20, 1976.

8   See Kate Davies, *The Rise of the U.S. Environmental Health Movement* (Lanham, MD: Rowman and Littlefield, 2013), p. 156. See also http://www.sier raclub.org/sierra/200103/conspiracy.asp.

9   Adrian Gross uncovered the IBT scandal, so he was held in high esteem by the government lawyers. He learned what he told me because of his privileged position during the trial. See also "Faking It: The Case Against Industrial Bio-Test Laboratories" and "IBT-Guilty: How Many Studies are No Good?," two articles by the *New York Times* reporter Keith Schneider published in spring 1983 in the *Amicus Journal*, http://planetwaves.net/contents/ibt_guity.html.

10 For more on the case, see https://bulk.resource.org/courts.gov/c/F2/776/776. F2d.678.84-1639.html.

11 Marcia Williams, "Quality Assurance Paper," decision memorandum to Edwin Johnson, January 12, 1981. Williams was a senior official.

12 "Fact Sheet—IBT Program," OPP, EPA [late 1981].

13 USDA Laboratory Audit / Inspection Issue; memo from Edwin L. Johnson to Steven D. Jellinek, July 17, 1979.

14 Laurence D. Chitlik, "Data validation of two Dimilin studies conducted at the Veterinary Toxicology and Entomology Research Laboratory, USDA, College Station, Texas," memorandum to Laurence Chloupek, March 1, 1979. Chitlik and Chloupek were EPA scientists.

15 Shoddy practices in labs were hardly unusual. One of my colleagues, whom I will call Robert Eagle, once worked for a major chemical company developing pesticides. The company, he told me, "used to hire former criminals, just out of jail, to formulate pesticides." "Those poor bastards would go about mixing the deadly chemicals blissfully ignorant of what they were doing," Eagle said. "And the company scientists creating pesticides never dream about anything else but how to keep their job and

make more money. To hell with public health, they say. So when the experimental animals develop tumors or other nasty effects because of their exposure to pesticides, the company toxicologists, or the toxicologists of commercial laboratories hired to test those poisons for chemical corporations, dump those animals in the trash can, replacing them with healthy animals in the middle of testing, and in a thousand other fraudulent ways they destroy any evidence [that] their product might cause what EPA defines as 'unreasonable adverse effect' on man or the environment. Then, to smooth their way into EPA, they go about inviting EPA scientists for a brief visit to the company headquarters, ostensibly for showing them all the fabulous scientific machinery, talent, money, and time the company uses in the development of pesticides. The purpose of the invitation, however, is to wine and dine and bribe, with booze and women, those bureaucrats. Having done that, the rest is easy. The 'kill and count studies' arrive at the gates of the EPA regulators to be quickly approved and, in the midst of one irregularity after another, the poison gets the government's blessing to start its deleterious Odyssey in the country's land, food, drinking water, and people."

16 Memo from Edward Johnson to Steven Jellinek, June 5, 1979.

17 James G. Touhey, "Status of Cannon Laboratories Testing Data," memorandum to Steve Schatzow, February 7, 1985. Touhey and Schatzow were senior officials in the EPA's Office of Pesticide Programs.

18 Cannon Lab audit report by EPA inspector Adrian Gross and FDA inspector Andrew J. Allen, August 15–19, 1983.

19 Anna Rena Phillips, "Relative Risk, One Result at a Time," *American Scientist*, January–February 2012.

20 March 1, 1978, letter from Johnson to A. E. Conroy, EPA's chief of pesticides enforcement, and Joan Z. Bernstein, EPA's top lawyer.

21 This accounting comes from the IBT studies EPA scientists reviewed from June 1980 to December 1981. See "Fact Sheet—IBT Program," OPP, EPA, late 1981.

22 "Looking into the Black Box: Factors Considered in Risk/Benefit Decision-Making" (briefing paper, OPP, late 1980s).

23 B. Ritz et al., "Dopamine transporter genetic variants and pesticides in Parkinson's disease," *Environmental Health Perspectives*, 117 (6) (June 2009), 964–69; "Genes and Pesticide Exposure Interact to Increase Men's Risk for Parkinson's Disease," *Science Daily*, June 14, 2010; Marianne van der Mark et al., "Is Pesticide Use Related to Parkinson's Disease? Some Clues to Heterogeneity," *Environmental Health Perspectives* 120 (3) (March 2012), 340–47.

CHAPTER 8: WHISTLE-BLOWERS AND WHAT THEY'RE UP AGAINST

1 April 29, 1984, letter from Regine Anderson of Austin, Texas, to Texas Attorney General Jim Mattox.

2 Dwight Welch, "Flammability Update and First Amendment Infringement" (memorandum to Janet Auerbach, November 4, 1982).

3 Only a fraction of these 2 billion spray cans list pesticides as the main

ingredient, but the rules are about the same for the regulation of all aerosols on the market.

4   Memo of April 26, 1985, from Ernest Regna to a senior EPA administrator in Arlington, Virginia.

5   To understand the memo, note the following: I.G., inspector general of EPA; William Ruckelshaus, the man who served as EPA's first administrator between 1970 and 1973 and then once again, at the request of Ronald Reagan, from 1983 to 1985; Steve Schatzow, another Reagan appointee who served as EPA's top pesticides chief from 1984 to 1986; and Herbert Harrison, a branch chief in the pesticides organization where Dwight Welch worked. (Memorandum to Janet Auerbach, November 4, 1985.)

6   Dwight Welch, "New Whistleblower Law—Same Old Office of Special Counsel," *Inside the Fishbowl*, April 1990, 5. (*Inside the Fishbowl* was a newsletter of the EPA employees union, National Federation of Federal Employees, Local 2050.) When I called Welch recently, he said he left all the EPA experience behind him and he did not want to remember any of it. "I have 14 boxes of documents, but don't ask me to search them. I will not do it. I live a different life now," he said. "Please don't call me back." He hung up. This reaction from a warm human being I remember so vividly shocked me. But I also understand it.

7   Memo of November 24, 1987, from Welch to Edwin Tinsworth.

8   Dwight A. Welch, "Management Retribution for Employee's Diligent Efforts to Protect the Public from Flammable Pesticide Aerosols" (grievance filed with Marita Llaverias, Management Relations Office, U.S. Department of Labor, October 7, 1988).

9   See Welch's article in the April 1990 issue of the EPA newsletter *Inside the Fishbowl*. See also Cate Jenkins, "Consultant Abuses at EPA and Cover-Up" (memorandum to Congressman John Dingell, Senator Max Baucus, Senator David Pryor, and Congressman Gerry Sikorski, October 7, 1989).

10   Jenkins's letter of April 30, 1989, was addressed to Congressman John D. Dingell, chairman of the Committee on Energy and Commerce; Senator Max Baucus, chairman of the Subcommittee on Hazardous Wastes and Toxic Substances, Committee on Environment and Public Works; Senator David Pryor, chairman of the Federal Services, Post Office, and Civil Service Committee; and Congressman Gerry Sikorski, chairman of the Human Resources Subcommittee, Post Office, and Civil Service Committee.

11   Jenkins memo to Reps. John Dingell and Gerry Sikorski and Sens. John Glenn and David Pryor, February 21, 1989.

12   The corruption of consultants and dioxin issues, 1978–90, were part of the suit Jenkins filed against the EPA. The U.S. Department of Labor adjudicated those issues in favor of Jenkins. See http://www.combat-monsanto.org/docs/doc%20scan/ Dioxine/Jenkins%20v.%20EPA/monsanto%20letters%20to%20EPA%20about%20 dioxin,%20Jenkins%20case.PDF. See also http://www.combat-monsanto.org/docs/ doc%20scan/Dioxine/Jenkins%20v.%20EPA/Jenkins%20vs%20EPA%20case.PDF.

13   Marsha Coleman-Adebayo, *NO FEAR: A Whistleblower's Triumph over*

Corruption and Retaliation at the EPA (Chicago: Lawrence Hill Books, 2011), 163.

14 Coleman-Adebayo, *NO FEAR*, 336–72.

CHAPTER 9: WHEN WILL THE WELL RUN DRY?

1 Richard Back of Union Carbide met Frank Sanders of EPA's pesticide program to break the news: aldicarb had been discovered in amounts ranging from 1 part per billion to 0.04 parts per million. See Frank Sanders's briefing paper on August 27, 1979.

2 Steven Jellinek letter to David Axelrod, health commissioner of New York, September 4, 1979.

3 We don't know whether certain fishes may be hypersensitive to malathion—a condition in which the behavior and health of the fish would change without any significant loss, reduction, or depression of the vital nerve enzyme cholinesterase, ChE, the clinical measurement of which confirms the poisoning of the animal. See David L. Coppage et al., "River Pollution by Anticholinesterase Agents," *Water Research* 10 (1) (1976): 19–24.

4 See the Biscardi memo of October 17, 1979, to Adrian Gross, who was then the chief of the toxicology branch. See also "Aldicaarb Information Paper," prepared by the following scientists of the Registration Division: Herbert Harrison, Charles Mitchell, and Frank Sanders, August 26, 1979; Douglas Campt, "Contamination of Ground (Drinking) Water from Aldicarb Crop Use" (memorandum to John Todhunter, April 28, 1982). Campt was director of the Registration Division, OPP, and Todhunter was the Reagan political appointee serving as the assistant administrator for pesticides and toxic substances at the EPA.

5 Maurie Semel, "History of the Colorado Potato Beetle in New York: Control and Development of Resistance to Insecticides on Long Island" (Long Island Horticultural Research Laboratory, Riverhead, New York, February 1980), pp. 1–19.

6 Letter from F. Eugene Hester, acting director of the Fish and Wildlife Service of the Department of the Interior, to Clayton Bushong, chief EPA ecologist, on January 22, 1982.

7 EPA, Office of Policy Analysis, "Agriculture and the Environment: Briefing for EPA Deputy Administrator" (June 22, 1988); Office of Pesticide Programs, Biological and Economic Analysis Division, "An Overview of Pesticide Usage, Groundwater Concerns, and Costs of Alternative Regulatory Options" (May 1989); Office of Pesticide Programs, "Pesticides and Ground-Water Strategy: A Survey of Potential Impacts" (February 1991).

8 EPA, Office of Pesticide Programs, "Combined Special Review of the Triazine Herbicides Atrazine, Simazine, Cyanazine: Briefing for the Assistant Administrator" (August 11, 1993).

9 Tyrone Hayes: www.atrazinelovers.com. Hayes lists his own articles and dozens of other similar articles documenting the devastating effects of atrazine.

10   Lindsey Konkel, "Atrazine in Water Tied to Menstrual Irregularities, Low
      Hormones," *Environmental Health News*, November 28, 2011.

11   Paul Taylor, "Weed Killer Linked to Gender-Bending in Animals," *Globe and
      Mail*, December 1, 2011.

12   Jeff Donn, Martha Mendoza, and Justin Pritchard, "What's in Our Drinking
      Water? For 41 million, Traces of Drugs," *Dayton Daily News*, March 10, 2008.

13   "Premature Births Peak Seasonally When Pesticides and Nitrates in Surface
      Water Are Highest," *Science Daily*, May 7, 2007.

14   Kathleen Blanchard, "Research Strongly Links Pesticides to Birth Defects,"
      EmaxHealth, October 22, 2011; P. Monica Lind et al., "New Research links
      Pesticides to cardiovascular Disease," *ENEWSPE*, October 14, 2011; EPA,
      Office of Policy Analysis, "Agriculture and the Environment: Briefing for EPA
      Deputy Administrator" (June 22, 1988).

15   According to a 2012 EPA report, fertilizer ends up in surface or groundwater
      because of bad farming practices and overuse: "excess fertilizer use and poor
      application methods can cause fertilizer movement into ground and surface
      waters." EPA, Office of Water, "Managing Agricultural Fertilizer Application to
      Prevent Contamination of Drinking Water," *Source Water Protection Practices
      Bulletin*, August 2010. See also George Hallberg, "Agricultural Chemicals and
      Groundwater Quality in Iowa" (Cooperative Extension Service, Iowa State
      University, December 1984).

16   Padma Datta," "Review of Hydrology, Water Quality and Land Management in
      the Big Spring Basin, Clayton County, Iowa" (Memorandum to David J. Severn
      and Carolyn K. Offutt, March 31, 1984).

17   See "Absorption of Pesticides in the Course of Occupational Exposure" (March
      1977), and "Cooperative Agreement Progress Report" (October 9, 1980), EPA
      report written in August 1980 by Kenneth W. Kirby and Leon Burmeister,
      University of Iowa School of Medicine, and John Kliewer and Gill Fuller,
      Medical University of South Carolina. See also Kenneth W. Kirby and Leon
      Burmeister, "Cancer Types Among Iowa Farmers" (August 4, 1980). This report
      says that "greater production of corn and soybeans may be associated with stom-
      ach cancer, while soybean production may be associated with multiple myeloma
      rates." See also Sheila H. Zahm, Division of Cancer Etiology, National Cancer
      Institute: there are "high cancer mortality rates among farmers in the midwest,"
      The Use and Regulation of Lawn Care Chemicals, Hearing, Subcommittee on
      Toxic Substances, Environmental Oversight, Research and Development,
      Senate Committee on Environment and Public Works, March 28, 1990
      (Washington, DC: Government Printing Office, 1990); D. M. Schreinemachers,
      "Birth Malformations and Other Adverse Perinatal Outcomes in Four U.S.
      Wheat-Producing States," *Environmental Health Perspectives* 111 (9) (2003):
      1259–64; M. Sanborn et al., *Systematic Review of Pesticides: Human Health
      Effects* (Ontario College of Family Physicians, 2004); U.S. National Cancer
      Institute, *Cancer Trends Progress Report*, 2007; Molly Jacobs and Dick Clapp,
      "Agriculture and Cancer: A Need for Action" (Lowell Center for Sustainable

Production, University of Massachusetts, and Boston University School of
Public Health, October 2008); S.-J. Lee et al., "Acute Pesticide Illnesses
Associated with Off-Target Pesticide Drift from Agricultural Applications—11
States, 1998–2006," *Environmental Health Perspectives* 119 (8), (2011):
1162–69; M. Antoniou et al., "Roundup and Birth Defects: Is the Public
Being Kept in the Dark?" *Earth Open Source*, June 2011; D. Brandli and S.
Reinacher, "Herbicides Found in Human Urine," *Ithaka Journal* 1/2012
(2012): 270–72.

CHAPTER 10: FALLOUT

1   Wiggins's speech was published in the spring of 1983 in the *Bulletin of the
    Entomological Society of America.*

2   George M. Woodwell, "The Challenge of Endangered Species," in *Extinction Is
    Forever: Threatened and Endangered Species of Plants in the Americas and Their
    Significance in Ecosystems Today and in the Future*, edited by Ghillian T. Prance
    and Thomas S. Elias (New York: New York Botanical Garden, 1977), 5–10.

3   David Pimentel, "Pesticides: Environmental and Social Costs," in *Pest Control:
    Cultural and Environmental Aspects*, edited by David Pimentel and John H.
    Perkins (Boulder, CO: Westview Press, 1980), 99–137; "Environmental and
    Economic Costs of the Application of Pesticides Primarily in the United States,"
    Environment, Development and Sustainability 7 (2005): 229–52; E. F. Knipling,
    "One Hundred Years of Entomology—Past and Future," *Journal of Economic
    Entomology* 47 (3), (June 1954): 545.

4   David Pimentel and Lois Levitan, "Pesticides: Amounts Applied and Amounts
    Reaching Pests," *BioScience* 36 (2), (February 1986): 86–91; Pimentel,
    "Amounts of Pesticides Reaching Target Pests: Environmental Impacts and
    Ethics," *Journal of Agricultural and Environmental Ethics* 8 (1995): 17–29.

5   David Pimentel and Michael Burgess, "Small Amounts of Pesticides Reaching
    Target Insects," *Environment, Development and Sustainability* 14 (2011): 1–2.

6   Meeting with David Pimentel, November 3, 1981, Crystal Square #4, Crystal
    City, Arlington, VA, OPP, EPA.

7   EPA position paper 2/3 on toxaphene, December 12, 1980.

8   Dave Severn, "Toxaphene" (note to Edwin Johnson, February 16, 1982, OPP,
    EPA); William Dickinson, "Toxaphene" (memorandum to Edwin Johnson,
    February 22, 1982, OPP, EPA).

9   In 1955, the U.S. Department of Agriculture's toxaphene scientists approved 7
    parts per million of toxaphene in crops. The government's decision on how
    much toxaphene people could "tolerate" in their food did not reflect some kind
    of scientific evaluation of toxaphene's toxicity; my guess is that they simply
    borrowed the number from the legal tolerance number of DDT.

10 Cited in a memorandum of William Dickinson, Deputy Director, Special
    Pesticide Review Division, to Edwin Johnson, Director, Office of Pesticide

Programs, EPA, February 22, 1982. See also EPA position document 2/3, dated December 12, 1980, stating that toxaphene ought to be banned for all uses except for cattle dip.

11 Memo from David Severn and Joseph Reinart, February 16, 1982.

12 Congressional Record, August 11, 1982, p. H5670. See also press release by the office of Congressman Yates: "Yates Reveals New Threat to Lake Michigan— Proposes Ban on Insecticide [Toxaphene] Found in Great Lakes Fish," July 23, 1982; Irvin Molotsky, "E.P.A. Plans to Curb Use of Toxaphene, a Pesticide," New York Times, October 17, 1982.

13 See Cook memo to his colleagues on September 21, 1983.

14 See Rosmarie von Rumker's July 1974 study, "Farmer's Pesticide Use Decisions and Attitudes on Alternate Crop Protection Methods."

CHAPTER 11: THE HUBRIS OF THE REAGAN ADMINISTRATION

1 See "Results of National Urban Pesticide Applicator Survey by EPA," 1984.

2 See EPA report, "National Household Pesticide Usage Study, 1976–1977."

3 Note from James Touhey to Edwin Johnson, September 7, 1983. Touhey was then the director of the Benefits and Use Division, OPP, EPA, and Johnson was the deputy assistant administrator or director, OPP, EPA.

4 Adrian Gross long ago showed that malathion and its oxygen analogue, malaoxon, cause cancer in both rats and mice. He also demonstrated that people eat five times more malathion per day than the maximum permissible level, and he warned that as many as four people per thousand are in the upper limit of possibly getting cancer from malathion. Adrian Gross, "Carcinogenicity of Malathion" (memorandum to Kevin Keeney through James Touhey, April 24, 1984, Office of Pesticides and Toxic Substances, U.S. EPA).

5 Joel A. Mintz, *Enforcement at the EPA: High Stakes and Hard Choices*, revised edition (Austin: University of Texas Press, 2012), 42.

6 William Sanjour, "In Name Only," *Sierra*, September/October 1992, 99.

7 "Anne Gorsuch Buford, 62, Dies; Reagan EPA Director," *Washington Post*, July 22, 2004.

8 *Sarasota Herald-Tribune*, May 19, 1983.

9 Richardson discussion with the author, September 22, 1983.

10 Martin Crutsinger, "Reagan Orders Full Probe of EPA," Associated Press, February 17, 1983.

11 See the August 1984 report "Investigation of the Environmental Protection Agency."

12 EPA, "National Nursery Pesticide Usage Survey" (1984).

13 EPA, "Health Assessment of Pesticide Applicators in an Enclosed Environment" (1984).

14 EPA, "A National Survey of Pesticide Usage of Golf Courses in the U.S." (1984).

15 Ibid.

16 EPA, Office of Pesticide Programs, "R.E.D. Facts: Thiram," September 2004.

17 National Corn Growers Association, "World of Corn," 2013.

18 See "Minutes for the First Meeting of the Interagency Task Force on Seed Treatment" (September 11, 1986, OPP, EPA); Edwin Tinsworth, "Note to Douglas Camp" ([1986], OPP, EPA); Eugene Wilson, Product Manager, Fungicide-Herbicide Branch, Registration Division, "Chronology of Recent Meetings Regarding Detreated Seed Corn" (memorandum to Frank Sanders, Chief, Fungicide-Herbicide Branch, Registration Division, OPP, EPA, January 27, 1987). Wilson wrote: "Illegal residues of heptachlor in milk reported by FDA [U.S. Food and Drug Administration] in 1986 were a result of feeding [the fungicide] captan and heptachlor detreated seed corn to dairy cows."

19 EPA, "Environmental News," September 10, 1976; testimony of Jack Griffith, Office of Pesticide Programs, to the Subcommittee on Health and Scientific Research, Committee on Human Resources, U.S. Senate, June 8, 1977.

20 EPA, "Pesticide and Toxic Substance Residues in Humans from the Second Health and Nutrition Examination Survey, 1976–1980," October 1983.

21 John A. Todhunter received a Ph.D. from Berkeley in 1976. According to the American Presidency Project, he was a fellow at the Roche Institute of Molecular Biology, Hoffmann La Roche, Inc. When appointed to EPA on November 13, 1981, to the EPA, he was an assistant professor of biology at the Catholic University of America. He was fired on March 25, 1983.

22 Edwin L. Johnson, "PCB's in Human Blood Serum," note to Don Clay, June 20, 1984. Johnson and Clay were senior officials at EPA.

23 See Nicole Ostrow, "Exposures to Pesticide in Utero Linked to Brain Abnormalities," *San Francisco Chronicle*, April 30, 2012.

24 John E. Davies, "Communities Studies and Pesticides" (progress report to EPA, December 20, 1971).

25 Mark R. Powell, *Science at EPA* (Washington, DC: Resources for the Future, 1999), 297.

26 See Philip Shabecoff, "U.S. Officials Faulted for Talks over Pesticide Ban," *New York Times*, January 30, 1984, http://www.nytimes.com/1984/01/31/us/us-officials-faulted-for-talks-over-pesticide-ban.html. See also "Possible Destruction of EPA Dagat Under Inquiry," *New York Times*, March 9, 1983, http://www.nytimes.com/1983/03/09/us/possible-destruction-of-epa-data-under-inquiry.html.

27 See Martin Crutsinger, "Three More EPA Officials Asked to Resign," Associated Press, March 25, 1983, http://news.google.com/newspapers?nid=1665&dat=19830325&id=5HEjAAAAIBAJ&sjid=NiQEAAAAIBAJ&pg=6636,3685204. See also http://www.nytimes.com/1983/03/25/us/acting-epa-chief-is-said-to-be-ready-to-quit-post-today.html. See also http://www.highbeam.com/doc/1G1-48 11096.html.

28 See "Ex-E.P.A. Official Says Pressure Didn't Delay Action on Pesticide," *New York Times*, September 27, 1983. See also "Possible Destruction of E.P.A. Data Under Inquiry," *New York Times*, March 9, 1983, http://www

.nytimes.com/1983/03/09/us/possible-destruction-of-epa-data-under-inquiry.html. See also Lloyd Tataran, *Formaldehyde on Trial: The Politics of Health in a Chemical Society* (Lorimer, 1983), p. 129. See also "The EPA Wasteland," *New York Times,* February 26, 1983, http://www.nytimes.com/1983/02/26/opinion/the-epa-wasteland.html.

CHAPTER 12: FROM REAGAN TO BUSH

1   For a link to a brief history of rice production in the Missouri Bootheel, see http://agebb.missouri.edu/rice/ricehist.htm.

2   The major source of PCB pollution, General Electric, while fighting every step of the way, was ultimately forced to engage in a massive cleanup of the Hudson.

3   Ambush is not a benign compound: Permethrin's links to cancer seemed to be "many-fold more 'significant' than indicated either in the superficial and flawed Hazard Evaluation Division's reviews or for a number of pesticide products which have in the past been suspended or canceled by the EPA," Adrian Gross wrote. EPA scientists who reviewed permethrin relied on "misleading" information they received from the owners of the insecticide, Gross said. Since the 1980s, we have learned that permethrin, a chemical belonging to the synthetic pyrethroids, combines the ecocidal effects of DDT with the crippling and dehumanizing power of a central nervous system toxin. January 19, 1981, letter from Adrian Gross to Patricia Critchlow of the Registration Division of the Office of Pesticide Programs of EPA.

4   Section 18 also opens another route for the expedited delivery of toxins: the so-called crisis exemption. With this rule, farmers (again represented by the governors of their states) are allowed to use untested and unregistered toxins, including poisons like DDT that EPA banned in 1972; some of these chemicals are suspected to be carcinogenic, or have been taken off the market by the EPA.

5   Douglas D. Campt, "Five Year Review of 40 CFR Part 166" (action memorandum to John A. Todhunter, March 4, 1983).

6   EPA, Office of Pesticide Programs, Registration Division, "Audit of Emergency Exemption and Special Local Needs Programs" (March 1983); "A Review of the Emergency Exemption Program" (March 1987).

7   Dodd letter to Clay, June 29, 1983.

8   See U.S. EPA, "Regional Environmental Management Reports," 1983.

9   U.S. Fish and Wildlife Service, Office of Migratory Bird Management, Pesticides and Birds, March 2000.

10 Rebecca Clarren, "Pesticide Drift," *Orion Magazine,* July/August 2008.

11 Lynne Peeples, "Pesticide Drift, Sick Rural Residents Force Face-Off with Big Agriculture," *Huffington Post,* July 23, 2012.

12 Brad Balukjian, "Pesticides found in frogs far from crops," *Los Angeles Times,* July 29, 2013.

13 Anne C. Mulkern, "Pesticide Industry Ramps Up Lobbying in Bid to Pare EPA Rules," *New York Times,* February 24, 2011.

14   PEER press release, "NJ DEP Employees Say Whitman Administration Soft on Polluters," December 22, 2000.

15   Schaeffer resignation letter, February 27, 2002.

16   Although federal and Supreme Court judges leaned on the EPA to enforce the law—especially the 1970 Clean Air Act—Bush's EPA remained firmly in the grip of the energy industry. Judges ordered the EPA to require factories under renovation to upgrade pollution control technologies and (in the case of coal-fired power plants) to reduce their emissions of mercury, a brain poison. The Supreme Court even ordered EPA to start regulating greenhouse gases from cars. See Schaeffer's article, "Clearing the Air," in the July/August 2002 issue of the *Washington Monthly*.

17   See note from Lyons Gray, EPA Chief Financial Officer, to his senior colleagues, June 8, 2006. Bush pulled similar tricks at the U.S. Forest Service, weakening or eliminating the government's protection of forests and easing restrictions on the timber industry.

18   Brian Litmans and Jeff Miller, "Silent Spring Revisited" (Center for Biological Diversity, San Francisco, 2004), 58–60.

19   Joe Eaton and Ron Sullivan, "Silent Spring for Bay Area Raptors?" *San Francisco Chronicle*, May 11, 2012.

CHAPTER 13: THE OBAMA ADMINISTRATION: YES, WE CAN?

1   Dina Cappiello, "EPA Tells Nation's Dirty Power Plants to Clean Up," Associated Press, December 21, 2011.

2   See letter, "Dear President-Elect Obama and Members of the Transition Team," signed by 102 organizations, dated January 9, 2009.

3   Bill Moyers and Company, "Crony Capitalism," January 20, 2012, PBS.

4   *Friends of the Earth Newsmagazine*, Fall 2009, p. 2.

5   See CBS News, "Critics Slam Obama for 'Protecting' Monsanto," March 28, 2013,http://www.cbsnews.com/8301-250_162-57576835/critics-slam-obama-for-protecting-monsanto/.

6   "Wikileaks Cables," *Democracy Now!* December 23, 2010.

7   In the Supreme Court of the United States, *Monsanto Company et al., Petitioners, v. Geertson Seed Farms et al.* On Writ of Certiorari to the U.S. Court of Appeals for the Ninth Circuit, Brief for the Federal Respondents Supporting Petitioners, Elena Kagan, Solicitor Genera, March 2010. See also "Elena Kagan: Toward a Pro-GM Supreme Court?" *The Atlantic*, May 12, 2010.

8   Michael Antoniou et al., "Roundup and Birth Defects: Is the Public Being Kept in the Dark?" *Earth Open Source*, June 2011; Carey Gillam, "Roundup Herbicide Research Shows Plant, Soil Problems," *Reuters*, August 12, 2011.

9   Carol Glatz, "GM Crops Breed Economic Dependence, a New Form of Slavery," *Catholic News Service*, January 5, 2012.

10   May 2, 2011, letter to Huber from Gregory Parham, Administrator of APHIS, USDA's Animal and Plant Health Inspection Service.

11   http://www.youtube.com/watch?v=ENmc9kHnvbo.

12   Huber met with Parham in the summer of 2011. Parham promised he might
     fund research proposals from Huber.

13   Don Huber letter, July 31, 2011.

14   Don M. Huber, "The effects of glyphosate (Roundup) on soils, crops and
     consumers" (presentation to the All-Party Parliamentary Group on Agroecology,
     House of Commons, UK, November 1, 2011).

15   Huber email to the author, August 2, 2012.

16   Carolyn Lochhead, "Genetically Modified Crops' Results Raise Concern," *San
     Francisco Chronicle*, April 30, 2012.

17   Ian Macleod, "'Big Farma' Companies Seek Federal Approval of 2,4-D-resistant
     corn, soybean seeds," *Ottawa Citizen*, May 12, 2012.

18   Michael Antoniou, Claire Robinson, and John Fagan, "Genetically-Modified
     Organisms, Myths and Truths: An Evidence-Based Examination of the Claims
     Made for Safety and Efficacy of Genetically Modified Crops," *Earth Open
     Source*, June 2012. See also Charles M. Benbrook, "Impacts of Genetically
     Engineered Crops on Pesticide Use in the U.S.—the First Sixteen Years,"
     Environmental Sciences Europe, September 28, 2012.

19   Center for Biological Diversity, "Lawsuit Initiated to Protect Hundreds of
     Endangered Species from Pesticide Impacts," January 28, 2010; Center for
     Biological Diversity, "Notice of Violation of the Endangered Species Act
     Related to the Registration of Pesticides," January 27, 2010.

20   Peter Galvin et al., "Ensure Pesticide Evaluations Protect Endangered Wildlife
     and Human Health," Letter to Lisa Jackson, EPA administrator, Washington,
     DC, early 2011.

21   Center for Biological Diversity, "Landmark Lawsuit Filed to Protect Hundreds of
     Rare Species from Pesticides," January 20, 2011. See http://www.biologicaldiver
     sity.org/campaigns/pesticides_reduction/pdfs/Jan_27_2010_ESA_NOI_CBD.pdf.

22   In the United States District Court for the Northern District of California, San
     Francisco Division, *Center for Biological Diversity and Pesticide Action
     Network North America, Plaintiffs, v. Environmental Protection Agency and
     Lisa Jackson, Administrator, U.S. EPA, Defendants*, Complaint for Declaratory
     and Injunctive Relief, January 19, 2011.

23   The former commissioner of environmental protection in New Jersey, Jackson
     was "not a viable candidate for redeeming a battered, politicized EPA," Jeff
     Ruch, director of the nonprofit Public Employees for Environmental
     Responsibility, wrote to Obama. Jackson embraced "a highly politicized
     approach to environmental decision-making that resulted in suppression of
     scientific information, issuance of gag orders restricting disclosures and threats
     against professional staff members who dared to voice concerns." See Ruch
     letter to Obama, December 5, 2008.

24   In the United States District Court for the Northern District of California, San
     Francisco Division, *Center for Biological Diversity and Pesticide Action
     Network North America, Plaintiffs, v. Environmental Protection Agency and*

Lisa Jackson, Administrator, U.S. EPA, Defendants, Complaint for Declaratory and Injunctive Relief, January 19, 2011.

25   Peter Galvin et al., "Ensure Pesticide Evaluations Protect Endangered Wildlife and Human Health," letter to Lisa Jackson, EPA administrator, Washington, DC, early 2011.

26   Kieran Suckling, "Help Stop Dangerous Pesticides from Killing Wildlife" (Center for Biological Diversity, September 27, 2011). Sadly, it wasn't just Obama's EPA ignoring endangered species. In fact, in January 2012, the Fish and Wildlife Service solicited comments on whether or not it should sharply limit the number of threatened animals and plants receiving any government protection under the Endangered Species Act. According to the Center for Biological Diversity, such a proposal "ignores entire populations of imperiled species." Center for Biological Diversity, January 23, 2012.

27   Lisa P. Jackson, "Too Dirty to Fail?" *Los Angeles Times*, October 21, 2011.

28   Environmental Integrity Project press release: "Pennsylvania, Ohio, Indiana, Kentucky and Texas are top states in terms of toxic power plant air pollution," Washington, DC, December 7, 2011.

29   Associated Press, "House approves bill to delay, scrap EPA rules," Washington, DC, September 24, 2011.

30   John M. Broder, "Re-election Strategy Is Tied to a Shift on Smog," *New York Times*, November 16, 2011.

31   Editorial in *New York Times*, May 27, 2012. Obama was elected with the Senate under Democratic control. Yet his indecisiveness, and his apparent ignorance about the country's environmental challenges, compromised the few promises he made to control the corporate abuse of public health and the natural world. It's not as if the environment was somewhere outside the public's gaze during his tenure: in 2010, BP poisoned the Gulf of Mexico, and a year later, Japan experienced the catastrophic Fukushima nuclear power plant meltdown. Suzanne Goldenberg, "Obama Administration Criticized over Failure to Disclose Coal Dump Locations," *The Guardian*, June 18, 2009.

32   "Poisoned Places," Center for Public Integrity, November 7, 2011.

33   Mark Guarino, "New EPA Guidelines on Soot," *Christian Science Monitor*, June 15, 2012.

34   Saundra Young, "Dirty 30 Want EPA Air Pollution Rule Repealed," WTNH. com, June 14, 2012.

35   Mark Guarino, "New EPA guidelines on soot," *Christian Science Monitor*, June 15, 2012.

CONCLUSION: BETTER LIVING AND A HEALTHIER NATURAL WORLD THROUGH SMALL FAMILY FARMS

1   Jerome A. Paulson et al., "Policy Statement Chemical-Management Policy: Prioritizing Children's Health," *Pediatrics*, April 25, 2011, 983–90.

2   Bob Herbert, *New York Times* (October 5, 2006).

3   *Legal Environmental Assistance Foundation vs. United States Environmental Protection Agency*, United States Court of Appeals for the Eleventh Circuit, No. 00-10381, EPA No. 65-02889, December 21, 2001.

4   Kate Sheppard, "For Pennsylvania's Doctors, a Gag Order on Fracking Chemicals," *Mother Jones*, March 13, 2012.

5   U.S. Environmental Protection Agency, Office of Water, "Evaluation of Impacts to Underground Sources of Drinking Water by Hydraulic Fracturing of Coalbed Methane Reservoirs" (Final, June 2004), ES-1.

6   Weston Wilson, "EPA Allows Hazardous Fluids to Be Injected into Ground Water: A report on EPA's failure to protect America's ground water from the impacts of oil and gas production" (October 8, 2004).

7   Josh Fox et al., "Affirming Gasland." See http://one.gaslandthemovie.com/whats-fracking/affirming-gasland.

8   Written testimony of Theo Colborn before the House Committee on Oversight and Government Reform, hearing on The Applicability of Federal Requirements to Protect Public Health and the Environment from Oil and Gas Development, October 31, 2007.

9   Ian Urbina, "Pressure Stifles Efforts to Police Drilling for Gas," *New York Times*, March 4, 2011, A1, A14.

10 Fox et al., "Affirming Gasland," 7, 9.

11 See Ian Urbina, "Pressure Limits Efforts to Police Drilling for Gas," *New York Times*, March 3, 2011. See also Abrahm Lustgarten, "Feds Link Water Contamination to Fracking for the First Time," *ProPublica*, December 8, 2011.

12 Abrahm Lustgarten, "Buried Secrets: Is Natural Gas Drilling Endangering U.S. Water Supplies?" *ProPublica*, November 13, 2008.

13 Fox et al., "Affirming Gasland," 6. See also Ian Urbina, "Pressure Limits Efforts to Police Drilling for Gas," *New York Times*, March 3, 2011.

14 "Obama's Support for Natural Gas Drilling 'A Painful Moment' for Communities Exposed to Fracking," *Democracy Now!* February 2, 2012.

15 John M. Broder, "New Proposal on Fracking Gives Ground to Industry," *New York Times*, May 4, 2012.

16 Sharon Hart, "An Approach to Solving Onion Production Problems in an Energy and Chemical Limited Future" (Department of Resource Development and Entomology, Michigan State University, February 1980). The report of Sharon Hart was part of an EPA-funded project at Michigan State University: "An Economic Analysis of an Agroecosystem for Pest Control," May 1980. EPA Grant R806065020. Principal Investigators: Thomas C. Edens and Dean L. Haynes.

17 Don Paarlberg, "The Land Grant Colleges and the Structure Issue," in *A Time to Choose: Summary Report on the Structure of Agriculture* (Washington, DC: U.S. Department of Agriculture, January 1981), p. 129.

18 Memo from David Menotti to Jodie Bernstein, September 23, 1977.

Index